SYSTEMS FOR STATE SCIENCE ASSESSMENT

Committee on Test Design for K–12 Science Achievement
Mark R. Wilson and Meryl W. Bertenthal, *editors*

Board on Testing and Assessment
Center for Education
Division of Behavioral and Social Sciences and Education

NATIONAL RESEARCH COUNCIL
OF THE NATIONAL ACADEMIES

THE NATIONAL ACADEMIES PRESS
Washington, D.C.
www.nap.edu

THE NATIONAL ACADEMIES PRESS   500 Fifth Street, N.W.   Washington, DC 20001

NOTICE: The project that is the subject of this report was approved by the Governing Board of the National Research Council, whose members are drawn from the councils of the National Academy of Sciences, the National Academy of Engineering, and the Institute of Medicine. The members of the committee responsible for the report were chosen for their special competences and with regard for appropriate balance.

This study was supported by Master Agreement No. 9911018 between the National Academy of Sciences and the National Science Foundation, Grant No. EHR-0237653. Any opinions, findings, conclusions or recommendations expressed in this publication are those of the authors and do not necessarily reflect the views of the National Science Foundation.

Library of Congress Cataloging-in-Publication Data

Systems for state science assessment / Committee on Test Design for K–12 Science Achievement ; Mark R. Wilson and Meryl W. Bertenthal, editors.
   p. cm.
   Includes bibliographical references and index.
   ISBN 0-309-09662-6 (hardcover) — ISBN 0-309-55060-2 (pdf) 1. Science—Study and teaching (Elementary)—United States—Evaluation. 2. Science—Study and teaching (Secondary)—United States—Evaluation. 3. Science—United States—Examinations, questions, etc. I. Wilson, Mark R. II. Bertenthal, Meryl W. III. National Research Council (U.S.). Committee on Test Design for K–12 Science Achievement.
   LB1585.3.S96 2005
   507.1'073—dc22
                              2005021294

Additional copies of this report are available from National Academies Press, 500 Fifth Street, N.W., Lockbox 285, Washington, DC 20055; (800) 624-6242 or (202) 334-3313 (in the Washington metropolitan area); Internet, http://www.nap.edu.

Printed in the United States of America

Suggested citation: National Research Council. (2006). *Systems for State Science Assessment.* Committee on Test Design for K–12 Science Achievement. M.R. Wilson and M.W. Bertenthal, eds. Board on Testing and Assessment, Center for Education, Division of Behavioral and Social Sciences and Education. Washington, DC: The National Academies Press.

THE NATIONAL ACADEMIES
Advisers to the Nation on Science, Engineering, and Medicine

The **National Academy of Sciences** is a private, nonprofit, self-perpetuating society of distinguished scholars engaged in scientific and engineering research, dedicated to the furtherance of science and technology and to their use for the general welfare. Upon the authority of the charter granted to it by the Congress in 1863, the Academy has a mandate that requires it to advise the federal government on scientific and technical matters. Dr. Ralph J. Cicerone is president of the National Academy of Sciences.

The **National Academy of Engineering** was established in 1964, under the charter of the National Academy of Sciences, as a parallel organization of outstanding engineers. It is autonomous in its administration and in the selection of its members, sharing with the National Academy of Sciences the responsibility for advising the federal government. The National Academy of Engineering also sponsors engineering programs aimed at meeting national needs, encourages education and research, and recognizes the superior achievements of engineers. Dr. Wm. A. Wulf is president of the National Academy of Engineering.

The **Institute of Medicine** was established in 1970 by the National Academy of Sciences to secure the services of eminent members of appropriate professions in the examination of policy matters pertaining to the health of the public. The Institute acts under the responsibility given to the National Academy of Sciences by its congressional charter to be an adviser to the federal government and, upon its own initiative, to identify issues of medical care, research, and education. Dr. Harvey V. Fineberg is president of the Institute of Medicine.

The **National Research Council** was organized by the National Academy of Sciences in 1916 to associate the broad community of science and technology with the Academy's purposes of furthering knowledge and advising the federal government. Functioning in accordance with general policies determined by the Academy, the Council has become the principal operating agency of both the National Academy of Sciences and the National Academy of Engineering in providing services to the government, the public, and the scientific and engineering communities. The Council is administered jointly by both Academies and the Institute of Medicine. Dr. Ralph J. Cicerone and Dr. Wm. A. Wulf are chair and vice chair, respectively, of the National Research Council.

www.national-academies.org

Working Group of Science Supervisors

THOMAS E. KELLER (*Chair*), Maine Department of Education
DIANE HERNANDEZ, California Department of Education
LINDA JORDAN, Tennessee Department of Education
SHELLEY A. LEE, Wisconsin Department of Public Instruction
BRETT MOULDING, Utah State Office of Education
MARSHA WINEGARNER, Florida Department of Education

Working Group of Science Teachers

VALDINE McLEAN (*Chair*), Pershing County High School, Lovelock, NV
AMITABHA BASU, George Washington Carver High School of Engineering
    and Science, Philadelphia, PA
CONNI CRITTENDEN, Williamston Explorer Elementary School,
    Williamston, MI
HECTOR IBARRA, West Branch Middle School, West Branch, IA
PATRICIA LeGRAND, Guilford County Middle College High School,
    Jamestown, NC
JOHN McKINNEY, Mountain Ridge Middle School, Castle Rock, CO
CAROL A. SHESTOK, Westford Public School System, Westford, MA

Acknowledgments

This report could not have been produced without the support of a number of people, and we are grateful for their contributions. First, we would like to acknowledge the support of our sponsor, the National Science Foundation, and, in particular, thank program officer Janice Earle for the encouragement she provided over the course of this study. Her belief in the importance of this project was highly valued by the committee.

We owe a debt of gratitude to the individuals who served on the working groups of state science supervisors, state directors of assessment, and science teachers, whose names are listed in this front matter. Members of these groups attended and contributed to committee meetings, participated in workshops, and reviewed drafts of the committee's and design teams' reports. Throughout the study they kept the committee informed about important practical issues related to No Child Left Behind (NCLB) and states' efforts to meet the legislative requirements for science standards and assessments. Several of the working group members also participated directly in the work of the design teams, providing the wisdom of practice to teams' work.

Our sincerest thanks go to state directors of assessment: Shelley Loving-Ryder, Virginia Department of Education; Herman W. Meyers, Vermont State Department of Education; Pat Roschewski, Nebraska Department of Education; Ann Smisko, Texas Education Agency; C. Scott Trimble (*retired*), Kentucky Department of Education; state science supervisors: Thomas E. Keller, Maine Department of Education; Diane Hernandez, California Department of Education; Linda Jordan, Tennessee Department of Education; Shelley A. Lee, Wisconsin Department of Public Instruction; Brett Moulding, Utah State Office of Education; Marsha Winegarner, Florida Department of Education; and outstanding science teachers: Valdine McLean, Pershing County High School, Lovelock, NV; Amitabha Basu, George Washington Carver High School of Engineering and Science, Philadelphia, PA; Conni Crittenden, Williamston Explorer Elementary School, Williamston, MI; Hector Ibarra, West Branch Middle School, West Branch, IA; Patricia LeGrand, Guilford County Middle College High School, Jamestown, NC; John McKinney, Mountain Ridge Middle School, Castle Rock, CO; and Carol A. Shestok, Westford Public School System, Westford, MA.

Because the committee wanted its findings to be based on a broad understanding of the ways in which science assessment systems could be designed and implemented, we asked six design teams of experts to help us conceptualize a variety of assessment system models. Individually and collectively, the members of the six groups provided great insight into the complexity of the issues involved in creating quality assessment systems. We are particularly grateful to the people who led four of these design teams: W. James Popham, University of California, Los Angeles (emeritus); Barbara Plake, Buros Institute, University of Nebraska; Edys Quellmalz, SRI International; Mark Moody, Hillcrest Associates; and Richard Patz, R.J. Patz, Inc. Also serving on these design teams were Mark Reckase, Michigan State University; Joseph Martineau, Michigan State University; Chad W. Buckendal, University of Nebraska–Lincoln; James C. Impara, University of Nebraska–Lincoln; Ian MacGregor, National Science Resources Center; Scott Marion, National Center for the Improvement in Educational Assessment; Carol Shestok, Westford Public School System; John McKinney, Mountain Ridge Middle School; Teresa Eckhout, Lincoln Public Schools; Cindy Gray, Elkhorn Public Schools; Thomas Neumann, Millard South High School; Arthur Zygielbaum, National Center for Information Technology in Education; Gwen Nugent, National Center for Information Technology in Education; Roger Bruning, University of Nebraska–Lincoln; Albert Steckelberg, University of Nebraska–Lincoln; Myron Atkin, Stanford University; James W. Pellegrino, University of Illinois at Chicago; Thomas E. Keller, Maine Department of Education; Brett Moulding, Utah Office of Education; Paul D. Sandifer, South Carolina Department of Education; James Beall, St. John's College, Annapolis; Henry Heikkinen, University of Northern Colorado; Smith Holt, Oklahoma State University; John Layman, University of Maryland; A. Truman Schwartz, Macalester College; and Christos Zahopolous, Northeastern University.

We also acknowledge with great appreciation the work done by Carol Smith, University of Massachusetts, Boston; Marianne Wiser, Clark University; Andy Anderson, Michigan State University; Brian Coppola, University of Michigan; Brian Reiser, Northwestern University; and Kefyn Catley, Vanderbilt University, who constituted the two design teams charged with developing assessments based on research on children's learning.

The committee was aided greatly by individuals who participated in our meetings and helped us to understand the complex issues involved in designing and implementing science assessment systems to meet the requirements of the No Child Left Behind Act of 2002. A portion of the committee's first meeting in August 2003 was an information gathering workshop at which Sue Rigney, U.S. Department of Education, Office of Elementary and Secondary Education, made a detailed presentation of the legislation and its requirements for science standards and assessments. Rolf Blank, Council of Chief State School Officers; Michael Hill, National Association of State Boards of Education; Bruce Hunter, American Association of School Administrators; Mary Kusler, American Association of Schools Administrators, Rural Schools Initiative; Michelle McGlaughlin, American Federation of Teachers; and Scott Young, National Conference of State Legislatures provided the committee with an overview of the challenges that states face in implementing science assessments under NCLB. We are grateful for the guidance these individuals provided.

We thank Robert Rothman, Annenberg Institute for School Reform, Brown University, for describing the many methods used by states for aligning their science standards and assessments, and Dylan Wiliam, Educational Testing Service, and Paul Black, Kings College, Cambridge, England, for providing the committee with a deeper understanding of international approaches to science education and assessment. We are also grateful to Mark Reckase and Joseph Martineau for sharing their thinking on the ways in which students' achievement in science might be measured over time and across grades, and to Stan Metzenberg, California State University, Northridge, for sharing early drafts of his paper "Improving State Science Assessments," with the committee. We also thank Alice Fu, a graduate student at Stanford University, for her assistance with gathering examples to illustrate state science standards.

At the committee's third meeting, Gerald Tindal, University of Oregon, and Mark Reckase helped the committee understand many of the issues involved in developing and implementing an assessment program that is highly inclusive. We are grateful for their perspectives and are appreciative of their participation in our work.

In May 2004, the committee held a workshop at which more than 100 participants representing educational organizations, states, test publishers, and educational researchers participated in detailed discussions of the design teams' work and gave their reactions to the usefulness of the various models. We are grateful to all of the design team members who participated and to the members of the working groups who served as discussion leaders at the workshop. At that same workshop, the committee also explored the ways in which technology could be used for improving the design, implementation, and administration of science assessments. We thank Randy Bennett, Educational Testing Service, and Edys Quellmalz for sharing their work on this topic. We also thank Geneva Haertel, SRI International, who coauthored the paper that Edys presented.

We have been most fortunate to have an outstanding staff working with us on this project. We are especially grateful to Alix Beatty, who joined the project just as we were beginning to write this report and whose assistance was invaluable in getting the volume ready for publication. Susan McCutchen and Andrew Tompkins have provided ongoing research support to the committee since its inception, and Judy Koenig helped us early on to organize the work of our design teams and to develop their charge. The committee benefited tremendously from having two excellent senior project assistants. Jane Phillips supported the committee extremely well until her retirement. We are very grateful to Teresia Wilmore, who joined the project after Jane left and who has served ever since, unflappably and flawlessly. She has dealt smoothly with the logistics of our meetings, with our enormous collections and distributions of materials, and with the many aspects of managing a committee, three working groups, six design teams, and multiple authors of commissioned papers.

The Board on Testing and Assessment (BOTA) and the Board on Science Education (BOSE) were instrumental in shaping early discussions about the project and in providing general guidance and support along the way. Their insights and knowledge at critical points in our work are much appreciated. We are especially grateful to BOTA members Lorrie Shepard, Eva Baker, and Bob Mislevy for their contributions to our thinking on possible assessment system models. We thank Stuart Elliott, BOTA director, and Jean Moon, BOSE director, for their support and encouragement. We note in particular our deep gratitude to Stuart, who attended all of our committee meetings and provided wise counsel at every stage of the committee's work.

Also at the National Research Council (NRC), many people contributed to the successful completion of this project. Martin Orland and Patricia Morison, director and associate director, respectively, of the Center for Education, provided the committee with encouragement and guidance along the way. Viola Horek, administrative coordinator for the center, and Lisa Alston, administrative coordinator for BOTA, were always there to ensure that the project ran smoothly and that the committee had everything it needed to do its work. We are extremely grateful to Kirsten Sampson Snyder who shepherded the committee's report through review and to Steve Olson and Christine McShane whose expert editing of the text of this report markedly improved its readability.

Above all, we would like to thank the committee members who gave enormous amounts of time and energy to this endeavor. The committee's work covered an exceedingly broad array of complex topics and issues, and committee members exhibited a deep commitment to learning from each other's expertise and producing a final report that reflects a consensus among all members. Everyone on the committee drafted text and contributed constructive, critical thinking to the deliberations. We are most grateful to them, as they made this report possible.

This report has been reviewed in draft form by individuals chosen for their diverse perspectives and technical expertise, in accordance with procedures approved by the NRC's Report Review Committee. The purpose of this independent review is to provide candid and critical comments that will assist the institution in making its published report as sound as possible and to ensure that the report meets institutional standards for objectivity, evidence, and responsiveness to the study charge. The review comments and draft manuscript remain confidential to protect the integrity of the deliberative process. We wish to thank the following individuals for their review of this report: Eva L. Baker, Center for the Study of Evaluation, University of California, Los Angeles; Glenn A. Crosby, Department of Chemistry (emeritus), Washington State University; David Hammer, Departments of Physics and Curriculum & Instruction, University of Maryland, College Park; Edward J. Hendry, Interdisciplinary Curriculum Specialist; Social Studies/Art/Music, Nashua School District, Nashua, NH; Norman G. Lederman, Department of Mathematics and Science Education, Illinois Institute of Technology, Chicago; Robert Linn, School of Education, University of Colorado; Stephen L. Pruitt, Science and Mathematics, Georgia State Department of Education; Edward D. Roeber, Office of Educational Assessment and Accountability, Michigan Department of Education, Lansing; Norman H. Sleep, Department of Geophysics, Stanford University; Nancy Butler Songer, Science Education and Learning Technologies, University of Michigan; Anne Tweed, Mathematics and Science Division, Mid-continent Research for Education and Learning, Aurora, CO; Carl E. Wieman, Department of Physics, University of Colorado; and Wendy M. Yen, Center for K–12 Research, Educational Testing Service, Monterey, CA.

Although the reviewers listed above have provided many constructive comments and suggestions, they were not asked to endorse the conclusions or recommendations nor did they see the final draft of the report before its release. The review of this report was overseen by Adam Gamoran, Department of Sociology, University of Wisconsin–Madison, and R. Duncan Luce, Institute for Mathematical Behavioral Science, University of California, Irvine. Appointed by the NRC, they were responsible for making certain that an independent examination of this report was carried out in accordance with institutional procedures and that all review comments were carefully considered. Responsibility for the final content of this report rests entirely with the authoring committee and the institution.

Mark R. Wilson, *Chair*
Meryl W. Bertenthal, *Study Director*
Committee on Test Design for K–12 Science Achievement

Contents

SYSTEMS FOR STATE SCIENCE ASSESSMENT

Executive Summary

Under the No Child Left Behind Act of 2002 (NCLB), states must develop challenging standards in science and assess students' achievement of those standards. The assessment requirement for science takes effect in the 2007–2008 school year, so states have an opportunity to carefully develop their response to the law's requirements.

The National Science Foundation, recognizing the importance of this opportunity, asked the National Research Council (NRC) to form a committee to help states prepare for the implementation of the law. The Committee on Test Design for K–12 Science Achievement was charged with two tasks: (1) providing advice and guidance and making recommendations that will be useful to states in designing, developing, and implementing quality science assessments to meet the 2007–2008 implementation requirements of the No Child Left Behind Act; and (2) fostering communication and collaboration between the NRC committee and key stakeholders in states and schools in order that the guidance provided by the NRC committee's report is responsive and can be practically implemented.

In conducting its study, the committee followed the fundamental position of the *National Science Education Standards*: science literacy should be the goal for K–12 science education. An essential element of science literacy is a strong foundation in the content knowledge of the life, physical, earth, and space sciences. It is also critically important for students to understand science as a specific way of knowing and to develop the skills necessary to both understand and appropriately apply the strategies of scientific inquiry. The states and the designers of assessments need to incorporate these fundamental aspects of science literacy in designing science assessments for NCLB.

This report is intended as a guide for states in making decisions about assessment to meet the NCLB requirements and in planning more broadly for assessment as a tool for supporting student learning. The committee recognizes that each state has its own goals for science education and assessment. This report, therefore, provides guidance that is specific enough to address the important issues raised by NCLB science requirements, but general enough to be adaptable to a wide range of contexts. The committee's advice to states is offered in the form of questions that all those responsible for designing and implementing state assessment programs should ask themselves as they develop science assessments. These questions are intended to focus state decision makers on important issues that need to be addressed as assessments are developed, implemented, and used. The questions appear throughout the report and are included in their entirety in Chapter 9. They are not included in the executive summary, which instead summarizes the findings that underlie the questions.

Although the science assessments that are developed to meet NCLB requirements will constitute but a small fraction of the science assessment that is conducted in schools across the nation, they are likely to exert a powerful influence on science curricula and instruction. It is therefore very important that the effects of states' NCLB science assessments be thoroughly explored before they are introduced and become mandatory.

STANDARDS

High-quality science standards are central to science education and assessment. They are the way that states articulate their goals for student learning and focus the attention of teachers, students, parents, and all others concerned with education on what students should know and be able to do. Content standards serve as the basis for developing curricula, selecting textbooks, setting instructional priorities, and developing assessments. Achievement standards make clear what information will be accepted as evidence that students have achieved the standards and how competence is defined.

Content standards should be clear, detailed, and complete; reasonable in scope; rigorous and scientifically correct; and built around a conceptual framework that reflects sound models of student learning. They should also describe examples of performance expectations for students in clear and specific terms so that all concerned will know what is expected of them. The committee found that although some state standards reflect many of these criteria, no current state standards meet all of them.

States should regularly review and revise standards documents at least every 10 years. Revisions to content standards documents should be mirrored by changes in curriculum, curricular materials, assessments, and instruction. In turn, ongoing teacher professional development will be required to ensure that the changes in the standards are reflected in classrooms and schools.

State standards should be organized and elaborated in ways that clearly specify what students need to know and be able to do and how their knowledge and skills will develop over time with instruction. Learning progressions and learning performance are two strategies that states can use in organizing and elaborating their standards to guide curriculum, instruction, and assessment. Learning progressions are descriptions of successively more sophisticated ways of thinking about an idea that follow one another as students learn: they lay out in words and examples what it means to move toward more expert understanding. Learning progressions should be developed around the organizing principles of science such as evolution and kinetic molecular theory. Such organizing principles—which are sometimes referred to as the big ideas of science—are the coherent foundation for the concepts, theories, principles, and explanatory schemes for phenomena in a discipline. Organizing standards around big ideas represents a fundamental shift from the more traditional organizational structure that many states use in which standards are grouped under discrete topic headings. A potentially positive outcome of a reorganization in state standards from discrete topics to big ideas is a shift from breadth of coverage to depth of coverage around a relatively small set of foundational principles and concepts. Those principles and concepts should be the target of instruction so that they can be progressively refined, elaborated, and extended over time.

Creating learning performances is a strategy for elaborating on content standards by specifying what students should be able to do if they have achieved a standard. Learning performances might indicate that students should be able to describe phenomena, use models to explain patterns in data, construct scientific explanations, or test hypotheses. A clear understanding of how students can demonstrate that they have attained a standard allows assessment developers to create items and tasks that are directed at these skills and provides teachers with targets for instruction. This approach helps build coherence between what is taught and what is tested.

ASSESSMENT

Assessment, which includes everything from classroom observations to national tests such as the National Assessment of Educational Progress, is a systematic process for gathering information about student achievement. It provides critical information for many parts of the education system, including guiding instructional decisions, holding schools accountable for meeting learning goals, and monitoring program effectiveness. Assessment is also a way that teachers, school administrators, and state and national education policy and decision makers exemplify their goals for student learning.

Although assessment can serve all of these purposes, no one assessment can do so. To support valid inferences, every assessment has to be designed specifically to serve its purpose. An assessment that is designed to provide information about students' difficulties with a single concept so that it can be addressed with instruction would be designed differently from an assessment that is to provide information to policy makers for evaluating the effectiveness of the overall education system. The former requires that students' understanding of a concept be tested deeply and thoroughly; the latter requires that the assessment cover broadly all of the topics deemed important by education policy makers. Results from either of these assessments would not be valid for the purposes of the other.

Assessment, by itself, cannot improve student learning—it is the appropriate use of assessment results that can accomplish that goal. Thus, the committee concluded that states should think about assessment in the context of the education system in which it functions. Assessment is one of a number of elements—which include curriculum, instruction, professional development, fiscal, and other resources—that interact in the classroom, school, school district, and state and that together support student learning. To serve its function well, assessment must be tightly linked to curriculum and instruction so that all three elements are directed toward the same goals. Assessment should measure what students are being taught, and what is taught should reflect the goals for student learning articulated in the standards. Thus, all of the elements in the education system have to be built on a shared vision of what is important for students to know and understand about science, how instruction affects that knowledge and understanding over time, and what can be taken as evidence that learning has occurred.

A SYSTEM OF ASSESSMENT

The committee concluded that a single assessment strategy would not, by itself, meet the requirements of NCLB. The committee therefore recommends that states develop a system of science assessment that can meet the various purposes of NCLB and provide education decision makers with assessment-based information that is appropriate for each specific purpose for which it will be used. The system should be comprised of a variety of assessment strategies, designed in ways that are fundamentally different from each other and which collectively would meet NCLB requirements. In particular, the law states that assessment must:

- be fully aligned with state standards;
- meet accepted professional standards for validity, reliability, and fairness for each purpose for which it will be used;
- be reported to parents, teachers, and administrators in ways that are diagnostic, interpretive, and descriptive so that the results can be used to address individual students' academic needs; and
- be reported in ways that provide evidence that all students in the state, regardless of race, ethnicity, economic status, or proficiency in English, are meeting the state's challenging academic standards.

The system that each state develops in response to NCLB will vary according to the state's goals and priorities for science education and its uses for assessment information. For example, a state might choose to develop a single hybrid test in which students take a core assessment that provides individual results along with an assessment with a matrix-sampling design that provides information about the achievement of groups of students across a broad content domain. Or a state might choose to combine standardized classroom assessments that provide diagnostic, descriptive, and interpretive information with an external assessment of progress that all students are making toward achieving state standards. Or a state may decide to eschew a statewide test and opt instead for one of many different models in which results from local, district, or state assessments are combined, aggregated, and reported for specific purposes.

Similarly, a single assessment strategy cannot provide all of the information that education decision makers in classrooms, schools, school districts, and states need to support student learning. Teachers need ongoing information on how well their students are learning so they can target instruction; students need timely feedback on how they are meeting expectations so they can adjust their learning strategies; districts need information on the effectiveness of their programs; and policy makers need to know how well their policies are working and where resources might best be targeted. Addressing all of these needs for assessment-based information requires multiple assessment strategies, each designed to serve its own specific purpose. These multiple assessment strategies should be designed from the beginning to function as part of a coherent system of assessment.

A successful system of standards-based science assessment is coherent in a variety of ways. It is *horizontally coherent*: curriculum, instruction, and assessment are all aligned with the standards; target the same goals for learning; and work together to support students' developing science literacy. It is *vertically coherent*: all levels of the education system—classroom, school, school district, and state—are based on a shared vision of the goals for science education, of the purposes and uses of assessment, and of what constitutes competent performance. The system is also *developmentally coherent*: it takes into account how students' science understanding develops over time and the scientific content knowledge, abilities, and understanding that are needed for learning to progress at each stage of the process.

DEVELOPING AND SUPPORTING A COHERENT ASSESSMENT SYSTEM

Coherent assessment systems do not develop by accident; they must be deliberately designed so that all of the measures work together both conceptually and operationally. To ensure coherence, states should develop a master plan for their assessment system, in which they clearly specify its purposes and the individual assessments that are needed to serve those purposes. The plan should document the constructs each assessment will measure; the ways in which the results of each assessment are to be used; who will be tested; where each component will be administered, and by whom; who is responsible for developing the component; when the assessment will be administered; and how the results will be scored, combined, and reported for specific purposes.

States should establish a system of interacting advisory groups that are in place before system design begins or as early in the process as possible. One of the advisory groups should advise the state about the technical measurement issues associated with a testing program; other groups should focus on the content areas that are part of the assessment program. Science content committees should include scientists, science educators, researchers who study science assessment, and individuals with expertise on how people learn science. There should be some overlapping members of the content and technical groups or structured interactions between them.

Reporting Assessment Results

The reports of assessments are a critical element of a coherent system. How and to whom results will be reported are questions that should be considered during the first stages of designing an assessment system because the answers will guide almost all subsequent decisions about assessment design.

Information about students' progress is needed at all levels of the education system, and reporting practices must meet the needs of parents, teachers, school and district administrators, policy makers, the public, and, of course, the students themselves. However, not all of these groups need the same information, and reports should be tailored to meet the needs of different users.

Professional Development

For assessment to function well, each of those who play a part in the interpretation and use of assessment results needs to have an understanding of assessment, the state's goals for assessment, the ways different assessments function, and how to interpret and use assessment results appropriately. Those who need the opportunity to develop their understanding of how assessment works range from students to elected officials to curriculum developers, but teachers are the group with the greatest need for understanding assessment.

Teachers play a pivotal role in the education system. The decisions that they make, the ways in which they interact with students, and their appropriate use of assessment affect the knowledge and attitudes that students acquire. Teachers cannot cultivate a deep conceptual understanding among their students unless they themselves have such understanding. A strong grounding in science subject matter knowledge as well as subject-specific pedagogical knowledge is fundamental to good teaching and assessment.

Teachers need to be able to use a variety of classroom assessment strategies and tools such as observation, student conferences, portfolios, performance tasks, rubrics, and student self-assessment. They must also understand the uses and limitations of external assessment and be cognizant of the ways in which such assessment affects their teaching.

Professional development strategies that involve the evaluation of student work are one important means for increasing teachers' understanding of assessment and for helping them to deepen their own understanding of science. In-service professional development opportunities, which schools and districts use for many different purposes, are not sufficient to provide teachers with the skills they need in order to use and understand assessment effectively. The committee therefore calls on colleges and universities that prepare teachers to include in their curricula courses on educational measurement that are both general and specific to science. Such courses should include information on the uses and limitations of state tests and on new and emerging assessment methods. In-service professional development could then build on this knowledge by including opportunities for teachers to refine or learn about and practice new assessment strategies.

Because the course requirements for teacher preparation programs are largely set by state licensure requirements, the committee calls on states to include in their standards for certification and recertification a provision that teachers demonstrate assessment competence as a condition for teacher licensure.

Opportunity to Learn

Excellence in science education embodies the idea that all students can achieve science literacy if they are given the opportunity to learn. Students will achieve understanding of science concepts in different ways and at different depths of understanding and at different rates of progress, but opportunity to learn implies that all students have the chance to the maximum extent possible. NCLB reflects this goal and mandates the interpretation of test-based information in ways that may highlight discrepancies in opportunity to learn among different groups of students, schools, and school districts within a state. Therefore, schools and school districts need to implement curricula and instructional approaches for all students that are aligned with both content and performance standards. States need to actively monitor and evaluate the effectiveness of schools' and school districts' efforts to provide all students with a sufficient opportunity to learn science. School-level data on the opportunity to learn will be critical in helping states to ensure that science education is accessible to all students.

The fairness of assessments and the validity of results depend on both the extent to which students have had the opportunity to learn the skills and material that are assessed and the use of assessments that are unbiased and accessible to a wide range of students with different abilities and disabilities. If students do not have the opportunity to learn the material or to demonstrate their knowledge in the context of appropriately designed assessments, it is impossible to know whether the results shed light on aspects of the curriculum, instructional strategies, or students' efforts or abilities, or whether they simply indicate that students have not been given a chance to learn what is being assessed or that the assessments are somehow not tapping into what they know in appropriate ways.

Inclusion

NCLB requires that all students, including students with disabilities and English language learners, participate in state accountability programs, and states are required to provide appropriate accommodations to these students. However, the effects of accommodations on test performance and on the inferences that can be made from test results are not well understood. As states make decisions about how to assess students' science literacy, they will need to consider the needs of English language learners and students with special needs and the challenges of devising technically sound accommodations for them. They will also need to consider the extent to which students with disabilities and English language learners have had an opportunity to learn the material covered by an assessment. These issues are particularly salient for states that make use of innovative assessment methods, for which there is little research about the effects of accommodations.

Resources

The allocation of time and money is an element in virtually every decision that education officials make. The assessment of science learning has resource implications for states and schools that could far outstrip the actual costs of the assessments themselves. New assessments may reveal inadequacies in the existing science education program in a state, as well as inequities in science education across schools and school districts. Such findings may trigger legal requirements to address inequities. As a state raises the stakes, the demand for high-quality science education may also increase. Financial incentives may be needed to encourage qualified science teachers to enter teaching or to remain in schools that serve disadvantaged students. Assessments also can reveal exemplary practices that contribute significantly to increased student learning: resources should be set aside to disseminate and implement these practices.

Monitoring and Evaluation

For an assessment system to achieve its goals, those responsible for it need to continuously monitor and periodically evaluate its effectiveness. NCLB holds states, districts, and schools accountable for student performance; it is equally important that they be held accountable for the quality, utility, and consequences of their assessment systems. States and districts should have a detailed plan for evaluating how well the assessment system is working, whether it is accomplishing its goals, and whether there are unanticipated effects. At the same time, states and districts need plans for continually refining their policies and procedures in response to evidence.

Assisting States

While the focus of this report is to provide advice and guidance to states, the committee recognizes that states cannot do all that is required on their own. Below we describe some important ways that scientists, science educators, professional societies, granting organizations, the federal government, and education policy organizations can assist states in their efforts to design, implement, and evaluate science assessment systems. The text below summarizes the text of the recommendations to these individuals and groups. The complete set of recommendations is contained in Chapter 9 of the report.

In its recommendations to others, the committee calls on federal granting agencies and others to support with funding and expertise the design and validation of prototype science assessment systems on which states could base their own efforts. These prototypes should include systems in which information that is used for accountability purposes is gathered in classrooms, as well as at the district and state levels. We also call on funding agencies to support research programs that can help states to develop and refine procedures for determining alignment, reliability, accuracy, fairness, and validity of assessment systems that are comprised of multiple measures and for setting achievement levels when multiple assessment strategies are used. Because the assessment of inquiry will be a key component in most states' science assessments, the committee recommends that expertise and funding also be provided to help states address issues related to the development, validation, and implementation of appropriate assessments of students' understanding and application of inquiry skills.

Standards are the heart of a science assessment system and we call on the U.S. Department of Education to take an active role in assuring that every state has high-quality standards. We recommend that it require every state to have an independent body evaluate the quality of its science content standards and procedures for developing and setting achievement levels. We recommend that the results of these evaluations be made public and that they be included in any review process that the Secretary of Education uses for evaluating and certifying compliance with key NCLB provisions.

The research base on which high-quality assessment systems should rest is incomplete. We call on the research community to propose and conduct studies on the ways in which students' understanding of the big ideas of science develop over time and the ways in which students represent their understanding of these ideas as they develop competence. Results of this research should be used to help states develop state science standards and create valid assessments of students' understanding of key scientific concepts as such understanding develops and changes over time.

1

Introduction

The No Child Left Behind Act of 2002 (NCLB, Public Law 110-107) extends the accountability provisions of the 1994 reauthorization of the Elementary and Secondary Education Act (Improving America's Schools Act) to all public schools and districts in states that receive federal Title I funds.[1] NCLB has two primary goals: improving student achievement overall and narrowing the achievement gap between students of different backgrounds. These goals are to be achieved by means of strong accountability measures for schools and districts and the imposition of sanctions on those that cannot demonstrate that their students are making adequate yearly progress in meeting challenging standards of academic achievement.

NCLB moves beyond the 1994 law both because it affects all public schools and districts and because it includes science in its requirements for standards and assessments. By including science in the requirements, Congress has signaled to the American public that science literacy is a national priority and schools should ensure that all students leave public education with the scientific knowledge, skills, and understandings that are necessary to be scientifically literate citizens.

---

[1]The 1994 law affected only schools and districts that served Title I students. NCLB, in contrast, affects all schools and districts that operate in a state that receives Title I funds. As this report went to press, all 50 states and affected territories were receiving Title I dollars. Thus, all U.S. schools and districts, even those that do not serve Title I students, must meet the same requirements.

NCLB REQUIREMENTS FOR SCIENCE

NCLB requires that all states must have challenging academic content and achievement standards for science in place by 2005–2006. They must begin measuring student attainment of those standards in 2007–2008 with assessments that are fully aligned with the standards and that meet accepted professional standards for technical quality for each purpose for which they will be used. The law further specifies that states' assessment systems must include multiple up-to-date measures of student achievement, including measures that assess higher order thinking skills and understanding of challenging content. Science assessments are to be administered annually to all students, including those with disabilities and those who are not fluent in English, at least once in each of three grade bands, 3–5, 6–9, and 10–12. At present, they need not be included in the calculation of adequate yearly progress that is used to monitor states' progress toward NCLB goals. States are required to make reasonable accommodations for students with disabilities and limited English proficiency to allow them to participate in the assessments, and they must have in place alternate assessments for students who cannot participate in the regular assessment even with accommodations.

In recognition of the decentralized nature of public education governance in the United States, as well as of the differences in states' circumstances and priorities, the legislation allows some flexibility in meeting the law's requirements. States may choose to include in their assessment systems either criterion-referenced assessments, augmented norm-referenced assessments, or both (assessments that support only norm-referenced interpretations are not acceptable).[2] Assessment systems, which can take many forms under NCLB, may be comprised of a uniform set of assessments statewide or a combination of state and local assessments. However, regardless of the form that the assessment system takes, the results must be reported publicly and be expressed in terms of the state's academic achievement standards. The results must be reported in the aggregate for the full group of test takers and be disaggregated for specified population groups and provide information that is descriptive, interpretive,[3] and diagnostic at the individual level. Box 1-1 includes excerpts from the assessment provisions of NCLB as they relate to science; they are referenced throughout this report.

Although NCLB requires states and districts that receive Title I funds to participate in the biennial state-level assessments in reading and mathematics conducted under the National Assessment of Educational Progress (NAEP), no such requirement for science is in place as this report goes to press. Thus, partici-

---

[2]Criterion-referenced tests are those that report student performance in terms of a defined body of skills and knowledge, while norm-referenced tests are those that report performance in terms of comparisons with the performance of groups of similar students. Both are discussed further in Chapter 5.

[3]Interpretive results provide guidance on what the results mean.

pation in state-level NAEP in science remains voluntary. Nonetheless, the committee sees the potential for the NAEP science assessment framework, which is currently under revision, to exert an indirect but important influence on the content of state science assessments and curricula.

STUDY CONTEXT

The Committee's Charge

Recognizing the challenges that states face in meeting NCLB requirements for the design and development of science assessments,[4] the National Science Foundation (NSF) asked the National Research Council (NRC) to form a committee to contribute in the following ways to the national effort:

(1) provide guidance and make recommendations that will be useful to states in designing, developing, and implementing quality science assessments to meet the 2007–2008 implementation requirement of the No Child Left Behind Act; and

(2) foster communication and collaboration between the NRC committee and key stakeholders in the states and in schools so that the guidance provided by the committee's report is responsive and can be practically implemented in states and schools.

The Committee on Test Design for K–12 Science Achievement was established, and this report is the result of our research, collaborations, and deliberations in response to this charge. Because states and localities across the nation vary widely in their goals and approaches to assessment and to science education, the advice in this report is targeted to policy makers and practitioners at a level that is specific enough to address the important issues raised by NCLB science requirements, yet adaptable to a wide range of contexts.

Committee Approach

In their initial discussions with the committee, the sponsors urged members not only to address the specific requirements of NCLB, but also to consider the design and development of high-quality science assessment more broadly. The committee was asked to consider the work of two earlier NRC committees, the

---

[4]When this study began in August 2003, only a few states had science assessment programs that would meet the requirements. A total of 23 of 56 states and territories had not administered any statewide science instruments during the 1999–2000 school year; of the 33 states and territories that did report testing students in science. Education Week reported that only 14 states were using assessments that met NCLB requirements in all three of the grade bands (Education Week, 2002).

BOX 1-1
Key Assessments of NCLB Requirements

Subpart 1—Basic Program Requirements
SEC. 1111. STATE PLANS
(b) ACADEMIC STANDARDS, ACADEMIC ASSESSMENTS, AND ACCOUNTABILITY
(3) ACADEMIC ASSESSMENTS

(A) IN GENERAL—Each State plan shall demonstrate that the State educational agency, in consultation with local educational agencies, has implemented a set of high-quality, yearly student academic assessments that include, at a minimum, academic assessments in mathematics, reading or language arts, and science that will be used as the primary means of determining the yearly performance of the State and of each local educational agency and school in the State in enabling all children to meet the State's challenging student academic achievement standards, except that no State shall be required to meet the requirements of this part relating to science assessments until the beginning of the 2007–2008 school year.

(C) REQUIREMENTS—Such assessments shall

(i) be the same academic assessments used to measure the achievement of all children;

(ii) be aligned with the State's challenging academic content and student academic achievement standards, and provide coherent information about student attainment of such standards;

(iii) be used for purposes for which such assessments are valid and reliable, and be consistent with relevant, nationally recognized professional and technical standards;

(iv) be used only if the State educational agency provides to the Secretary evidence from the test publisher or other relevant sources that the assessments used are of adequate technical quality for each purpose required under this Act and are consistent with the requirements of this section, and such evidence is made public by the Secretary upon request;

(II) beginning not later than school year 2007–2008, measure the proficiency of all students in science and be administered not less than one time during
(aa) grades 3 through 5;
(bb) grades 6 through 9; and
(cc) grades 10 through 12;

(vi) involve multiple up-to-date measures of student academic achievement, including measures that assess higher-order thinking skills and understanding;

(ix) provide for

(I) the participation in such assessments of all students;

(II) the reasonable adaptations and accommodations for students with disabilities (as defined under section 602(3) of the Individuals with Disabilities Education Act) necessary to measure the academic achievement of such students relative to State academic content and State student academic achievement standards; and

    (III) the inclusion of limited English proficient students, who shall be assessed in a valid and reliable manner and provided reasonable accommodations on assessments administered to such students under this paragraph, including, to the extent practicable, assessments in the language and form most likely to yield accurate data on what such students know and can do in academic content areas, until such students have achieved English language proficiency as determined under paragraph (7);

(xii) produce individual student interpretive, descriptive, and diagnostic reports, consistent with clause (iii) that allow parents, teachers, and principals to understand and address the specific academic needs of students, and include information regarding achievement on academic assessments aligned with State academic achievement standards, and that are provided to parents, teachers, and principals, as soon as is practicably possible after the assessment is given, in an understandable and uniform format, and to the extent practicable, in a language that parents can understand;

(xiii) enable results to be disaggregated within each State, local educational agency, and school by gender, by each major racial and ethnic group, by English proficiency status, by migrant status, by students with disabilities as compared to nondisabled students, and by economically disadvantaged students as compared to students who are not economically disadvantaged, except that, in the case of a local educational agency or a school, such disaggregation shall not be required in a case in which the number of students in a category is insufficient to yield statistically reliable information or the results would reveal personally identifiable information about an individual student;

(xiv) be consistent with widely accepted professional testing standards, objectively measure academic achievement, knowledge, and skills, and be tests that do not evaluate or assess personal or family beliefs and attitudes, or publicly disclose personally identifiable information; and

(xv) enable itemized score analyses to be produced and reported, consistent with clause (iii), to local educational agencies and schools, so that parents, teachers, principals, and administrators can interpret and address the specific academic needs of students as indicated by the students' achievement on assessment items.

(c) ACADEMIC STANDARDS, ACADEMIC ASSESSMENTS, AND ACCOUNTABILITY

  (5) STATE AUTHORITY

    (A) adopting academic standards and academic assessments that meet the requirements of this subsection, on a statewide basis, and limiting their applicability to students served under this part; or

continues

BOX 1-1 Continued

(B) adopting and implementing policies that ensure that each local educational agency in the State that receives grants under this part will adopt curriculum content and student academic achievement standards, and academic assessments aligned with such standards, which
  (i)   meet all of the criteria in this subsection and any regulations regarding such standards and assessments that the Secretary may publish; and
  (ii) are applicable to all students served by each such local educational agency.

SOURCE: P.L. 107-110, No Child Left Behind Act of 2002, Title I Part A, Subpart I, Basic Program Requirements, Section 1111, State Plans.

Committee on the Cognitive Foundations of Assessment (National Research Council, 2001b) and the Committee on Assessment in Support of Instruction and Learning (National Research Council, 2003). Both of these committees called for the creation of balanced assessment systems that are supported by the larger education system and are based on what is known about how people learn and gain expertise in a specific domain of knowledge. These ideas provided the foundation for the committee's thinking.

In this report, the term assessment is used to mean a process for collecting information that can be used for a variety of purposes—for example, to exemplify the state's learning goals, to categorize the achievement of individual students, to provide the basis for instructional decisions or decisions about resources, or to monitor and evaluate the success of instructional programs. High-quality assessment is critical to science education because it is both the way in which states exemplify the goals for science education embodied in the standards and a major source of the information that states use in making important decisions about education.

Based on our review of relevant research and extensive practical experience with the design of assessment programs, the committee decided to take a systems approach in thinking about the nature and role of science assessment in education. This approach explicitly recognizes that the elements that make up the education system are independent but also interrelated and interacting, so that changes in one element necessarily create changes in others. Indeed, this is the premise on which NCLB is based—set high standards, implement assessments aligned to those standards, hold schools and districts accountable for the assessment results, and use the improvement of assessment results as a lever to foster changes in curriculum and instruction in ways that will lead to better student outcomes.

Many of the points made in this report may apply equally well to assessment in other areas. The measurement principles that have guided the committee's thinking about science assessment could guide assessment in other domains as well. However, there are aspects of science as a discipline—the abstract nature of many of the concepts that students are expected to learn and the emphasis on scientific inquiry and investigation in many state standards, for example—that present specific challenges for assessment. Thus, to design high-quality science assessment, states will need to focus on both the general precepts of sound educational measurement and the features that are unique to science assessment. The report as a whole presents goals for states to consider in developing science assessments that meet high technical standards and are tailored to the demands of science as a discipline, but much of the discussion has a wider application.

Gathering the Evidence

The committee used many sources of information to prepare this report. We looked for evidence in the scientific and professional literature on science assessment and on science education and in policy reports on the implementation and effects of NCLB. We reviewed the body of work that has been done on science assessment by scientific disciplinary societies, such as the American Association for the Advancement of Science, the National Science Teachers Association, the American Chemical Society, the American Physics Society, and others. We examined state science standards and considered others' evaluations of both science standards and science assessments that are currently being used in states, even though it was clear, in the context of the looming NCLB deadlines, that these things would be changing quite rapidly. We also relied on the work of earlier NRC committees that synthesized research on how people learn, what is known about the cognitive foundations of assessment, and the uses and potential of technologies for assessment. We considered at length many reports and analyses of science curricula, textbooks, and instructional approaches that have been conducted by Project 2061 (American Association for the Advancement of Science) and NSF-supported curriculum and instructional projects.

To ensure that our advice would be practical and responsive to states' concerns, we also relied on the experience of experts who have had responsibility for testing programs in states and districts, as well as others with relevant practical experience. The committee formed and collaborated with three working groups, consisting of state assessment directors, state-level science supervisors, and science teachers. We relied heavily on their experiences and knowledge in considering the design of science assessment systems. Biographical information about the working group members appears in Appendix C.

In order to base our conclusions on a broad understanding of the possible conceptual models for the design of assessment systems, the committee asked four design teams to develop plans for science assessment systems that would meet the requirements of NCLB, but also move beyond them in ways they thought most likely to improve students' science learning. Each had a specific focus, selected to be consistent with different approaches that states may use in the design of their science assessments. These models are summarized in Chapter 2 and additional information about the design teams and their work appears in Appendix B.

The committee also asked two additional teams of experts to develop designs for assessments that would reflect current research on the ways in which students learn and represent knowledge in a given domain. These teams were made up of scientists, science educators, cognitive scientists, and teacher educators (see Appendix B). Using research on children's learning, they developed learning progressions to depict the ways in which students might acquire knowledge over time, as well as ways in which that knowledge might be assessed. The models developed by these teams are summarized in Chapter 5.

The committee held a workshop at which representatives of education and policy organizations discussed the challenges related to science assessment facing legislatures, governors, chief state school officers, school administrators, school boards, teachers, and others. A second workshop provided the committee and design teams with stakeholders' reactions to the model science assessment system designs described above. Discussions at the workshop helped the committee to conceptualize some of the important issues states would face in implementing any of these proposed designs.

Finally, the committee commissioned several papers to develop greater depth of understanding on particular topics. These papers addressed a range of topics: an analysis of frequently used procedures for gauging the alignment of assessments with standards; advances in the roles of technology in assessment systems; international approaches to science assessment; and the ways in which science assessments can be vertically scaled to better represent students' achievement over time (see Appendix B). The papers as well as those written by the design teams are available at the committee's web site at www7.nationalacademies.org/BOTA/Test_Design_K-12_Science.html.

ABOUT THIS REPORT

Limitations

While research suggests principles to guide the development and operation of assessment systems and provides some guidance to states in choosing among available options, the design of assessment systems is not an exact science and has not been thoroughly researched. Therefore, the committee's advice to states is in some cases based on our combined judgment and the experiences of our working group members. Although the research base is not complete, the range of ideas from which states can benefit is growing, as more states implement innovative approaches to assessment. Nevertheless, additional research on the design, implementation, validity, and uses of assessment systems that reflect new thinking on the ways in which students develop scientific knowledge, skills, and understanding is needed. We call attention to specific areas of need throughout the report, but note that in many cases research-based methodologies for accomplishing the particular goals discussed in this report have not yet been developed. We acknowledge that we are calling on states to consider some ideas that are not yet supported by a well-developed empirical base, as well as some that have been tried only in relatively confined settings. However, taken together, the existing research literature and the innovative work that has been done in some states provide key means of meeting the challenges of developing NCLB science assessments that are technically sound and support high-quality science education.

In carrying out our charge, the committee did not make recommendations about the science content that should be included in state science standards or represented in assessment, because we view standards as a state responsibility. For this report we turned to the standards that have been developed by the National Research Council (1996) and the American Association for the Advancement of Science (1993) as a good starting place, noting that these too could be improved to make them more useful in the design of curriculum materials and assessments. While we lay out a process for developing and criteria for evaluating the quality of science content and performance standards, and we recommend that states use these criteria to review their own science standards, we did not systematically evaluate existing state standards, because doing so would require a deep understanding of individual states' goals and purposes and would have been outside the scope of our charge.

There is no single science test that would be equally useful in all the states and territories affected by the NCLB requirements, and the committee did not try either to develop a model assessment system or to break new ground in assessment development. Instead, we examined how what is currently being done could be improved in the context of an assessment system. The committee chose not to recommend that states include or not include particular item types in their assessments or to provide exemplary items for states to emulate. We recognize that no individual item or test would be universally admired, and we note that while the improvement of items and tests is important, it will require more than that to improve the quality and utility of science assessment more generally.

Finally, the committee thinks that the results of science assessment should be publicly reported in a timely manner to all interested stakeholders, along with all other data about student achievement. However, we did not take a stance on future decisions to include or exclude science assessment results from accountability decisions, including measures of adequate yearly progress, as is required by NCLB for reading and mathematics; this policy decision is beyond the committee's charge.

Structure

The report begins with a discussion of the nature of an assessment system. This is followed by a discussion of the goals for science literacy and the insights provided by research on learning that shed light on how students' understanding of important science concepts can be assessed. Subsequent chapters address the nature and structure of science standards and the design of assessments that reflect the foundations that have guided the committee. The report continues with an examination of strategies for building, operating, and supporting an assessment system and with discussions of issues related to fairness and adequacy. Chapter 8 covers monitoring and evaluation of the system to ensure that it is functioning as intended. The report closes with a discussion of the ways in which the federal government, agencies that fund research, researchers, and others can assist states in their efforts to improve science assessment.

Three appendixes complete the report. Appendix A is a set of practical tips that came from our discussions with participants in the state assessment process. Appendix B is a list of the background papers and design teams that provided valuable information to aid the committee in its work. Appendix C contains biographical sketches of the committee, staff, and working group members.

Using This Report

A major goal for this study was that the committee's report be practical and be presented in such a way that individual elements can easily be considered and implemented by states. The report is also intended to be useful to states that are at different stages in designing and modifying their science assessment programs. Some states, for example, may already have developed high-quality science standards that meet the criteria laid out in Chapter 4, but they may find in other chapters suggestions for improvements they have not considered. Moreover, most states are not in a position to rethink completely the ways in which they assess students in science, but are more likely to view the process of change and improvement as ongoing. While the report underscores the importance of considering the assessment system as a whole, states might begin by targeting their areas of greatest need and using some of the ideas contained in the report to do so.

For each of the major topics addressed, the committee presents a set of questions that states can use to review elements of their systems for science education and assessment and consider aspects they may want to change. The committee's overarching recommendation to states is that they think carefully about the issues raised by these questions and consider the extent to which their assessment system attends to them.

2

A Systems Approach to Assessment

Although the science assessment that is put in place by states specifically to meet the No Child Left Behind (NCLB) requirements will constitute but a small fraction of all of the science assessment that is conducted in schools and classrooms across a state, it will exert a powerful effect on all aspects of science education. The committee concludes that carefully considering the potential nature of this effect up front, as NCLB assessment strategies are being developed, would help states meet the requirements of the law and, at the same time, lessen the unintended and possibly undesired effects on students' science education. Thus, the committee recommends that states take a systems approach and consider the design of science assessment in its context as part of the larger education system, not as an entity that operates in isolation.

This chapter begins with a discussion of what a system is and what it means to take a systems approach to assessment. It then describes the reasoning that underlies the committee's conclusion that states should meet NCLB requirements by developing a system of assessment that incorporates multiple measures and a range of assessment strategies. We then discuss the importance of coherence in the science education system and, within it, in the science assessment system. The chapter concludes with summaries of some possible configurations for assessment systems to meet NCLB requirements.

CHARACTERISTICS OF SYSTEMS

The term "system" is used frequently in discussions of education; people speak of educational systems, instructional systems, assessment systems, and others, but it is often unclear what they actually mean by the term. In recommending that states take a systems approach to science assessment, the committee means that assessment must be understood in terms of the ways it works within the education system and the ways in which the parts of the assessment system interact.

Systems have several key characteristics:

- Systems are organized around a specific goal;
- Systems are composed of subsystems, or parts, that each serve their own purposes but also interact with other parts in ways that help the larger system to function as intended;
- The subsystems that comprise the whole must work well *both* independently and together for the system to function as intended;
- The parts working together can perform functions that individual components cannot perform on their own; and
- A missing or poorly operating part may cause a system to function poorly, or not at all.

Systems and subsystems interact so that changes in one element will necessarily lead to changes in others. Systems must work to strike a balance between stability and change, and they need to have well-developed feedback loops to keep the system from over- or underreacting to changes in a single element. Feedback loops occur whenever part of an output of some system is connected back to one of its inputs. For example, when teachers identify difficulties students are having with a concept and adjust their instructional strategies in response, which in turn causes students to approach the concept in a different way, a feedback loop has worked effectively. As we will discuss in Chapter 8, evaluation and monitoring—which are essentially assessment of the assessment system—provide another source of feedback that can shape the ways in which the assessment system functions within the education system.

THE SCIENCE EDUCATION SYSTEM

The goal of a science education system is to provide all students with the opportunity to acquire the knowledge, understanding, and skills that they will need to become scientifically literate adults (science literacy is discussed further in Chapter 3). In a standards-based education system, the state goals are articulated in the standards. Thus, well-conceived standards are key if the science education system is to achieve its goals and we discuss the nature of high-quality standards in Chapter 4.

The science education system is part of a larger system of K–12 education and is, itself, comprised of multiple interacting systems. These other systems include science curriculum, which describes what students will be taught; science instruction, which specifies the conditions under which learning should take place; and

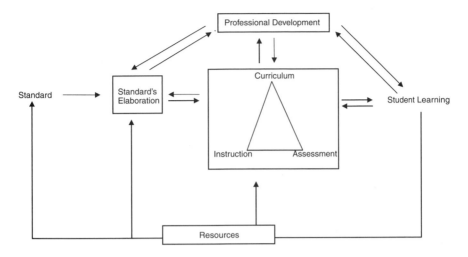

FIGURE 2-1 Conceptual scheme of a science education system.

teacher preparation and professional development, which are critical for the proper functioning of many other elements. Each of these systems is also subject to other influences—as for example when teacher preparation policies are influenced by professional societies, accrediting agencies, institutions of higher education, and governmental agencies or when legislators pass laws to influence what is taught in the schools. The committee's conception of a science education system is illustrated in Figure 2-1.

An additional source of complexity is that science education systems function at multiple levels—classroom, school, school district, state, and national levels. Moreover, because comparisons among educational priorities and achievement results around the world are often sought, international influences also affect science education. Public reactions to results from international comparisons of educational achievement, such as the Third International Mathematics and Science Study or the Programme for International Student Assessment highlight the influence of the international community on science education in the United States.[1]

---

[1]The committee commissioned a paper from Dylan Wiliam, Educational Testing Service, and Paul Black, Kings College, England, to explore the nature of science education in other countries and its effects on science assessment and achievement. The paper, "International Approaches to Science Assessment," is available at http://www7.nationalacademies.org/bota/Test_Design_K-12_Science.html.

A science education system is thus responsive to a variety of influences—some that emanate from the top down, and others that work from the bottom up. States and school districts generally exert considerable influence over science curricula, while classroom teachers have more latitude in instruction. The federal govenment and states tend to determine policies on assessment for program evaluation and accountability, while teachers have greater influence over assessment for learning. Thus for the education system to maintain proper balance, adjustments must continually be made among curriculum, instruction, and assessment not only horizontally, within the same level (such as within school districts), but also vertically, through all levels of the system. For example, a change in state standards would require adjustments in assessment and instruction at the classroom, school, and school district levels.

Coherence in the Science Education System

A successful system of standards-based science education is coherent in a variety of ways. It is *horizontally coherent* in the sense that curriculum, instruction, and assessment are all aligned with the standards, target the same goals for learning, and work together to support students' developing science literacy. It is *vertically coherent* in the sense that there is a shared understanding at all levels of the system (classroom, school, school district, and state) of the goals for science education that underlie the standards, as well as consensus about the purposes and uses of assessment. The system is also *developmentally coherent*, in the sense that it takes into account what is known about how students' science understanding develops over time and the scientific content knowledge, abilities, and understanding that are needed for learning to progress at each stage of the process.

Coherence is necessary in the interrelationship of all the elements of the system. For example, the preparation of beginning teachers and the ongoing professional development of experienced ones should be guided by the same understanding of what is being attempted in the classroom as are the development of curriculum, establishing goals for instruction, and designing assessments. The reporting of assessment results to parents and other stakeholders should reflect these same understandings, as should the evaluations of effectiveness built into all systems. Each student should have an equivalent opportunity to achieve the defined goals, and the allocation of resources should reflect those goals. Each of these issues is addressed in greater detail later in the report, but we mention them here to emphasize that a system of science education and assessment is only as good as the effectiveness—and alignment—of all of its components.

While state standards should be the basis for coherence, and should serve to establish a target for coordination of action within the system, many state standards are so general that they do not provide sufficient guidance about what is expected. Thus, each teacher, student, and assessment developer is left to decide independently what it means to attain a standard[2]—a situation that could lead to curriculum, instruction, and assessment working at cross purposes. As will be discussed in Chapter 4, better specified standards can assist states in achieving coherence among curriculum, instruction, and assessment.

THE SCIENCE ASSESSMENT SYSTEM

Science assessment is a primary feedback mechanism in the science education system. It provides information to support decisions and highlight needed adjustments. Assessment-based information, for example, provides students with feedback on how well they are meeting expectations so they can adjust their learning strategies; provides teachers with feedback on how well students are learning so that they can more appropriately target instruction; provides districts with feedback on the effectiveness of their programs so they can abandon ineffective programs and promulgate effective ones; and provides policy makers with feedback on how well policies are working and where resources might best be targeted so appropriate decisions can be made. Assessment practices also communicate what is important and what is valued in science education and, in this way, exert a powerful influence on all other elements in the science education system.

Collecting data about student achievement is very important to states, and the results must be accurate and valid for the specific purposes for which they will be used (American Educational Research Association, American Psychological Association, and National Council on Measurement in Education, 1999). Researchers in educational measurement have established that, in general, the results from a single assessment cannot provide results to support valid interpretations for a variety of purposes equally well. Given this reality, multiple assessment strategies, or a single assessment consisting of multiple components, are required to supply the assessment-based information needed within the system. Incorporating multiple assessment strategies into a system is important, but a set of strategies does not, as Coladarci et al. (2001)[3] note, necessarily constitute a system any more than a pile of bricks constitutes a house. Just as the science education system must be coherent, the assessment system must be coherent as well.

Coherence in the Science Assessment System

Educators at each level of the education system use a variety of assessment strategies to obtain the information they need, and these strategies can take many

---

[2]Many state standards are written using terms such as "students will understand," "students will know" (see Chapter 4 of this report).

[3]Downloaded on April 15, 2005 at: http://mainegov-images.informe.org/education/g2000/measured.pdf.

forms and can serve both summative and formative purposes. Formative assessment provides diagnostic feedback to teachers and students over the course of instruction and is used to adapt teaching and learning to meet student needs. Formative assessment stands in contrast to summative assessment, which generally takes place after a period of instruction and requires that someone make a judgment about the learning that has occurred.

While any assessment can provide valuable information, the multiple forms of assessment that are used within a district or state are typically designed separately and thus do not cohere. This situation can yield conflicting or incomplete information and send confusing messages about student achievement that are difficult to untangle (National Research Council, 2000a). If discrepancies in achievement are evident, it is difficult to determine whether the tests in question are measuring different aspects of student achievement—and are useful as different indicators of student learning—or whether the discrepancy is an artifact of assessment procedures that are not designed to work together. Gaps in the information provided by the assessment system can lead to inaccurate assumptions about the quality of student learning or the effectiveness of schools and teachers.

For a science assessment system to support the goals of the science education system, it must be coherent within itself and with the larger system of which it is a part. Thus, it must be tightly linked to curriculum and instruction so that all three elements are directed toward the same goals. Moreover, assessment should measure what students are being taught, and what is taught should reflect the goals for student learning articulated in the standards. The assessment system must be characterized by the same three kinds of coherence—horizontal, vertical, and developmental—that are needed in the system as a whole.

In a coherent assessment system, assessment strategies that are designed to answer different kinds of questions, and provide different degrees of specificity, can provide results that complement one another. For example, a classroom assessment designed by a teacher might provide immediate feedback on a student's understanding of a particular concept, while an assessment given throughout the state might address mastery of larger sets of related concepts achieved by all students at a particular grade level. The results might look different in the way they are expressed, but because they would both be linked to the shared goals that underlie the assessment system, they would not cause confusion. In a coherent system, even information that seems contradictory is useful as it may be shedding light on an important aspect of achievement not tapped by other measures.

When there is no system to guide the interpretation of assessment results, data from any one assessment can be taken out of context as justification for action. This may cause the education system to over- or underreact to assessment results in ways that are disruptive to the education system and student learning. For example, if the state indicates that it values the results of a particular test and makes known its plans to base important decisions on the results, school and school district education systems are likely to adjust their efforts to make sure that scores on that test improve. Teachers and administrators may focus on teaching the knowledge and skills that are assessed while deemphasizing those that are not tested. Similarly, students may focus on mastering those things that will lead to better test performance. The result may be to turn a single, narrowly focused assessment into the de facto curriculum. This situation is undesirable, even when the assessment is aligned with the standards because no single assessment, no matter how well designed, can tap into the complexity of knowledge and skills that are necessary for developing students' science understanding. Evidence that teaching to a single test has contributed to the narrowing of curricula in many jurisdictions is discussed in Chapter 9. Box 2-1 outlines some important characteristics of a high-quality science assessment system.

MULTIPLE MEASURES AND A RANGE OF MEASUREMENT APPROACHES

The committee recommends that states take a systems approach to science assessment, by developing a system of assessment that incorporates multiple measures and a range of assessment strategies. Box 2-2 describes some of the possible approaches states could incorporate into their systems. The list is not meant to be exhaustive, and the committee does not specify which of these strategies would be most useful for states to use, rather states must determine which strategies are most likely to produce the information that they need to fully assess students' achievement of the state goals.

NCLB requirements support the committee's position that multiple assessment strategies should be iused (see Box 1-1). While the use of the terms "multiple measures" and "range of measurement approaches" is advocated, these terms can mean different things in different contexts. For example, the term multiple measures is used in the context of high-stakes testing to mean that when important decisions about individuals are to be based on test results, they should not be made on the basis of the results of a single test. The concept of multiple measures has expanded over the years and now also is used to refer to the array of assessment approaches that are included in an assessment program rather than the number or kinds of tests that any one student is asked to take.

The committee recommends that states should incorporate both multiple measures and a variety of measurement approaches in their science assessment systems for two primary reasons, the second of which has several components. *First*, as discussed above, different kinds of information are needed at each level of the education system to support the many decisions that educators and policy makers need to make, for example, assessing the status or level of student achievement for the purposes of monitoring progress in the classroom, evaluating programs at the district level, or providing information for accountability purposes at the state level. No one assessment instrument could reasonably supply, for example, long-term trend data regarding the achievement of population sub-

---

BOX 2-1
Characteristics of a High-Quality Assessment System

The following are characteristics of an assessment system that could provide valid and reliable information to the multiple levels of the education system and support the ongoing development of students' science understanding:

(1) incorporates assessments that are closely aligned to the standards that guide the system, and is structured so that all elements are coherent with the goals, curriculum materials, and instructional strategies of the science education system of which it is a part;

(2) includes a range of measurement approaches and multiple measures of achievement that provide a variety of evidence to support educational decision making at different levels of the system;

(3) contains measures that assess student progress over time rather than relying solely on one-time, large-scale testing opportunities;

(4) is useful in the sense that the assessment results are made accessible and are reported in a timely manner to those who need them;

(5) fits into a larger education system that provides the necessary resources for the development, operation, and continued improvement of both the assessment system and the education system when assessment results indicate improvement is necessary;

(6) provides systematic, ongoing professional development for teachers and others on current science assessment practices, the uses and limitations of assessment results, and processes for developing and using sound assessments; and

(7) is systemically valid—that is, it promotes in the education system desired curricular and instructional changes that result in increased learning and not just improvement in test scores. (NOTE: This concept is described in greater depth by Frederiksen and Collins, 1989.)

---

groups statewide, ongoing feedback to support instruction and learning in the classroom, information about students' mastery of a topic they have just been taught, and comparative data that could be used to evaluate a new instructional strategy—yet these are only a few of the types of information needed within the system.

NCLB requires that assessment-based information be used for multiple purposes. Explicitly, it is to be used both to hold schools and districts accountable for student achievement and to provide interpretive, descriptive, and diagnostic information that can be used by parents, teachers, and principals to understand and address individual students' specific academic needs. Tests intended to serve diagnostic functions for individuals are likely to include kinds of items and tasks different from those tests designed to monitor a system's progress toward system goals (Millman and Greene, 1993). Thus, while both individual and group-level information may be needed to achieve the overarching goals of NCLB, it is not

BOX 2-2
Assessment Strategies: Examples

Observations: Watching work in progress shows student attitudes, communication, and process skills.

Written tests: Tests can show the extent of students' scientific knowledge and ability to apply it.

Questioning: Questioning can check the depth of student understanding, shown in other assessments, and show science attitudes. Open questions can show ability to apply knowledge to new situations.

Research projects: Students working on projects can show planning, organizing, and investigative skills. Project products can show analyzing, interpreting, and communication skills.

Presentations: Oral or written presentations allow students to show their ability to communicate scientifically and their understanding and application of scientific knowledge.

Practical investigations: In practical activities, students show investigation, research, prediction, and manipulative skills. Reports can show skill in communication and drawing conclusions.

Fieldwork: Fieldwork allows students to show planning, investigating, and data-collection skills and the application of their scientific knowledge.

Practical tests: Practical tests can provide information on students' process skills and their ability to apply their scientific knowledge.

Self-assessments: Students reflect on their learning, listing what they know and their concerns.

Peer assessments: Peer assessments can show students' ability to communicate to an audience.

Modeling/simulations: Modeling activities allow students to clarify and show the depth of their understanding and to communicate scientifically.

Creative writing: Creative writing can show students' depth of understanding, application of scientific knowledge, and communication skills.

Student portfolios: Samples of work selected by students show the range of their understanding and their progress over time.

Student profiles: Samples of student work annotated with teacher comments on outcomes demonstrated can show progress over time.

Problem solving: Problem solving activities can show students' investigating and analyzing skills and ability to apply scientific knowledge.

Bundling activities: Collecting, analyzing and organizing activities can assist student understanding and show process skills.

Concept mapping: Identifying and linking key words can show students' level of understanding of a topic.

Drawing: Drawing and labeling can show students' depth of understanding and communication skills.

SOURCE: Adapted from *Science Assessment and Reporting Support Materials*, 1997, Department of Education, Victoria. Available: http://www.eduweb.vic.gov.au/curriculumatwork/science/sc_assess.htm.

likely that a single assessment, consisting of a single component, could provide this information and meet professional technical standards for validity and fairness for each purpose for which the results will be used.

The *second* reason is that, as discussed in Chapter 3, science achievement is dependent on students' developing a broad and diverse set of knowledge and skills that cannot be adequately assessed with a single assessment or a single type of assessment strategy. Indeed, some critical aspects of science, such as the ability to conduct a sustained scientific investigation, cannot be tested using traditional paper-and-pencil tests (Quellmalz and Haertel, 2004; Champagne, Kouba, and Hurley, 2000; Duschl, 2003). Furthermore, learning science requires different kinds of knowledge and applications of knowledge. A growing body of evidence indicates that some types of measurement approaches may be better suited than others for tapping into these different aspects of knowing. For example, creating multiple-choice items that are indicators of the reasoning that students use in arriving at their answers can be very difficult, while this aspect of learning may be measured more easily using other formats.

Another concern that is raised by the complexity of the domain of science is related to the importance of assessment for signaling to teachers, students, and the public what is valued in science and what should be the focus of teaching and learning. A single assessment, no matter how well designed, cannot capture the breadth and depth of the science that is included in most state standards. Similarly, it would be difficult for a single assessment to be fully aligned with states' content and performance standards, as is required by NCLB. There is also some suggestion that a single state standard may be too complicated to assess with a single assessment strategy.

Some states, such as Maryland, California, and Kentucky, tried to develop assessment systems that are more fully aligned with their goals for student learning than previous assessments. All three used a matrix sample design in which all students take the test, but each student is only tested on a small subset of all of the items. This allows a larger sample of the instructional program to be assessed, which helps states both to align the assessment with the full breadth and depth of their standards and to discourage narrowing of the science curriculum. These states also included multiple measurement strategies, such as performance tasks and student collaborative work into the system. However, we note that state programs such as these that have instituted this design have been forced, by public pressure for individual scores, to abandon these programs. For a similar reason a model that only included a matrix-sample test could not, by itself, be used by a state to meet NCLB requirements which require the reporting of individual results that are diagnostic, descriptive, and interpretive.

Finally, multiple measures are needed to provide a complete and accurate picture of students' science achievement. Any one test, task, or assessment situation is an imperfect measure of what students understand and can do. Including different types of measures in the system also can provide opportunities for different types of learners to demonstrate their achievement. In addition, multiple measures directed at the same standard can paint a richer picture of student achievement and can tap into the complexity of each science standard more fully.

THE NEED FOR AN ASSESSMENT SYSTEM
TO MEET NCLB REQUIREMENTS

The committee concludes that meeting NCLB requirements will necessitate that states develop either one test with multiple components or a set of assessment strategies that collectively can provide assessment-based information. The components necessarily will vary according to state priorities and goals. For example, some states may choose to develop a single hybrid test in which students take both an individual core assessment and also participate in large-scale assessment with a matrix sample design that provides information about groups of students. Other states may choose to combine standardized classroom assessment with a large-scale assessment with a matrix sample design. Still others may decide not to develop a statewide test at all and may opt instead for one of many local, district, or mixed models of assessment that combine local, district, and state assessments.

Some states may decide to meet NCLB requirements by allowing districts to develop their own content standards and assessments. In this model, districts adopt or develop challenging academic content standards, develop or use existing assessments that are aligned to these standards, and set achievement standards. Other states may choose to use a mixed approach by creating mechanisms whereby the state and school district work together to create and implement assessment that fills in the information that is lacking in the state test.

The specific components of a science assessment system will vary for many reasons, including available resources, political influences, the purposes for which the system is being created, and the needs of the audiences that will use the results.

FOUR SAMPLE ASSESSMENT SYSTEM DESIGNS

Recognizing that no one conception of an assessment system would fit every state, the committee commissioned four different groups of science educators and researchers to develop the outlines of assessment systems that would not only meet the criteria laid out in NCLB, but also meet a variety of other criteria. These designs are just a few of the many possible configurations that states could adopt. The charge to these design teams is included in Appendix B. For consistency, each team was instructed to use the *National Science Education Standards* (*NSES*) as the basis for its model, though the committee recognizes that state standards are designed to meet somewhat different goals than those that guided the development of the *NSES*. Appendix B provides lists of the participants in these design teams. We summarize here their key findings.

Instructionally Supportive Accountability Tests

One of the four teams was asked to develop a system with a focus on the application of the 2001 recommendations of the Commission on Instructionally Supportive Assessments. That commission determined that a significant problem with most high-stakes tests is that they are expected to provide information on student mastery of exhaustive science standards—an expectation that is unreasonable and will lead to a variety of serious deficiencies in the assessment. In brief, the commission advocated that tests:

- Measure students' mastery of only a modest number of extraordinarily important curricular aims,
- Describe what was to be assessed in language that is entirely accessible to teachers, and
- Report results for every assessed curricular aim.

The design team chose to apply these three principles just in the context of the *NSES* standards for science-as-inquiry in physical science, which could serve as an example for the way it might be done for an entire set of science standards. With guidance from educators, physicists, and chemists, the team developed a set of strategies for implementing the commission's recommendations. Their strategies were based on the assumption that states would use a 90- to 100-minute assessment once in each grade band to meet the NCLB requirements.

The team found that it could winnow the curricular aims in the *NSES* related to physical science considerably, and it organized them in a matrix of cognitive skills (such as identifying questions, designing and conducting an investigation, etc.) and significant concepts (such as forces and motion, forms of energy and energy transfer, etc.). The team recognized that some of the elements on the matrix would overlap with those for other science disciplines, such as life sciences, which would help streamline the ultimate results. Each cell in the matrix would include examples of test items or other assessment tactics that could measure the concepts and skills well, in addition to suggested instructional strategies.

While the interrelationships in the matrix helped the team reduce the total number of critical concepts, they were not able to winnow the set of critical concepts down to a number that could be assessed with reasonable accuracy using an annual test; since they were addressing only one aspect of one scientific discipline, a strategy for assessing the "genuinely irreducible" number of key concepts was needed.

The team's solution was to recommend that the key concepts be rotated on an unpredictable basis, so that each would be eligible for inclusion on the assessment in any given year, though no single assessment would include all of them. In this way, teachers would continue to view all of them as important. The team recognized, however, that student progress toward mastery of the crucial concepts should be monitored in other ways as well, and included optional classroom assessments of key concepts and skills, perhaps standardized instruments developed at the state level, in their model.

Other characteristics of the model included an emphasis on the assessment of concepts over skills, a reliance on multiple-choice items supplemented by a small proportion of constructed-response items, and the incorporation of targeted professional development designed to assist teachers in gaining optimal instructional insights from the assessments.

A Classroom-Based Assessment System for Science

Another design team was asked to develop a strategy for building a coherent, instructionally useful, teacher-led assessment program that would meet the NCLB requirements. Their principal goal was that assessment should have the effect of informing instruction and improving student achievement. The team took as its starting point the Nebraska STARS assessment system, which uses classroom-based assessments for accountability purposes. The team identified professional development as the critical component in the system, with the following specific goals:

- Teachers must understand the state content standards and incorporate them into their work,
- Teachers must be able to develop instruments to gather information about their students' performance relative to the standards at the classroom level, and
- Teachers' reports of their students' achievement can be collected and used in meeting NCLB's accountability requirements.

The model includes criterion-referenced assessments administered in the classroom and developed by teachers, with guidance provided through peer groups and other supports. These assessments, while embedded in regular classroom activities, would yield classifications of students into at least the three categories required by NCLB: basic, proficient, and advanced. Because the results would be reported in terms of these predetermined performance categories, they could be aggregated across the state, and could be disaggregated by student subgroups. The assessments would also yield diagnostic information about individual students that could be immediately useful to students and teachers, as well as other kinds of information needed by stakeholders at each level of the system.

While the team saw considerable potential benefits to a classroom-based system led by teachers—ranging from the potential for integrating standards, instruction, and assessment to empowerment of teachers, to potential cost savings—they noted challenges as well. Calibrating the expectations for achievement of different districts and teachers is not easily done. Some costs may be reduced, but others—particularly for professional development—will likely be higher. They also acknowledged that this assessment model is not, as they put it, "psychometrically pristine." They noted that in a system where districts and teachers are given considerable freedom to devise assessment strategies on their own, a system for evaluating and documenting the technical quality, and the content validity, of classroom-based assessments is critical to the integrity of the enterprise. Despite these and other challenges, however, the team was convinced that such a system could meet NCLB requirements, and provide significant other benefits as well.

Models for Multilevel State Science Assessment Systems

A third design team was asked to explore two possible means of meeting the NCLB requirements for science: using collaboration among states to minimize the burden of developing new strategies, and using technology in new ways to streamline and improve tasks ranging from developing innovative assessment tasks to scoring and data analysis. The team focused on identifying key ways in which intrastate collaboration and technology could be harnessed, and went on to develop two models that illustrate different ways of implementing the features they identified.

The team described its plan as a multilevel, articulated science assessment system that would build and draw upon banks of items and tasks designed according to common specifications. States that chose to participate would share resources to build the banks and draw from them to build individual or shared state science assessments. The item and task pools would be aligned with separate state standards, yet represent joint efforts to address individual standards identified as high priority. Teachers and professional development teams would share responsibility for the pools and work together both to maintain their quality and utility and to engage in a process of ongoing professional development.

Model 1, the State Coalition for Assessment of Learning Environments Using Technology (SCALE Tech), focuses on collective development of means to measure the full range of challenging science standards, and the use of technology throughout the system. Skills and concepts that are particularly difficult to measure could be targeted using strategies—such as simulations and other advanced technologies, tailored reporting of results, and tasks that call on students to design investigations and do other scientific work—that might seem out of reach to a single state on its own.

Model 2, the Classroom Focused Multi-Level Assessment Model, by contrast, focuses on assessments that are embedded in classroom activities. Again drawing on both collaboration, to spread out resources and costs, and technology, to increase efficiency, this model allows teachers to use assessment flexibly, as a formative tool. The program would offer modules that teachers could adapt to meet their own instructional needs as well as administrators' needs for information to support decision making.

The team provides examples of ways technology can support assessment, and, for both models, presents ways to implement them incrementally, to suit states' individual needs. They stressed as essential elements for success in collaboration: a clear, shared mission that meets the needs of each participating state; realistic expectations of what is to be accomplished; a governing board with decision-making authority; and expert advisors to assist in maintaining quality.

Psychometric and Practical Considerations

The fourth design team was asked to consider the design of a science assessment to meet the requirements of NCLB in the context of psychometric and practical considerations that states are likely to face. This team's job was to think about the choices states would have—and the constraints they would face—in trying to adapt a fairly typical assessment program to the NCLB requirements, while maintaining validity and reliability. The team assumed that the basic elements of the program that could be reconfigured would include content standards, test blueprints, test items, scoring methods, measurement models, scaling and equating procedures, standard-setting methods, and reporting procedures.

After reviewing each of these elements and their implications for the outcome, the team developed a hybrid test design that incorporates a variety of elements in common use. Their aim was to develop a model that would bring simplicity and clarity to a complex domain. While the design calls for innovative items that target significant aspects of science learning, it focuses on the collection of summative information of the kind typically used for accountability, with the proviso that classroom assessments and other tools for collecting formative data would be collected separately.

The design uses a matrix-sampling model similar to that used in the National Assessment of Educational Progress, in which students are given a variety of combinations of test forms so that a broad content domain can be covered. This design also allows for the inclusion of sets of items that can be used to compare performance among schools and districts over time. A version of vertical scaling, in which assessment can be linked by measures of common content across grades, allows for monitoring of growth over time. Moreover, a subset of the test forms could focus on different aspects of the entire domain; as a result, no one test administration would cover the whole domain, but that fact would not be license for teachers or schools to neglect the content not included in any one year.

The team acknowledges that the design is complex, and that it entails demanding statistical analysis procedures, but it believes it successfully balances the need for broad content coverage with the demands for strict comparability that arise when a significant purpose of the testing is accountability.

INTERNATIONAL EXAMPLES

In addition to the models described above, the committee sought insight from approaches to assessment that have been developed in other countries. In a study of the structure and functioning of science assessment systems in seven countries, Wiliam and Black (2004) point to an almost complete absence of pattern in the science assessment systems of the eight countries they investigated. This team reviewed assessment systems in Australia (Queensland), France, Germany, Japan, New Zealand, Sweden, and England—a set that illustrates both important differences from practices in the United States and a wide range of practices in general—in an effort to identify critical design issues.

Wiliam and Black concluded that while there is no one right assessment system for all jurisdictions, nine major issues provide the greatest insight into a particular assessment system, and merit careful consideration as systems are designed. These issues are:

- Which purposes of assessment are emphasized—accountability, certifying individual achievement, or supporting learning.
- The structure of the assessment system, including the articulation between the assessments taken by students at different ages, and the way achievement results are reported.
- The locus of assessment, that is, who creates the assessments, when and where they are administered, and who scores them.
- The extensiveness of assessment, that is, questions of who will be assessed at which times, and on what basis these decisions are made.
- The assessment format, that is, multiple-choice or constructed-response test, portfolios, or other kinds of assessments.
- Scoring models, the way in which results are combined, aggregated, reconciled, and reported.
- Issues of quality, including standards for validity, fairness, and reliability.
- The role of teachers in assessment.
- Contextual issues, that is, the relationship between assessment strategies and beliefs and assumptions about learning, education, the value of numerical data, and other issues.

As the four models and the insights from abroad presented above suggest, views of what is fundamental to an assessment system do not vary dramatically, but the forms they take are more variable. At the same time, the models presented in this and other chapters offer many valuable ideas for states to consider.

QUESTIONS FOR STATES

Having laid out the case for taking a systems approach to assessment, the committee proposes two questions for the states to consider.

Question 2-1: Does the state take a system approach to assessment? Are assessments at various levels of the system (classroom, school district, state) coherent with each other and built around shared goals for science education and the student learning outcomes described in the state standard?

Question 2-2: Does the state have in place mechanisms for maintaining coherence among its standards, assessments, curricula, and instructional practices? For example, does the state have in place a regular cycle for reviewing and revising curriculum materials, instructional practices, and assessments to ensure that they are coherent with each other and with the state science standards, and that they adhere to the principles of learning and teaching outlined in this report? Does the state conduct studies to formally monitor and evaluate the alignment between its standards and assessments?

3

Science Literacy:
Implications for Assessment

Every assessment is designed to measure a construct. Science achievement, Newtonian mechanics, and understanding inquiry are examples of constructs that might be measured by a science assessment. A necessary first step in the development of any assessment is defining the construct that it is intended to measure. In this chapter we discuss the construct of science literacy, which many organizations—the National Research Council (1990, 1996), the National Science Teachers Association (1992), the American Association for the Advancement of Science (1989, 1993), and the National Science Board (1983)—have identified as a goal for K–12 science education. Given this goal, K–12 science assessment should be designed to measure how well and to what degree students are gaining the knowledge, understanding, and skills that are necessary for science literacy.

This chapter discusses three elements of science literacy that are widely represented in state science standards, some of the challenges they pose for assessment design, and ways that research on learning might help states in addressing those challenges.

SCIENCE LITERACY

While the definitions of science literacy that have been proposed by professional societies and others vary in their specifics, three elements are commonly found in most state science standards:

- knowledge of science content,
- understanding science as a way of knowing, and
- understanding and conducting scientific inquiry.

Other aspects of science literacy are also important, but they are not included in this discussion because they are not often mentioned in state science standards or assessments. These include, among other things, the history of science, scientific habits of mind, science in social and personal perspectives, and the nature of the scientific enterprise.

Knowledge of Science Content

A strong foundation of science content knowledge is a necessary component of the ability to think scientifically. The ability to plan a task, to notice patterns, to generate reasonable arguments and explanations, and to draw analogies to other problems—all key elements of science literacy—are dependent on factual knowledge (National Research Council, 1999a).

A review of both state and national standards and benchmarks calls attention to the considerable breadth of content knowledge in the natural sciences that K–12 students are expected to attain. For example, the *National Science Education Standards* (National Research Council, 1996) includes eight dimensions of science content: Inquiry, Physical Science, Biological Science, Earth and Space Science, Unifying Concepts and Processes, Science and Technology, Science in Social and Personal Perspectives, and History and Nature of Science. The authors of the *NSES* indicate that "the standards are a complete set of outcomes for students . . . [and that] the implementation of these standards cannot be successful if only a subset of the content standards is used (such as implementing only the subject matter standards for physical, life, and earth science)" (p.103).

The framework for organizing curriculum put forth in the *Benchmarks for Science Literacy* (American Association for the Advancement of Science (AAAS), 1993) describes 12 topical areas: Nature of Science, Nature of Mathematics, Nature of Technology, The Physical Setting, The Living Environment, The Human Organism, Human Society, The Designed World, The Mathematical World, Historical Perspectives, Common Themes, and Habits of Mind. The authors used five major criteria in determining what should be included as science content in their recommendations. These are utility, social responsibility, intrinsic value of the knowledge, philosophical value, and childhood enrichment (AAAS, 1989).

Although these documents include a considerable body of content knowledge, they also emphasize that students are expected to *understand* science principles and *be able to apply* their science knowledge, not just absorb it. To do this, students cannot learn science as a series of facts, formulas, and procedures disconnected from any context.

Organizing Knowledge

Scientific knowledge has been characterized as hierarchical and highly organized, with many connections and interrelationships among ideas. Scientists do not just mentally store long lists of facts, procedures, formulas, or even connections; rather, they have a mental map of the major concepts within a discipline that guides the way new information is used and assessed. For example, when asked how they would solve various problems, professional physicists used major principles of physics, such as Newton's laws, to classify them and devise solutions. Individuals with less expertise used superficial features, such as isolated memories related to inclined planes or individual formulas, to classify the problems and consider ways to respond (Larkin 1981; Chi, Feltovich, and Glaser, 1981; Chi, Glaser, and Rees, 1982). As Bransford, Brown, and Cocking (NRC, 2000b) have observed, knowing is less the accumulation of facts than the capacity to integrate knowledge, skills, and procedures in responding to new situations and addressing new tasks. Thus, it is important for students to develop a structure for organizing what they learn so that it is accessible when it is needed. One way to help them develop this structure is to organize science instruction in much the same way that expert scientists organize their knowledge—around the organizing principles, or big ideas, of the discipline.

Big ideas are central to a scientific discipline and have broad explanatory scope. They are the source of coherence among the various concepts, theories, principles and explanatory schemes within a discipline. They also provide insight into the development of the field, and provide links between disciplines. Big ideas can be understood in progressively more sophisticated ways as students gain in cognitive abilities and experiences. Big ideas underlie the acquisition and development of concepts central to a discipline and lay the foundation for continual learning.

Organizing information around core principles helps students see similarities and patterns across scientific ideas and disciplines, enabling them to understand that the principles that underpin one scientific discipline also apply to others. For example, the ideas of scale and structure, models, stability and change, systems and interactions, and energy are all applicable in the biological, physical, and earth and space sciences. However, they are generally taught and retaught as separate topics and related only to the discipline under consideration at the time. This approach may hinder students from making important connections that could help them integrate new learning more effectively.

In Chapter 4, we discuss the need for content standards to be organized around big ideas and for the curriculum, instruction, and assessment that are aligned with standards to be organized this way as well.

Context and Access to Knowledge

Research that compares the performance of experts and novices demonstrates that experts are good at knowing which knowledge is relevant to a particular task, but novices are not. Expert knowledge is conditionalized; that is, it is organized and linked to a specification for when it might be useful (Simon, 1980;

Glaser, 1992). Students' knowledge is not. In fact, there is evidence to suggest that students' knowledge is context bound, that is, it is tied to the context of the original learning. Bransford (1979) showed that students' knowledge is so tied to the context of learning that including items on a final examination, with no clue as to the textbook chapter with which they are associated, creates problems for students (even those who answered the same types of questions correctly on unit tests). That is because students do not know what information is relevant for solving them. Experts know when and how to use their knowledge because they have had multiple experiences with applying it across related contexts. To conditionalize their knowledge, students need to have multiple experiences applying the same principle in different contexts. The abilities to apply a principle to an unfamiliar problem, to combine ideas that were originally learned separately, and to use knowledge to construct new products are evidence that robust understanding has been achieved (Hoz, Bowman, and Chacham, 1997; Perkins, 1992). The concept of applying what is learned in one context to others is frequently referred to as transfer (see Mestre, 2005, for a discussion of some contemporary views on this topic).

Helping students develop an understanding of when and how to use what they know is an important key to the development of science literacy. Yet, many science assessments fail to help teachers and students assess the degree to which the student's knowledge is conditionalized and rarely ask students to demonstrate that they know when, where, and how to apply what they know.

Science as a Way of Knowing

Each of the sciences has its own unique way of knowing, but all scientists share certain basic beliefs and attitudes about what they do. They approach their work with the belief that the world is understandable, that scientific ideas are subject to change yet durable over time, and that science involves the collection of verifiable evidence. All scientists ask questions about what happens in the world around them. Scientists share the goal of explaining the phenomena they observe and making predictions about what will happen in the context of their observations. To make these predictions and explanations, scientists develop detailed explanations of how the world works. The hallmark of any scientific theory is that it can explain current and previous observations and helps scientists predict new events. For instance, the theory of plate tectonics provides a detailed explanation of the origin of the ocean basins. It also explains other, related phenomena such as earthquakes and volcanic activity, which allows scientists to make valuable predictions about possible future events.

Scientists create theories through careful, systematic study and observation, and they base their work on the assumption that the world has order and is understandable. Although scientists and philosophers of science agree that there is no one single scientific method, and although different scientific fields use various approaches and methods, empirical verification of theories is a critical aspect of science. Scientists continually test their theories by subjecting them to new empirical challenges. When empirical evidence does not support claims, the underlying theories will change. Science, then, is not about finding absolute truth, but rather about constructing theories that provide better means of predicting and explaining phenomena.

Scientists use data and existing hypotheses, theories, models, and principles to create logical, consistent explanations of what they observe. To be classified as scientific, observations, measurements, explanations, and conclusions must be verifiable by other scientists. Thus, the understandings that result from scientific investigations are modified or changed with new observations and the further testing of ideas. For instance, chemists once thought that atoms were small, indivisible spheres. However, this model of the atom could not explain later findings, made possible through observations of macroscopic phenomena such as spectra. Chemists thus replaced the concept of the indivisible atom with that of an atom that has subcomponents. The replacement of old hypotheses and theories with new ones illustrates the dynamic nature of science.

Assessment of students' understanding of this aspect of science literacy should focus on ascertaining whether students can use their knowledge of science content to reason, make and justify predictions, develop explanations, and revise explanations in light of additional information.

Inquiry

Scientific inquiry is difficult to define and different organizations have taken slightly different approaches in describing it. In general, scientific inquiry can be thought of as the set of skills and approaches that scientists use in conducting their work.[1] Conducting inquiry allows students to experience the ways in which scientists study the world and encourages an understanding of the nature of science and scientific knowledge. Central to inquiry is a view of science as an ongoing cyclical process of constructing and modifying ideas and models through the systematic gathering of evidence, the application of logical argument, and the questioning of assumptions, procedures, and conclusions.

Scientifically literate adults should understand both how scientific evidence is obtained and how it is used to support explanations. Both the *National Science Education Standards* and the *Benchmarks for Science Literacy* recommend that students both *understand* and *develop* the skills related to inquiry, although the

---

[1]Inquiry is also used to refer to the activities of students in classrooms in which they develop knowledge and understanding of scientific ideas, as well as an understanding of how scientists study the world. The *National Science Education Standards* includes inquiry as both a content area and an instructional strategy.

former places more emphasis on students' acquisition of the ability to conduct an inquiry, while the latter emphasizes the importance of students knowing about inquiry (Kouba and Champagne, 2002). Both the *Benchmarks for Science Literacy* and the *National Science Education Standards* suggest that before students graduate from high school they should have the opportunity to conduct a scientific investigation from start to finish, from identifying the question to presenting the results of the investigation and responding to criticism.

The majority of state science content standards include science inquiry as an important aspect of what students should learn. However, state standards (like their national counterparts) vary somewhat in their approaches to inquiry, with some states focusing on developing students' abilities to conduct inquiry, while others focus on developing students' understanding and appreciation for the process of scientific inquiry as practiced by scientists. Still others require that students demonstrate competence in both ways (see Box 3-1). Despite these differences there is general agreement that including inquiry in the science curriculum gives students not only an understanding of what scientists have accomplished but also how they have learned what they know.

The way in which a state's standards describe what students are expected to know and be able to do relative to inquiry is important, as it influences what is

---

BOX 3-1
Illustrative State Standards for Scientific Inquiry

The following state standard emphasizes that students understand and appreciate the nature of inquiry.

Example #1

A student should possess and understand the skills of scientific inquiry.

Example #2

All students will develop problem-solving, decision-making, and inquiry skills, reflected by formulating usable questions and hypotheses, planning experiments, conducting systematic observations, interpreting and analyzing data, drawing conclusions, and communicating results.

Example #3

Students understand the processes of scientific investigation and design, conduct, communicate about, and evaluate such investigations.

SOURCE: Adapted from multiple state standards documents.

taught, what should be expected from teachers and students, and what should be taken as evidence that students have attained the defined goal. Considering the abilities that comprise inquiry, such as observing, controlling variables, hypothesizing, thinking critically, and developing well-reasoned arguments further illustrates its complexity. While there is little question that inquiry should be measured in state science assessments (if it is included in the state content standards), each state will need to link decisions about which elements of inquiry will be measured, and how they will be measured, to their standards.

Assessment developers will need explicit guidance from states on what students are expected to know and be able to do relative to inquiry. Does the state have the goal that graduates will be able to use methods of scientific inquiry to develop new scientific knowledge, or that they will have an understanding of inquiry that enables them to make well-founded decisions about scientific issues that affect their daily lives? A precise understanding of what is meant by science inquiry in a state's standards is a necessary condition for developing tasks to assess it; if a state does not make it explicit, the items and tasks included in the state assessment program will come to define its meaning to teachers and students (Champagne and Kouba, 1996; Gummer and Champagne, 2005).

We note than many abilities associated with inquiry can be assessed using paper-and-pencil test items, including:

- identifying questions that can be answered through scientific investigations;
- developing descriptions, explanations, predictions, and models using evidence;
- thinking critically and logically to link evidence and explanations;
- recognizing and analyzing alternative explanations and models; and
- communicating and defending a scientific argument.

While it is possible for paper-and-pencil tests to provide a snapshot of students' abilities in these areas, these snapshots may miss the mark by not addressing the iterative nature of inquiry and the revisions in thinking that occur as scientific inquiry unfolds. Few large-scale assessments, even performance assessments, probe in detail the fundamental ways that individuals process and use information in tasks that require extended lines of reasoning (Baxter, Elder, and Glaser, 1996; Quellmalz, 1984). Moreover, studies such as the Validities of Science Inquiry Assessments study lend empirical support to claims that many science inquiry standards, such as formulating scientific explanations or communicating scientific understanding, cannot be adequately measured using a multiple-choice format (see Quellmalz and Haertel, 2004).

It is also the case that paper-and-pencil items cannot assess students' ability to conduct a scientific inquiry from beginning to end. This process entails generating a question, designing the approach, running trials, gathering and analyzing the data, writing a report, presenting the results to others, and responding to criticism. The ability to complete this complex task may best be evaluated by teachers or others observing students as they are engaged in sustained investigations (Neill and Medina, 1989; Raizen and Kaser, 1989; Baron, 1990). It is possible, with careful planning, to incorporate these kinds of evaluations into the states' science assessment system. For example, in New York teachers administer a standardized classroom inquiry assessment, score student work using rubrics that include samples of student work, and report scores as part of the state science assessment program.[2] In other states—Connecticut for example—a separate test that is developed by the state is administered in the classroom after the students have engaged in inquiry activities (see Box 3-2).

State assessment systems that include a classroom assessment component, or that are based almost completely on teacher-led assessments (for example, Nebraska), have the advantage of being able to measure the conduct of inquiry in the classroom over time with multiple tasks and opportunities for observing student growth in understanding. Maine and Vermont, two states that have developed multilevel assessment systems, collect information about students' ability to inquire through classroom- and district-level assessment (see web sites).

Assessing students' understanding of inquiry *as it is described in the state standards* is important in itself, and is also critical to alignment. If alignment between a state's science standards and its assessments is to be sustained, as is required both by the No Child Left Behind Act and the principles of standards-based education, inquiry must be assessed. If the state standards require that students be able to conduct an investigation, then building such opportunities into a state science assessment system is important. On the other hand, if the standards require only that students demonstrate an appreciation for the role inquiry plays in the work of scientists, or that students demonstrate an understanding of the nature of inquiry, including opportunities to assess students as they conduct an investigation could be less important. States should look to their standards for guidance on the role inquiry should play in their state science assessment system.

DEVELOPMENTAL NATURE OF SCIENCE LEARNING

While individuals who study learning do not believe that there is a single trajectory that all students follow, they recognize that some scientific ideas and concepts have to be learned so that more sophisticated understandings can be built on them. For example, before students can understand that organisms get energy from oxidizing their food, they must understand that energy can change

---

[2]Information about the New York assessment is available at: http://www.emsc.nysed.gov/ciai/mst.html.

BOX 3-2
Assessing Experimentation

To assess student's ability to use inquiry skills, Connecticut requires students to participate in a hands-on laboratory activity several weeks prior to the written test. This performance task asks students to design and carry out their own experiment to solve a problem and write about their results in an authentic format. Students are not scored on their actual performance on this task at the state level. Rather, teachers are encouraged to score their own students' work and provide students with feedback about their performance. On the written test, students are given follow-up questions that relate directly to the hands-on task. These questions are scored at the state level and become part of the student's score on the science portion of the CAPT.

CAPT Science Performance Task: Soapy Water
Grade 10

Scenario:

Local water treatment plants often remove environmentally harmful impurities, such as soap, from wastewater before returning it to the environment.

One way to remove soap from water is to have it react with other substances. When these reactions occur, a solid called a *precipitate* is sometimes formed. The precipitate can be filtered out of the water.

Student's Task:

The students will design and conduct an experiment to explore the use of several substances in removing soap from water. During this activity they will work with a lab partner (or possibly two partners). The students must keep their own individual lab notes because after they finish, they will work independently to write a lab report about the experiment.

The materials listed below should be provided for each lab group. It may not be necessary for the students to use all of the equipment that is provided. You may use additional materials or equipment if they are available.

Powdered soap	Splash-proof goggles and apron
Table salt	for each student
Epsom salt	4 test tubes
Sugar	Test tube rack
4 paper cups	Test tube brush
8 clear plastic cups	Parafilm (to cover test tubes)
4 white plastic spoons/stirring rods	Marking pencil
Graduated cylinder	5 paper cones
Access to tap water	5 pieces of filter paper
Access to a balance	Ruler
Access to a clock or watch with a	Scissors
second hand	1 beaker
Paper towels for cleanup	Labeling dots

SOAPY WATER

Item 1

This item assess students' understanding of conclusions drawn from scientific investigations and factors that affect their validity. The results of the experiment seem to indicate that soap has been removed from the water by the Epsom salt; however, this conclusion should be questioned. The color of the filtrate and presence of a precipitate do not mean that all of the soap has been removed. The group did not include a control in their experiment for comparison purposes. The groups also could have performed a shake test on the filtrate to see if suds formed, indicating the presence of soap. It is also unclear if important variables that affect the validity of the conclusion have been controlled in the experiment.

CAPT Framework
Experimentation: Draw valid conclusions and discuss their validity.

Item 2

This item assess students' understanding of what constitutes a complete experimental design. In this case, students do not have all of the information they need to replicate the experiment. Students are given some information, such as the substances added to the soapy water, and general procedures that were followed. However, other important information, such as the amount of soap added to the water, the amount of soapy water added to each cup, and the amount of each substance added to the cups, is needed.

CAPT Framework
Experimentation: Design and conduct appropriate experiments.

Item 3

This item assess students' understanding of what makes an appropriate control in an experiment. In Group B's experiment, an appropriate control would have been a cup containing 50 mL of soapy water in which nothing was added. The control should have been filtered and the filtrate shaken, just as with the other samples. The control would improve the experiment because it would serve as a basis of comparison to determine if any of the substances removed soap from the water. The control would show if filtering alone removes soap.

CAPT Framework
Experimentation: Design and conduct appropriate experiments.

Item 4

This item assess students' understanding of what constitutes an appropriate experimental design. Group B's experiment is somewhat better although each experiment has its flaws. Group B specifies the amount of each material used (soapy water, salts, sugar) and uses a shake test as a quantitative measure of soap left in the water. Neither group included a control in their experiment, neither performed multiple trials, and it is not clear if all variables have been controlled in either experiment. (NOTE: Downloaded from http://pals.sri.com/pals/tasks/9-12/Soapy-Water/admin.html. Connecticut is revising its science assessment and may no longer require students to participate in this assessment activity. Information about the new assessment can be found on the Connecticut Department of Education's web site.)

from one form to another. This concept can be represented in the form of *learning progressions*. Learning progressions are descriptions of the successively more sophisticated ways of thinking about an idea that follow one another as students learn.[3]

A learning progression lays out in words and examples what it means to move toward more expert understanding in an area of interest. Ideally, learning progressions should be based on research about how competence develops in the domain; however, for many aspects of science learning the research literature is incomplete. Thus, research findings may need to be supplemented with the experience of expert teachers and others with knowledge of how students learn science. In such cases, basic principles of cognition and learning that can be applied more generally, such as the importance of how scientists organize and retrieve their knowledge in approaching new questions and solving new problems, can be used to develop the learning progressions.

More than one path leads to competence. The pathways that individual students follow depend on many things, including the knowledge and experience that they bring to the task, the quality of the instruction that supports their learning, and the nature of the specific tasks that are part of the experience. Nonetheless, some paths are followed more often than others. Using these typical paths as a foundation for describing learning and the ways in which deeper understanding develops can provide the basis for developing learning progressions. It also can provide clues about the types of assessment tasks that will elicit evidence to support inferences about student achievement at different points along the progression.

Prior Knowledge

Contemporary theories of learning emphasize that learning is a process of constructing understanding that involves ongoing revision and reorganization of current thinking as new knowledge is acquired. Thus, one very important aspect of science knowledge that should be considered is students' prior knowledge. To focus their instruction, teachers need a clear idea of the depth of knowledge, skills, and experiences their students bring to the classroom. Teachers must draw out and work with the prior understandings that students have. To do this, the teacher must actively inquire into students' reasoning, creating tasks and opportunities in which students' thinking can be revealed. Ongoing classroom assessment conducted prior to and during instruction can help teachers develop instructional strategies that link new knowledge to existing knowledge. For example, asking students to describe their reasoning as they tackle tasks is a strategy that provides

---

[3]Learning progressions have been referred to by many different names, including progress variables, learning trajectories, progressions of developmental competence, and profile strands.

insight into their thinking and the ways they are using what they have previously learned. It also provides teachers and students with opportunities to correct any misunderstandings.

The assessment of prior knowledge is most usefully accomplished in the classroom where students can receive timely feedback and further instruction that can help to reconstruct their alternate or naïve conceptions so that learning can proceed. Large-scale state and district tests can also help identify students' alternate conceptions, but because the results of these assessments come too late to assist students in reconstructing their flawed beliefs, they may be more useful for improving future instruction than for helping current students learn.

IMPLICATIONS FOR ASSESSMENT

Practice and Feedback

The domain of science is complex and multifaceted, requiring sustained effort and focused instruction for learning to progress. Students need multiple opportunities to practice what they have learned and to receive timely feedback with which to adjust their learning strategies—to reinforce successful ones and to modify and refine unsuccessful ones (Senge, 1990; Shepard, 2000; Sylvester, 1995). Classroom assessment strategies that provide timely feedback are an important tool for this purpose and should be included in any science assessment system, even when the results are not used as part of the state testing system for accountability purposes.

Because different assessment strategies tap into different aspects of students' knowledge and understanding, students should be provided with multiple opportunities to get feedback. For example, during a unit on cell structure, students might be asked to participate in an oral examination after completing a reading assignment and receive feedback from the teacher on their understanding of key concepts. As part of the same unit, the teacher may use a check sheet during microscope work to assess skills and share the results with the student. Laboratory data records might be evaluated individually as students are working on investigations, and the teacher can provide immediate feedback to students as they work. A short multiple-choice test on identifying and naming cell parts could also be given, graded, and discussed in class. Students could be asked to prepare concept maps illustrating the relationship between cell structure and function, and also be asked to explain their thinking to a small group. The group could give feedback, and each student could perform a self-assessment of the quality of his or her concept map. The class might develop a rubric that will be used to score an essay question comparing prokaryotic and eukaryotic cell structure that is part of a unit test. The results of the unit test would be returned to the student in a timely manner. This variety of measures provides students and teachers with a richer picture of what students know and are able to do in multiple contexts, and provides students with the feedback they need to progress.

Assessing Science Literacy

In a content-rich domain such as science, selecting the specific content to include as part of any one assessment activity is always a challenge. Even teachers cannot assess every aspect of learning that is important, but these decisions should not be made lightly. Assessment and learning are so tightly linked that both students and teachers likely will refine their expectations for student learning only to the outcomes that are assessed. This is particularly true when the results earned on any one test are valued more than the information provided by the others.

If the goal of science education is to develop science literacy, then science assessments, and the standards on which they are based, must be consistent with that goal and must reflect the intellectual and cultural traditions that characterize the practice of contemporary science. Science assessments that reflect what is valued in the domain should include opportunities for students to demonstrate their science literacy by asking them, for example, to read and interpret scientific articles as they might appear in newspapers and the popular press, or to interpret graphs and charts and to use the information to support a claim. Science assessment that reflects the practice of science should focus not on the retention of discrete knowledge of facts or procedures but on assessing students' abilities to use scientific theories to explain phenomena, to make predictions in light of evidence, and to apply their science-related knowledge in approaching new and unfamiliar situations. Assessments designed with these ideas in mind might, for example, ask students to describe, using Newton's law, why seat belts should be used in cars, rather than asking them to state Newton's law of motion. Such an assessment might ask them to explain why veins and arteries have particular properties rather than asking students to list the properties of arteries, or to use what they know to create an artificial artery and to justify why particular features were included in the model or not. In other words, such assessments will focus on assessing students' ability to use what they know—to show evidence of transfer. Box 3-3 contains two questions from an examination given to first-year physics students (Mazur, 1997). The first question requires students to think scientifically and apply what they know about circuits, while the second question requires only that they use a frequently used formula to calculate an answer. Assessment strategies that rely most heavily on questions such as the one in the second example send a message that application is not as important as memorization.

Science assessment should include opportunities for students to demonstrate their reasoning and conceptual understanding; their ability to build and revise logically consistent explanations using theories and evidence; and their ability to justify and explain their answers. Science assessment should be designed so that

BOX 3-3
Memorization Versus Understanding

Below are two assessment questions on DC circuits: one conceptual (top) and one conventional (bottom). The questions were given on a physics examination at Harvard University in 1991. Although the second question required more advanced calcualtions than the first, students performed better on the second question.

1. A series circuit consists of three identical light bulbs connected to a battery as shown here. When the switch S is closed, do the following increase, decrease, or stay the same?

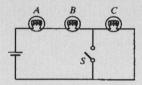

   a. The intensities of bulbs A and B
   b. The intensity of bulb C
   c. The current drawn from the battery
   d. The voltage drop across each bulb
   e. The power dissipated in the circuit

5. For the circuit shown, calculate α the current in the 2-Ω resistor and (b) the potential difference between points P and Q.

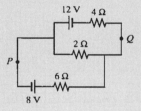

SOURCE: Mazur (1997, p. 5). Reprinted by permission of Pearson Education, Inc., Upper Saddle River, NJ.

students are asked to perform tasks such as using theories, principles, and models to link data to claims; communicating and defending scientific explanations; and critiquing the reasoning in arguments in which fact and opinion are intermingled and the conclusions do not follow logically from the evidence.

To assess students' abilities to use what they have learned about science, states will need to use a variety of assessment approaches including, but not limited to, well-designed multiple-choice questions, open-ended items, performance assessments, and classroom assessment that can provide opportunities for students to demonstrate deeper understanding and complex skills that cannot easily be captured by time-limited tests, regardless of their quality.

An assessment system provides opportunities to gather information about students' understanding and abilities using a variety of sources, both proximate and distal from instruction, and to combine and reconcile results to paint a richer picture of student achievement. In such a system, not only could content knowledge be assessed more completely but it could also be assessed in ways that indicate whether students can apply their knowledge and reasoning to situations similar to those they will encounter outside the classroom, as well as to situations that are similar to how scientists work.

QUESTIONS FOR STATES

In designing a science assessment system that is consistent with the goals of science literacy and the ways in which students develop their understandings and abilities relative to science, states should ask themselves the following questions.

Question 3-1: Does the state's science assessment system target the knowledge, skills, and habits of mind that are necessary for science literacy? For example, does it include items, tasks, or tests that require students to describe, explain, and predict natural phenomena based on scientific principles, laws, and theories; understand articles about science; distinguish questions that can be answered scientifically from those that cannot; evaluate the quality of information on the basis of its source; pose and evaluate arguments based on evidence; and apply conclusions appropriately?

Question 3-2: Does the state's science assessment system reflect current scientific knowledge and understanding? For example, does the state have in place mechanisms to ensure that all of the measures that comprise the assessment system are scientifically accurate?

Question 3-3: Does the state's science assessment system measure students' understanding and ability to apply important scientific content knowledge and scientific practices and processes? For example, does it include a focus on assessing students' understanding of the big ideas of science as opposed to recall of isolated facts, formulas, and procedures?

Question 3-4: Has the state conducted an independent review of its content standards to ensure that they articulate both the skills and the content knowledge students need to achieve science literacy?

Question 3-5: Does the state's science assessment system reflect contemporary understandings of how people learn science?

Question 3-6: Is the state's science assessment system consistent with the nature of scientific inquiry and practice as it is outlined in the state standards? For example, are opportunities built into the assessment system to assess students' abilities to conduct extended scientific investigations, if such abilities are included in the state's science standards?

4

The Centrality of Standards

S tandards are the most important element in the science education system because they make explicit the goals around which the system is organized, thus providing the basis for coherence among the various elements. They guide the development of curriculum, the selection of instructional resources, and the choices of teachers in setting instructional priorities and planning lessons. They are the basis for developing assessments, setting performance levels, and judging student and school performance. Standards are also the reference point for reporting performance to educators and the public and for focusing school improvement efforts. The No Child Left Behind Act (NCLB) requires states to have science standards of high quality, although it says relatively little about what characterizes standards of high quality.

Under NCLB the word "standards" refers to both content standards and achievement standards. NCLB requires states to develop challenging academic standards of both types, and the law describes them as follows (U.S. Department of Education, 2004, p. 1):

> Academic *content* standards must specify what all students are expected to know and be able to do; contain coherent and rigorous content; and encourage the teaching of advanced skills.

> Academic *achievement* standards must be aligned with the State's academic content standards. For each content area, a State's academic achievement standards must include at least two levels of achievement (proficient and advanced) that reflect mastery of the material in the State's academic content standards, and a third level of achievement (basic) to provide information about the progress of lower-achieving students toward mastering the proficient and advanced levels

of achievement. For each achievement level, a State must provide descriptions of the competencies associated with that achievement level and must determine the assessment scores ("cut scores") that differentiate among the achievement levels.

Thus, content standards describe the knowledge and skills students should attain, and achievement levels indicate the adequacy of performance that is expected at different levels of competence.

It is important to note that the role of standards in the NCLB context differs somewhat from the role envisioned for standards by those who developed national standards for science education. The *National Science Education Standards* (*NSES*) and the *Benchmarks for Science Literacy* (American Association for the Advancement of Science, 1993) were written to present "a vision of science education that will make scientific literacy for all a reality in the 21st century" (National Research Council, 1996, p. ix).

To serve as the basis for curriculum materials, instructional strategies, and assessments at the classroom, district, and state levels, state standards must provide richer, more focused, and more detailed descriptions than those contained in either the *NSES* or the benchmarks.[1] The standards contained in these documents—and those in most state standards documents—are written primarily as lists of propositional statements that describe the scientific ideas students should learn. They rarely articulate the knowledge and skills that students need to understand them. To fulfill their role of guiding curriculum, instruction, and assessment, standards need to better describe the knowledge, understandings, and abilities that are necessary to attain the standard, the prerequisite standards on which each standard is built, and the subsequent standards to which each contributes.

This chapter begins with an overview of existing state science content standards. It continues with an examination of key features of high-quality content standards and research-based strategies for organizing and elaborating the standards for practitioners. The chapter concludes with an overview of achievement standards and issues related to setting achievement levels for systems of assessment.

STATE SCIENCE STANDARDS

To obtain an overview of current state science standards, the committee examined samples of science standards from states that had developed them as of January 2004. We also reviewed the work of other organizations, such as the Council of Chief State School Officers, Mid-continent Research for Education

---

[1]Two National Research Council reports explore applications of the *NSES* and provide examples of elaboration: *Classroom Assessment and the National Science Education Standards* (2001a) and *Inquiry and the National Science Education Standards* (2000c).

and Learning, Achieve, Inc., the Fordham Foundation, the American Federation of Teachers, and Editorial Projects in Education, which produces the annual *Quality Counts* reports for *Education Week.*

Variation Among States

In our review, we found that existing state science standards vary widely in organization, format, breadth, and depth. Many standards do not reflect current knowledge of how students learn and develop scientific understanding or the fact that science is a network of mutually supporting ideas and practices that develop cumulatively. Indeed, it is difficult to compare one set of standards to another because they are organized and presented in such different ways. This occurs because, as Archibald (1998, p. 4) notes, "There is no standard language or model for content standards."

State standards vary considerably in terms of features that affect their usefulness for developing curriculum materials, planning instruction, and creating assessments. While all state standards contain recognizable descriptions of academic content, these descriptions differ in important ways. One of the most important differences is in the specific content that states expect students to know. Some state standards focus on declarative and procedural knowledge— that is, knowing scientific facts, formulas, and principles and making accurate measurements and computations. These standards usually include such words as "define," "describe," "identify," or "state." Other standards include schematic or strategic knowledge—that is, posing scientific questions, designing investigations, and developing explanations and arguments. These standards may include such words as "explain," "analyze," "justify," "predict," "compare," and "support."

Another important difference is the scope of the basic content units that are included. Some standards describe topics broadly; others describe content in more specific, small units. Standards also differ in terms of the grade ranges that are used to locate content. Some descriptions are specific to a single grade level; others cover two- or three-year grade spans. States that use the latter approach must, under NCLB, specify grade-level content expectations for every grade in the span. The committee concurs with this requirement, noting that without it there could be a tendency for curriculum and instruction to focus more heavily on topics covered in years in which students would be assessed rather than on the full range of knowledge and skills contained in the standards.

The descriptions of content have many other differences. For example, some state standards establish priorities by identifying selected concepts or topics as of greatest importance, but most states give no guidance about the relative importance of topics, tacitly implying that everything mentioned is of equal importance. Likewise, few states make any attempt to limit the scope of their standards on the basis of an analysis of available instructional time. Some standards documents indicate interconnections among topics and attempt to integrate related components of science, but this is not the norm. Illinois explicitly attends to these interconnections in organizing its standards; state goal 12 reads, "[Students will] understand the fundamental concepts, principles and interconnections of the life, physical and earth/space sciences."[2] Only a few state standards attempt to show how scientific topics are related to material in other disciplines, such as mathematics. New Jersey science standard number 5.3, for example, states: "All students will integrate mathematics as a tool for problem-solving in science, and as a means of expressing and/or modeling scientific theories."[3]

While most state science standards are limited to descriptions of science content, some go further to describe aspects of content that are relevant to teaching and learning. For example, some standards give suggestions regarding lesson structure (how scientific information is organized and presented) or instructional approach (how teachers interact with students about science content). Some standards include helpful information about the structure and transmittal of scientific knowledge, and a few describe desired student attitudes toward science. In addition, some standards contain assessment-related information, such as conditions for student performance (how students demonstrate their scientific understanding). This information is helpful both for teachers and assessment designers. Box 4-1 includes a small portion of the Rhode Island science standards that illustrates this point.

Finally, there are some useful features that the committee found in only a few state standards, such as examples of real-world contexts in which scientific principles apply. Many of these examples are found in the elementary or early middle grades. Delaware and Nevada both provide such contexts in their science standards. The standards of one or two states contain lists of required or expected scientific terminology. For example, Utah's standards include lists of science language that students should understand and use in meeting specific standards. Box 4-2 includes a portion of the Utah state science standards in which guidance is given to teachers on important terminology that students should learn and be able to use. Some states make explicit the connections between the science standards and the curriculum. For example, Florida requires publishers to align textbooks with the state standards. An increasing number of states, including Alaska, Florida, and Indiana, also include in their standards student understanding about the history of science or the role of science in contemporary society.

The one general principle that emerged from the committee's review of state science standards is the importance of clear, thorough, understandable descriptions. For standards to play a central role in assessment and accountability systems, they must communicate clearly to all the stakeholders in the system—

---

[2]See http://www.isbe.state.il.us/ils/science/word/goal12.doc [12/12/04].
[3]See http://www.state.nj.us/njded/cccs/s5_science.htm#53 [12/8/04].

BOX 4-1
Assessment-Related Information
in the Rhode Island Science Standards

Here is an example of a state science standard that includes examples of classroom work and assignments that might be suitable. Performance expectations are suggested, and each standard includes an "embedded assessment" and a summative assessment.

By the end of the eighth grade, all students will know that the sun is a medium-sized star located near the edge of a disk-shaped galaxy (Milky Way) of stars, part of which can be seen as a glowing band of light that spans the sky on a very clear night. The universe contains many billions of galaxies, and each galaxy contains many billions of stars. To the naked eye, even the closest of these galaxies is no more than a dim, fuzzy spot.

Suggested Activity: Visit planetarium, contact NASA for computer program, pictures, etc. Help students locate the Milky Way and prominent galaxies in the night sky.

Embedded Assessment: Look at photographs, identify the differences between a galaxy and a star.

Summative Assessment: Using a diagram of our own galaxy and the approximate position of our solar system, explain the phenomenon known as the Milky Way.

Theme: Systems

Process: Developing Explanatory Frameworks

NASA Space Grant Program Center located at Brown University (863-2889) has celestial maps and other resources available for teachers.

SOURCE: http://ridoe.net/standards/frameworks/science/default.htm.

---

teachers, assessment developers, students, parents, and policy makers—what students are expected to know and be able to do. In other words, they must be elaborated.

Other Evaluations of State Science Standards

Besides conducting our own examination of sample science standards, the committee relied on two comprehensive reviews by other groups that provide a good starting point for thinking about the features of high-quality standards. The reviews were conducted by the American Federation of Teachers (AFT) and the Fordham Foundation; each used its own criteria for making judgments about the quality of standards.[4] The AFT reviewed state content standards in English, mathematics, science, and social studies in 1996 and updated this review in 1999 and 2001 (American Federation of Teachers, 1996, 1999, 2001). The AFT review criteria have evolved from one review to the next, but they typically involve a small number of broad themes that are applicable to all four subject areas. The principal criteria are that standards should define core content, be organized by grade level, provide sufficient detail, and address both content and skills. The AFT reviews also examine curricula, assessments, and accountability systems separately, and some of the evaluative criteria that are applied to these other components are also relevant to standards.

The Fordham Foundation commissioned content experts to review content standards in English, history, geography, mathematics, and science using subject-specific criteria (Finn and Petrilli, 2000). Instead of the few, broad criteria used by the AFT, the Fordham Foundation used 25 detailed criteria, ranging from the structure and organization of the standards to the specific science content and cognitive demand—what, exactly, students were expected to do (Lerner, 1998, 2000). The Fordham review was done from the perspective of a scientist "who has no official connection with K–12 education," whereas the AFT reports were written from the perspective of science educators.

These reviews produced markedly different results. In some cases, the same state received a top grade in one review and a bottom grade in another, according to an *Education Week* story (Olson, 1998). This contradiction points to a divergence of views about what students should know and be able to do, as well as to a divergence of views about how this information should be communicated to educators and the public.

Regardless of the criteria that were used, all the evaluations found considerable variation in quality among state standards. While the reviews showed that the states made progress in improving their standards over time, the most recent evaluations still found room for improvement. In a paper written for the National Education Goals Panel, Archibald (1998) described the state of content standards as one of "startling variety."

Other groups have suggested criteria for developing or reviewing content standards and frameworks (Education Week, 2004; the National Education Goals Panel, 1993; Blank and Pechman, 1995; Pacific Research Institute, 2004, available athttp://www.pacificresearch.org/pub/sab/educat/ac_standards/main.html). Although these efforts provide additional ideas about the features of good standards, they do not lead to any convergence of opinion.

---

[4]The Council for Basic Education also commissioned a review of state standards, but this review focused only on English/language arts and mathematics, not science.

BOX 4-2
Guidance for Teachers on Science Terminology in the
Utah Science Standards

This standard for a first-year biology course provides guidance to teachers on the specific terminology that students need to learn and use to indicate mastery of a set of standards.

Objective 1: Summarize how energy flows through an ecosystem.

a. Arrange components of a food chain according to energy flow.

b. Compare the quantity of energy in the steps of an energy pyramid.

c. Describe strategies used by organisms to balance the energy expended to obtain food to the energy gained from the food (e.g., migration to areas of seasonal abundance, switching type of prey based upon availability, hibernation or dormancy).

d. Compare the relative energy output expended by an organism in obtaining food to the energy gained from the food (e.g., hummingbird energy expended hovering at a flower compared to the amount of energy gained from the nectar, coyote chasing mice to the energy gained from catching one, energy expended in migration of birds to a location with seasonal abundance compared to energy gained by staying in a cold climate with limited food).

e. Research food production in various parts of the world (e.g., industrialized societies' greater use of fossil fuel in food production, human health related to food product).

Objective 2: Explain relationships between matter cycles and organisms.

a. Use diagrams to trace the movement of matter through a cycle (i.e., carbon, oxygen, nitrogen, water) in a variety of biological communities and ecosystems.

b. Explain how water is a limiting factor in various ecosystems.

HIGH-QUALITY SCIENCE STANDARDS

What should effective standards look like? NCLB contains no specific requirements concerning the format in which science standards should be presented, what topics they should emphasize, or how detailed they should be. The law leaves to states the prerogative to develop standards in their own ways and to develop their own consensus views of what students should know and be able to do in science. Because of the central role of standards in both the education and the assessment systems, review and revision of standards documents should be the impetus for substantive discussion among educators, parents, and others, about priorities for science learning.

c. Distinguish between inference and evidence in a newspaper, magazine, journal, or Internet article that addresses an issue related to human impact on cycles of matter in an ecosystem and determine the bias in the article.

d. Evaluate the impact of personal choices in relation to the cycling of matter within an ecosystem (e.g., impact of automobiles on the carbon cycle, impact on landfills of processed and packaged foods).

Objective 3: Describe how interactions among organisms and their environment help shape ecosystems.

a. Categorize relationships among living things according to predator-prey, competition, and symbiosis.

b. Formulate and test a hypothesis specific to the effect of changing one variable upon another in a small ecosystem.

c. Use data to interpret interactions among biotic and abiotic factors (e.g., pH, temperature, precipitation, populations, diversity) within an ecosystem.

d. Investigate an ecosystem using methods of science to gather quantitative and qualitative data that describe the ecosystem in detail.

e. Research and evaluate local and global practices that affect ecosystems.

Science language that students should use:

—predator-prey, symbiosis, competition, ecosystem, carbon cycle, nitrogen cycle,

—oxygen cycle, population, diversity, energy pyramid, consumers, producers,

—limiting factor, competition, decomposers, food chain, biotic, abiotic, community,

—variable, evidence, inference, quantitative, qualitative.

SOURCE: http://www.uen.org/core/core.do?courseNum=3520.

After reviewing the evaluations of the AFT, the Fordham Foundation, and the Council for Basic Education, Archibald (1998, p. 5) proposed that the evaluation of standards needs a "theory of design for content standards that would link purpose, content and organization." While this remains an unrealized goal, the committee suggests that a first step in this direction is to derive a set of guidelines for standards that can help identify the essential features that standards should possess. It would be very inefficient for each state to develop such a theory of design on its own. Education policy and research organizations could assist states by bringing together experts and state education leaders to develop guidance on the structure of quality science standards. The U.S. Department of Education also might provide some guidance to states, not on the content of their science standards, which they are prohibited by law from doing, but on the nature and characteristics of well-formulated science standards. We note here that this discussion relates primarily to content standards; issues specific to achievement standards are discussed at the end of the chapter.

Content Standards Must Support Accountability Actions

In a standards-based accountability system such as NCLB, content standards are the explicit reference point for action. Rather than serving as loose guides, content standards must be a consistent reference point, as the U.S. Constitution is for the nation's judicial system. State content standards define what students should know and, therefore, what teachers should teach. They also are used for developing assessments and setting achievement targets that will be used to judge student achievement, identifying successful and unsuccessful schools and districts, reporting to the public, triggering interventions (including reorganizations and reconstitutions), and issuing sanctions and rewards. In addition, standards are the reference point for developing improvement strategies to enhance curriculum and instruction and to make school and district operations more effective. Although science is not currently included in the NCLB accountability requirements, it may be in the future; moreover, states may use results from science assessments for their own accountability purposes. The committee assumes that because the results from state science assessments will be publicly reported, they will become part of the accountability system, even if the results are not included in calculations of adequate yearly progress.

Key Features of Content Standards

The committee has compiled a list of characteristics that science content standards should have. Science content should:

- be clear, detailed, and complete;
- be reasonable in scope;
- be rigorously and scientifically correct;
- have a clear conceptual framework;
- be based on sound models of student learning; and
- describe performance expectations and identify proficiency levels.

Each of the characteristics is described below, and examples of current state standards are used to illustrate many of them.[5] We were unable to identify any complete set of state science standards that meets all of the criteria we describe. We did, however, find examples of standards that embody one or more of these

---

[5]State standards are continually being revised, and it may be that exemplars used in this report are no longer part of the identified state's curriculum framework.

features, and we use them to illustrate some key points, although they may fall short in other regards. It was not possible to include examples from all of the state standards that meet a particular criterion, and many examples could be found of other state standards that meet many of the criteria we discuss. Similarly, our including a state's standards in this document does not constitute an endorsement by the committee of that state's standards as a whole.

Clear, Detailed, and Complete

To serve as the basis for curriculum development, the selection of instructional resources, and related activities, science standards must describe the desired outcomes of instruction in clear, detailed, and complete terms. Clarity is important because curriculum developers, textbook and materials selection committees, and others need to develop a shared understanding of the outcomes their efforts are designed to promote. If the standards are incomplete—for example, if they omit important aspects of science—the curriculum will contain similar gaps. We do not suggest that, to be complete, standards should include everything that is known about student learning in this area. That would be both impractical (since it would lead to encyclopedic standards documents) and impossible (since understanding of student science learning is still developing). Rather, we suggest that the standards should reflect careful judgment about which aspects of science students need to learn. One means of paring this very large domain down to a manageable size to serve as targets for instruction and assessment is described by Popham et al. (2004) (see Chapter 2, the instructionally supportive design team model).

However, completeness means more than covering the important science content. It also means providing enough information to communicate a standard well. For example, a complete description of a standard should include as much information as possible about related concepts and principles that are necessary for students to develop an understanding of the standard, prerequisite knowledge that students will need, subsequent knowledge that will build on the standard, expectations for student performance that demonstrates mastery of the standard, and connections to related standards. Sufficient detail is necessary to enable educators to determine whether potential curriculum units and materials promote the goals that the standards are supposed to represent. This is best communicated by concrete examples of student work at all levels of achievement.

In addition, the standards must provide a complete description of the domain of science as a school subject. If standards are incomplete, they will not provide a common reference for all users. One way that standards can be incomplete is by using broad, general, or vague language that leaves interpretation to the individual. This defeats the purpose of having standards. When describing student performance objectives, if standards use precise terms, indicating whether students are expected to know, explain, communicate about, compare, differentiate among, analyze, explore, design, construct, debate, or measure, they are far more useful. California's science standards, although they describe the content to which students should be exposed, do not make clear what it is that students must be able to do to demonstrate mastery of the standards (see Box 4-3). Merely indicating that students will "know" a given topic is not enough.

Science standards must be clearly written so that they are understandable to science educators, parents, and policy makers. The American Federation of Teachers (1996) said standards should use "clear explicit language . . . firmly rooted in the content of the subject area, and . . . detailed enough to provide significant guidance to teachers, curriculum and assessment developers, parents, students

---

BOX 4-3
Lack of Clarity in the California Science Standards

The California standards are specific about content, but the language and the lack of clarification about what it means to "know" make the standards an inadequate guide for curriculum or assessment.

Plate Tectonics and Earth's Structure

1. Plate tectonics accounts for important features of Earth's surface and major geologic events. As a basis for understanding this concept:

   a. *Students know* evidence of plate tectonics is derived from the fit of the continents; the location of earthquakes, volcanoes, and midocean ridges; and the distribution of fossils, rock types, and ancient climatic zones.

   b. *Students know* Earth is composed of several layers: a cold, brittle lithosphere; a hot, convecting mantle; and a dense, metallic core.

   c. *Students know* lithospheric plates the size of continents and oceans move at rates of centimeters per year in response to movements in the mantle.

   d. *Students know* that earthquakes are sudden motions along breaks in the crust called faults and that volcanoes and fissures are locations where magma reaches the surface.

   e. *Students know* major geologic events, such as earthquakes, volcanic eruptions, and mountain building, result from plate motions.

   f. *Students know* how to explain major features of California geology (including mountains, faults, volcanoes) in terms of plate tectonics.

   g. *Students know* how to determine the epicenter of an earthquake and know that the effects of an earthquake on any region vary, depending on the size of the earthquake, the distance of the region from the epicenter, the local geology, and the type of construction in the region.

SOURCE: http://www.human-landscaping.com/BA_collaboratory/standards.html.

and others who will be using them." The Consortium for Policy Research in Education (1993) described this quality as "sufficient precision" to be used for the intended functions.

Reasonable in Scope

The pressure for clarity and completeness has to be balanced against the reality of the school day and year. The consensus-building process that is used to develop standards can result in an unrealistically large document. The tendency to resolve disagreements about priorities by including more things in the standards should be counterbalanced by a realistic appraisal of the limitations dictated by the length of the school day and year. If the standards contain more material than can be covered in a year, administrators and teachers become de facto standard setters by virtue of their choice of textbooks, curriculum materials, and lessons.

Efforts should be made to restrict the scope of standards. Furthermore, since it is difficult to know exactly how much content can be covered in the available time, it is important to indicate priorities among topics to give guidance to teachers and assessment developers who have to make choices.

If the scope of science content has to be limited, it should favor overarching principles and powerful ideas that have explanatory power within and across scientific disciplines—the "big ideas" of science discussed in earlier chapters. Standards developers should not let content area specifics overwhelm broader understandings. An example from the Washington state standards demonstrates a good way to meet this criterion (see Box 4-4).

Rigorous and Scientifically Correct

To support curriculum-related functions, science standards must be rigorous and scientifically correct. Since standards are the reference point that guides other elements of the system, errors and omissions in the standards will be replicated in curricula, instruction, and assessments. Rigor also entails a focus on important scientific understandings rather than trivial facts or formulas in isolation. The standards should reflect the manner in which scientific knowledge is organized, so that curricula can be structured in appropriate ways.

State science content standards should be accurate in describing the nature of science and scientific investigation, and they should be thorough in covering the basic principles in the fields they address. Lerner (1998, p. 3) objects to standards that are mere lists of facts because "lists tend to obscure the profound importance of the theoretical structure of science."

A Clear Conceptual Framework

Standards should embody a clear conceptual framework that shows how scientific knowledge is organized into disciplines, how large principles subsume

BOX 4-4
Thoroughness in Covering Basic Principles in the Washington Science Standards

These standards specify precisely what students should be expected to do to demonstrate mastery of the standards.

EALR 1—Systems: The student knows and applies scientific concepts and principles to understand the properties, structures and changes in physical, earth/space, and living systems.

Component 1.1 Properties: Understand how properties are used to identify, describe, and categorize substances, materials, and objects and how characteristics are used to categorize living things.

GLE	6	7	8	9	10
1.1.3	Understand sound waves, water waves, and light waves, using wave properties including amplitude, wavelength, and speed. Understand wave behaviors including reflection, refraction, transmission, and absorption.			Analyze sound waves, water waves, and light waves, using wave properties including frequency and energy. Understand wave interference.	

Physical Systems

• (6) Describe how sound waves and/or water waves affect the motion of the particles in the substance through which the wave is traveling (e.g., air molecules vibrate back and forth as sound waves move through air).

• (6) Describe the behavior of sound and water waves as the waves are reflected and/or absorbed by a substance.

• (8) Describe how the observed properties of light, sound, and water are related to amplitude, frequency, wavelength, and speed of waves (e.g., color and brightness of light, pitch and volume of sound, height of water waves, light waves are faster than sound waves).

Wave Behavior

• (8) Describe the behavior of light waves when light interacts with transparent, translucent, and opaque substances (e.g., blue objects appear blue in color because the object reflects mostly blue light and absorbs the other colors of light, transparent objects transmit most light through them, lenses refract light).

• (8) Describe the changes in speed and direction as a wave goes from one substance into another.

• (10) Describe the relationship between the wave properties of amplitude and frequency and the energy of a wave (e.g., loud vs. soft sound, high vs. low pitch sound, bright vs. dim light, blue light vs. red light).

• (10) Explain the relationship between a wave's speed and the properties of the substance through which the wave travels (e.g., all sound regardless of loudness and pitch travels at the same speed in the same air, a wave changes speed only when traveling from one substance to another).

• (10) Predict and explain what happens to the pitch of sound and color of light as the wave frequency increases or decreases.

• (10) Compare the properties of light waves, sound waves, and water waves.

• (10) Describe the effects of wave interference (constructive and destructive).

SOURCE: Office of Superintendent of Public Instruction, http://www.k12.wa.us/curriculumInstruct/Science/default.aspx.

smaller concepts, and how facts and observations support scientific theories. The framework also should reflect the way science is understood by students and how their understanding develops over time. In addition, the framework should be coherent—the content should be presented in a logical order; there should be connections between the standards for one year and the next (whether standards are written at every grade level or in grade-level bands); there should be connections among curriculum, instruction, and assessment and the standards; and the progression of content should be developmentally appropriate for the students.

Standards should have a clear internal structure to provide a framework for developing curriculum and organizing instruction, as well as to provide a reference point for reporting student results. Topics should be organized into conceptually coherent units that make sense to stakeholders. Standards also should convey which subscores are meaningful in terms of the content domain. It may be adequate to report a single judgment for all of science, but more detailed information about subtopics or subdomains can shed more light on the developmental trajectory of a student. Subtopic results can show where a student is having difficulty, and they also can reveal patterns of difficulty among individuals or groups of students that point to a need for curricular or instructional improvements. If results are to be used by teachers to improve instruction, their content has to be organized in ways that will be helpful to them.

Sound Models of Student Learning

Effective standards should reflect what is known about how students learn science. For example, content should be organized in the standards to match the way students actually develop scientific understanding. Similarly, it would be a mistake to establish a standard that research had shown was inaccessible to most students of a given age.

To the extent possible, the standards should reflect what is known about how students learn science. For example, standards should clarify the way understanding builds on prior knowledge and experience. Similarly, standards can illustrate the way ideas are applied in multiple contexts as a basis for developing deeper understanding. When appropriate, standards should explicitly mention the kinds of cognitive tools that characterize the work of scientists and the ways in which students learn science. As states begin to elaborate standards for specific audiences, they should think about other learning principles that are particularly relevant for instructional planning, such as the importance of interactions with peers and experts in developing understanding through collaborative work.

Another function of standards is to support instructional planning and the setting of instructional priorities. In a standards-based system, teachers should refer directly to standards documents, as well as to the curriculum and instructional resources, to decide what to teach and how to teach it. Thus, standards become directly relevant to instructional decisions.

Describe Performance Expectations and Identify Proficiency Levels

If content standards are to fulfill their role of supporting assessment development and the setting of achievement standards, they must describe examples of performance expectations for students in clear and specific terms. Moreover, it is helpful if the central standards document suggests the basis on which distinctions between levels of proficiency can be made, even before specific decisions are made about how the achievement standards will be set. An exhaustive description of every performance level for every standard is unrealistic. However, if the developers of content standards have clear beliefs about aspects of scientific knowledge and skills that should be associated with basic, proficient, and advanced performance, they should indicate this as a guideline for the setting of achievement levels.

ELABORATING STANDARDS FOR PRACTITIONERS

To be effective, state science standards need to be more thorough and thoughtful than most are at present. However, that does not mean that science content standards alone would be adequate to serve the needs of teachers, test developers, students, parents, and policy makers. Supplementary material must be developed to help communicate the standards widely and to elaborate on them for practitioners, policy makers, and others. Users of the standards need guidance in applying them, in part because research has not answered every conceivable question; standards will, and should, inevitably leave room for judgment at the school district, school, and classroom levels. Each state will develop its own strategy for elaboration, based on its existing resources, but it is important that the elaboration process be as inclusive as possible, so that all relevant stakeholders become familiar with the standards. It is also important that the supplementary materials be designed to "stretch" the standards to meet the needs of different audiences. A few examples illustrate the type of materials we have in mind.

The state may need to elaborate on the standards to help teachers apply the curriculum and develop instructional plans that link the standards. These materials may contain references to approved curricula, suggested lesson activities, and sources of supplemental lesson materials, and they would certainly contain examples of student work that satisfy the standards. They may also contain information about the prior knowledge and experiences that students need to learn the information embodied in a given standard, sources of difficulty that students commonly encounter with the content, common misconceptions that they hold about the topic, connections between this standard and others in science, and connections between this standard and standards in other disciplines. There is no common label to describe such elaborations, but a good descriptive term might be *standards-based lesson support.* As teachers work with students, particularly as they assess student understanding in class, they will learn more about the prior knowledge and experience students need to master a given standard, the sources of difficulty students have, and relevant misconceptions. This knowledge should be shared with others as part of an ongoing process of elaboration. Ultimately, it should find its way back into revisions of the standards themselves.

For test developers, the state may need to provide a measurement-oriented document that focuses on the content that has high priority for assessment, the manner in which student understanding should be determined, the balance among presentation options, constraints regarding test administration and scoring, and reporting requirements. *Standards-based assessment guidelines* would be a suitable label for such a document. It would contain information on which to build more detailed assessment blueprints or specifications. It also would contain necessary background information required to develop a request for proposals for an assessment contractor.

The committee suggests that states consider, as they elaborate on their standards, a model that can be used not only for organizing and elaborating standards but also as the conceptual framework for assessment. We have described why systems for science education and assessment should be organized around the big ideas of science. These central principles can be introduced early and progressively refined, elaborated, and extended throughout schooling. Organizing standards around these central principles and developing learning progressions make clear what could be taken as evidence at different grade levels that students are developing as expected and building a foundation for future learning.

Organizing standards around big ideas represents a fundamental shift from the more traditional organizational structure that many states now use, in which standards are grouped under discrete topic headings. In reorganizing their standards, states may find that they will need to add to, elaborate on, delete, or revise some standards to better represent the kinds of scientific knowledge and understandings that are the basis for these big ideas. This process is likely to mean a shift in state standards from broad coverage to deep coverage around a relatively small set of foundational concepts that can be progressively refined, elaborated, and extended.

The committee recognizes the challenges inherent in trying to organize standards in this way. It is a time-consuming process that requires the combined expertise of science teachers, scientists, curriculum developers, and experts with knowledge of how children learn in specific domains of science. The strand maps in the *Atlas for Science Literacy* (American Association for the Advancement of Science, 2001) may provide a useful starting place for thinking about state-level learning progressions (Figure 4-1). These maps show how students' understanding of the ideas and skills that lead to literacy in science, mathematics, and technology grow over time. Each map contains explicit connections to ideas represented on other maps, as understanding these connections is a critical part of developing science literacy.

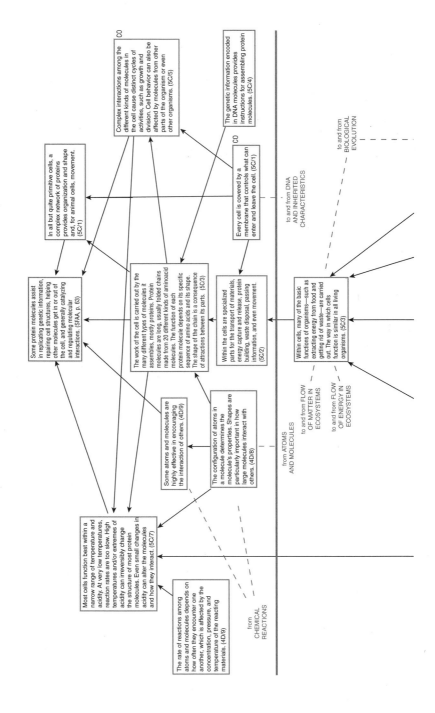

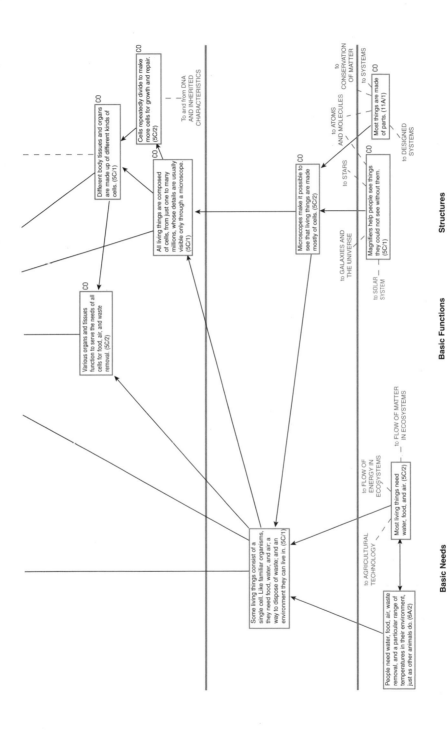

FIGURE 4-1 A strand map for cell functions. SOURCE: LaPointe, Mead, and Phillips (1989). Reprinted by permission of the Educational Testing Service.

ACHIEVEMENT STANDARDS

The term "standards" is often used loosely in a way that does not distinguish between content and achievement standards. However, both kinds of standards are important, and they must work together. We turn now to some issues that relate to the setting and use of achievement standards. Achievement standards are means of defining levels of performance. Because there are a variety of ways to set them, they can take a variety of forms. In some contexts—licensure tests for airline pilots and surgeons, for example—they are used to mark a minimum level of acceptable performance. In other settings, more general descriptions of performance that sort students into achievement levels, such as basic, proficient, and advanced, are used. Achievement standards are important for many reasons:

• They provide teachers with targets for instruction by specifying what, and how much, students must be able to do to demonstrate mastery of the content standards and the achievement level that is called for.

• They provide clear directions to test developers about the kinds of performance situations and tasks that will be used to make judgments about student proficiency.

• They provide a tool for evaluating the alignment between standards and assessments that is more precise than an analysis of the content match between the two.

• They help standard setters by suggesting the basis on which judgments about levels of proficiency should be made.

• They provide a framework for aggregating data drawn from different sources of information to document performance.

• They help to clarify for the public what it means for a student to be classified at a particular level.

Before considering the NCLB requirements for achievement standards, it is useful to note the different ways in which the term "achievement standard" is used. To test developers and psychometricians, an achievement standard is represented by the point on a test score scale that separates one level of achievement from another (a passing score from a failing one, for example). To educators involved in the development of curriculum and instruction, the term can mean a description of what a student knows and can do to demonstrate proficiency on a standard. To others, it can mean examples of student work that illustrate a particular level of performance. Hansche (1998) defines achievement standards (which he refers to as performance standards) as a system that includes performance levels (labels for each level of achievement), performance descriptors (narrative descriptions of performance at each level), exemplars of student work that illustrate the full range of performance at each level of achievement, and cut scores that differentiate among the achievement levels. The key characteristics

---

BOX 4-5
Criteria for Good Performance (Achievement) Standards

Performance standards clearly differentiate among levels. Performance descriptors should be easy to apply to collections of student work. When they apply the descriptors for the performance levels, teachers, parents, and students should clearly see why certain sets of student exemplars or student profiles are assigned to one performance level and not to another.

Performance standards are grounded in student work but not tied to the status quo. The system should reflect the major concepts and accomplishments that are essential for describing each level of performance. Student work that reflects the diverse ways in which various students demonstrate their achievement should be used to inform the descriptions during various stages of development, illustrating where students should be as a result of the educational process rather than where they are now.

Performance standards are built by consensus. The system of standards must be arrived at by the constituency who will use them. It must be built around agreed-upon statements of a range of achievement with regard to student performances. Not only should teachers and students understand the standards, but the "end users," such as colleges and universities, technical schools, and employers, should also understand what performance standards mean for them.

Performance standards are focused on learning. Performance descriptors should provide a clear sense of increased knowledge and sophistication of skills. Descriptors that simply specify "more advanced" at each successive level are not particularly useful. The "more" should be clearly described or defined to show progression of learning. Cut scores on assessments must be based on this learning, and exemplars of student work should illustrate learning at each level.

SOURCE: Hansche (1998). Reprinted by permission of the Council of Chief State School Officers.

---

that systems of achievement standards should have, as conceived by Hansche, are shown in Box 4-5.

Three of the four components of the assessment system—labels, descriptors, and exemplars—should be created before assessments are developed. Bond (2000) argues that test development can be improved if test developers are given copies of the achievement standard descriptors and exemplars of what satisfactory performance looks like before test development begins. Test developers can use the content specifications, the assessment framework, and the performance descriptors to create items that assess all levels of performance.

The cut score—the numerical cutoff marking the divide between levels of performance deemed acceptable for particular purposes—is defined in the context of a particular instrument and is usually developed after the assessment is administered and scored. NCLB requires that states develop science achievement standards by the 2005–2006 school year, but does not require states to set cut scores until after they administer their first science assessments in 2007–2008.

Establishing Achievement Levels

Current methods for setting achievement levels fall into two categories: test-based methods and student-based methods. Test-based methods are those in which judgments are based on close examination of individual items or tasks that help to refine understanding of the performance of students who fall close to the border between two achievement levels. Student-based methods, by contrast, are procedures by which judgments are made about the skills or knowledge (or both) displayed by sample groups of students, generally by teachers who know them well. Methods that combine the test-based and student-based approaches also have been developed (Haertel and Lorie, 2004; Wilson and Draney, 2002). Each is likely to yield somewhat different results and no single method is recognized as the best for all circumstances (Jaeger, 1989).

Variability in Achievement Standards

While the language of standards-based reform has focused on setting high standards and helping all students move toward those levels, definitions of proficiency are not consistent from state to state or, in some cases, from district to district. For example, one study found that definitions of proficiency range from the 70th percentile or higher to as low as the 7th percentile. In other words, in one state, 30 percent of students in a particular grade may be identified as proficient in a subject, while in a neighboring state, 93 percent are identified as proficient. Such stark contrasts are likely to indicate that expectations—and perhaps the purposes of testing—are different in the two states, not that students in one state are vastly more competent in the assessed domain than students in the other. Judgment is a key part of the standard-setting process, and the variability this introduces must be factored into planning. Different groups of human beings will not produce exactly comparable results using the same process, and this source of error variance must be taken into account in the process by which the results are validated (Linn, 2003). In one study in which the standards set by independent but comparable panels of judges were evaluated, the percentages of students identified as failing ranged from 9 to 30 percent on the reading assessment and from 14 to 17 percent on the mathematics assessment (Jaeger, Cole, Irwin, and Pratto, 1980).

The method chosen to set achievement standards will also have an impact on the standards. An early study in which independent samples of teachers set standards using one of four methods showed considerable variability in the levels set (Poggio, Glasnapp, and Eros, 1981). On a 60-item reading test, the percentage of students who would have failed ranged from 2 to 29 percent across the standard-setting methods. Some researchers have suggested that variability can be minimized if multiple methods are used in setting achievement standards and a panel then uses these results to set the final standards.

Establishing the Validity of Achievement Standards

A critical aspect of the standard-setting process is the collection of evidence to support the validity of the standards and the decisions that are made in using them (Kane, 2001). A first step in doing this is to examine the coherence of the standard-setting process—that is, the standard-setting methods should be consistent with the design of the assessment and the model of achievement underlying the assessment program (Kane, 2001). Evidence regarding the soundness of the design and implementation of the standard-setting study is needed; this could include reviews of the procedures used for selecting and training judges and for crafting descriptors for the achievement levels. Researchers advocate that descriptors for the achievement levels be developed before the cut scores are established so that the judges have a clear definition of each of the levels.

Evidence of the extent of internal inconsistency, or variability, in judgments is needed as well. Variability among judges can be examined at the different stages of the standard-setting process. For example, after training, judges can be asked to independently set cut scores in the first round of the process. Each judge can then be provided with information on the cut scores set by other judges; after a group discussion, the judges can be asked to review their own cut scores and make any modifications they deem necessary. The variability of the judges can also be examined after this second round. Judges can be shown impact data (demonstrating the effects of setting cut scores at particular levels, for example) and then be asked to discuss how this affects their chosen cut scores. Afterward they could have another opportunity to make modifications to their cut scores if they wish. The variability can be examined again at this point.

The consistency of the standards set by independent sets of judges representing the same constituencies should also be evaluated. This would require forming independent panels of comparably qualified judges to set standards under the direction of comparable leaders using the same method, procedures, instructions, and materials. The variance in the standards set by the independent panels provides a measure of the error present with panels and standard-setting leaders (Linn, 2003). Supplementary data should also be collected regarding the judges' level of satisfaction with the standard-setting process as well as their degree of confidence in the resulting cut scores. Surveys and interviews can provide these data.

Evidence of external validity is also needed. NCLB requires states to participate in biennial administrations of the state-level National Assessment of Educational Progress (NAEP) in reading and mathematics at grades 4 and 8. In the near future, states will also be able to participate in administrations of NAEP in science, which will allow them to use these results in evaluating the stringency of their achievement standards.

Setting Achievement Standards for a System of Assessments

Although there are many different ways to set achievement standards, further options are needed. The most common methods used to set achievement levels, such as the modified Angoff or bookmark methods, were designed for use on a single test. Although the committee did not evaluate them, we identified several methods for setting achievement standards when multiple measures are used. These methods include the body of work method (Kingston, Kahl, Sweeney, and Bay, 2001); the judgmental policy capturing method (Jaeger, 1995) and the construct mapping method (Wilson and Draney, 2002). All of these methods have been tried with some success on a limited scale; however, this is an area in which research is clearly needed, as states will need help in implementing standard-setting strategies or systems of assessment that include multiple measures of student achievement.

QUESTIONS FOR STATES

In responding to the requirements of NCLB, states will need to review their science standards and the documents that serve to elaborate the standards, and they may need to modify them in significant ways. We urge states to use the principles outlined in this chapter as a guide, and we pose questions that states can use as they consider possible improvements to their science standards.

Question 4-1: Have the state's science standards been elaborated to provide explicit guidance to teachers, curriculum developers, and the state testing contractors about the skills and knowledge that are required?

Question 4-2: Have the state's science standards been reviewed by an independent body to ensure that they are reasonable in scope, accurate, clear, and attainable; reflect the current state of scientific knowledge; focus on ideas of significance; and reflect current understanding of the ways in which students learn science?

Question 4-3: Does the state have in place a regular cycle (preferably no longer than 8 to 10 years) for reviewing and revising its standards, during which time is allowed for development of new standards as needed; implementation of those standards; and then evaluation by a panel of experts to inform the next iteration of review and revision? Has the state set aside resources and developed both long- and short-term strategies for this to occur?

5

Designing Science Assessments

In this report the committee has stressed the importance of considering the assessment system as a whole. However, as was discussed in Chapter 2, the success of a system depends heavily on the nature and quality of the elements that comprise it, in this case, the items, strategies, tasks, situations, or observations that are used to gather evidence of student learning and the methods used to interpret the meaning of students' performance on those measures.

In keeping with the committee's conclusion that science education and assessment should be based on a foundation of how students' understanding of science develops over time with competent instruction, we have taken a developmental approach to science assessment. This approach considers that science learning is not simply a process of acquiring more knowledge and skills, but rather a process of progressing toward greater levels of competence as new knowledge is linked to existing knowledge, and as new understandings build on and replace earlier, naïve conceptions.

This chapter begins with a brief overview of the principal influences on the committee's thinking about assessment. It concludes with a summary of the work of two design teams that used the strategies and tools outlined in this report to develop assessment frameworks around two scientific ideas: atomic-molecular theory and the concepts underlying evolutionary biology and natural selection.

The chapter does not offer a comprehensive examination of test design, nor a how-to manual for building a test; a number of excellent books provide that kind of information (see, for example, Downing and Haladyna, in press; Irvine and Kyllonen, 2002). Rather, the purpose of this chapter is to help those concerned with the design of science assessments to conceptualize the process in ways that may be somewhat different from their current thinking. The committee emphasizes that in reshaping their approaches to assessment design states should, at all times, adhere to the *Standards for Educational and Psychological Testing* (American Educational Research Association, American Psychological Association, and the National Council on Measurement in Education, 1999).

DEVELOPMENTAL APPROACH TO ASSESSMENT

A developmental approach to assessment is the process of monitoring students' progress through an area of learning over time so that decisions can be made about the best ways to facilitate their further learning. It involves knowing what students know now, and what they need to know in order to progress. This approach to assessment uses a learning progression (see Chapter 3), or some other continuum to provide a frame of reference for monitoring students' progress over time.[1] Box 5-1 is an example of a science progress map, a continuum that describes in broad strokes a possible path for the development of science understanding over the course of 13 years of education. It can also be used for tracking and reporting students' progress in ways that are similar to those used by physicians or parents for tracking changes in height and weight over time (see Box 5-2).

Box 5-3 illustrates another conception of a progress map for science learning. The chart that accompanies it describes expectations for student attainment at each level along the continuum in four domains of science subject matter: Earth and Beyond (EB); Energy and Change (EC); Life and Living (LL); and Natural and Processed Materials (NPM). The creators of this learning progression (and the committee) emphasize that any conception of a learning continuum is always hypothetical and should be continuously verified and refined by empirical research and the experiences of master teachers who observe the progress of actual students.

A developmental approach implies the use of multiple sources of information, gathered in a variety of contexts, that can help shed light on student progress over time. These approaches can take a variety of forms ranging from large-scale externally developed and administered tests to informal classroom observations and conversations, or any of the many strategies described throughout this report. Some of the measures could be standardized and thus provide comparable information about student achievement that could be used for accountability purposes; others might only be useful to a student and his or her classroom teacher. A developmental approach provides a framework for thinking about what to assess and when particular constructs might be assessed, and how evi-

---

[1]These may also be referred to as progress variables, progress maps, developmental progress maps, or strands.

BOX 5-1
Science Progress Map

Interprets experimental data involving several variables. Interrelates information represented in text, graphs, figures, diagrams. Makes predictions based on data and observations. Demonstrates a growing understanding of more advanced scientific knowledge and concepts (e.g., calorie chemical change).	Level 5
Demonstrates an understanding of intermediate scientific facts and principles and applies this in designing experiments and interpreting data. Interprets figures and diagrams used to convey scientific information. Infers relationships and draws conclusions by applying facts and principles, especially from the physical sciences.	Level 4
Has a grasp of experimental procedures used in science, such as designing experiments, controlling variables, and using equipment. Identifies the best conclusions drawn from data on a graph and the best explanation for observed phenomena. Understands some concepts in a variety of science content areas, including the Life, Physical, Earth, and Space Sciences.	Level 3
Exhibits a growing knowledge in the Life Sciences, particularly human biological systems, and applies some basic principles from the Physical Sciences, including force. Also displays a beginning understanding of some of the basic methods of reasoning used in science, including classification, and interpretation of statements.	Level 2
Knows some general scientific facts of the type that can be learned from everyday experiences. For example, exhibits some rudimentary knowledge concerning the environment and animals.	Level 1

Increasing Science Achievement →

SOURCE: LaPointe, Mead, and Phillips (1989). Reprinted by permission of the Educational Testing Service.

---

dence of understanding would differ as students gain more content knowledge, higher-order and more complex thinking skills, and greater depth of understanding about the concepts and how they can be applied in a variety of contexts.

For example, kinetic molecular theory is a big idea that does not usually appear in state standards or assessments until high school. However, important concepts that are essential to understanding this theory should develop earlier. Champagne et al. (National Assessment Governing Board, 2004)[2] provide the

---

[2]Available at http://www.nagb.org/release/iss_paper11_22_04.doc.

BOX 5-2
Details for a Progress Map

	Interprets experimental data involving several variables. Interrelates information represented in text, graphs, figures, diagrams. Makes predictions based on data and observations. Demonstrates a growing understanding of more advanced scientific knowledge and concepts (e.g., calorie chemical change).	Level 5
	Demonstrates an understanding of intermediate scientific facts and principles and applies this in designing experiments and interpreting data. Interprets figures and diagrams used to convey scientific information. Infers relationships and draws conclusions by applying facts and principles, especially from the physical sciences.	Level 4
John—June 1993 John—December 1992 John—May 1991	Has a grasp of experimental procedures used in science, such as designing experiments, controlling variables, and using equipment. Identifies the best conclusions drawn from data on a graph and the best explanation for observed phenomena. Understands some concepts in a variety of science content areas, including the Life, Physical, Earth, and Space Sciences.	Level 3
	Exhibits a growing knowledge in the Life Sciences, particularly human biological systems, and applies some basic principles from the Physical Sciences, including force. Also displays a beginning understanding of some of the basic methods of reasoning used in science, including classification, and interpretation of statements.	Level 2
	Knows some general scientific facts of the type that can be learned from everyday experiences. For example, exhibits some rudimentary knowledge concerning the environment and animals.	Level 1

NOTE: This represents a learning progression for science literacy over 13 years of instruction. The arrow on the left indicates increasing expertise. The center of the progression provides a general description of the kinds of understandings and practices that students at each level would demonstrate. To be of use for assessment development, these descriptions must be broken down more specifically.
SOURCE: LaPointe et al. (1989). Reprinted by permission of the Educational Testing Service.

following illustration of how early understandings underpin more sophisticated ways of understanding big ideas.

> Children observe water "disappearing" from a pan being heated on the stove and water droplets "appearing" on the outside of glasses of ice water. They notice the relationships between warm and cold and the behavior of water. They develop models of water, warmth, and cold that they use to make sense of their observations. They reason that the water on the outside of the glass came from inside the glass. But their reasoning is challenged by the observation that droplets don't form on a glass of water that is room temperature. Does the water really disappear? If so, where did the water droplets come from when a cover is put on the pot, and why doesn't the water continue disappearing when the cover is on?

> These observations, models of matter, warmth and cold, are foundations of the sophisticated understandings of kinetic-molecular theory. Water is composed of molecules, they are in motion, and some have sufficient energy to escape from the surface of the water. This model of matter allows us to explain the observation that water evaporates from open containers. Understanding temperature as a measure of the average kinetic energy of the molecules provides a model for explaining why the rate at which water evaporates is temperature dependent. The higher the temperature of water the greater is the rate of evaporation.

This simple description illustrates that at different points along the learning continuum the understandings and skills that need to be addressed through instruction and assessed are fundamentally different.

INFLUENCES ON THE COMMITTEE'S THINKING

The committee drew on a variety of sources in thinking about the design of developmental science assessments, including the work of the design teams described in Chapter 2 and those described below. We also reviewed work conducted by a variety of others interested in this type of assessment (Wiggins and McTighe, 1998; CASEL, 2005; Wilson 2005; Wilson and Sloane 2000; Wilson and Draney 2004), the work of the Australian Council for Educational Research (Masters and Forster, 1996), and the work that guided the creation of the strand maps included in the *Atlas of Science Literacy* (AAAS, 2001).[3]

The Assessment Triangle

Measurement specialists describe assessment as a process of reasoning from evidence—of using a representative performance to infer a wider set of skills or

---

[3]See Figure 4-1.

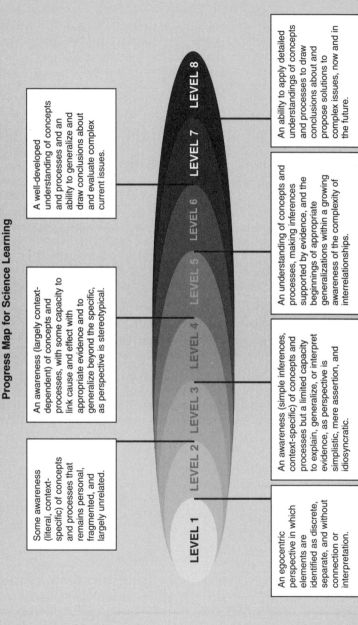

BOX 5-3
Elaborated Progress Map for Energy and Change

Progress Map for Science Learning

An ability to apply detailed understandings of concepts and processes to draw conclusions about and propose solutions to complex issues, now and in the future.

A well-developed understanding of concepts and processes and an ability to generalize and draw conclusions about and evaluate complex current issues.

An understanding of concepts and processes, making inferences supported by evidence, and the beginnings of appropriate generalizations within a growing awareness of the complexity of interrelationships.

An awareness (largely context-dependent) of concepts and processes, with some capacity to link cause and effect with appropriate evidence and to generalize beyond the specific, as perspective is stereotypical.

An awareness (simple inferences, context-specific) of concepts and processes but a limited capacity to explain, generalize, or interpret evidence, as perspective is simplistic, mere assertion, and idiosyncratic.

Some awareness (literal, context-specific) of concepts and processes that remains personal, fragmented, and largely unrelated.

An egocentric perspective in which elements are identified as discrete, separate, and without connection or interpretation.

LEVEL 8 LEVEL 7 LEVEL 6 LEVEL 5 LEVEL 4 LEVEL 3 LEVEL 2 LEVEL 1

Elaborated Framework

Science > Earth and Beyond, Energy and Change, Life and Living, Natural and Processed Materials

	FOUNDATION	LEVEL 1	LEVEL 2	LEVEL 3
Earth and Beyond Students understand how the physical environment on Earth and its position in the universe impact on the way we live.	**EB F** **The student:** Attends and responds to local environmental features.	**EB 1** **The student:** Understands that easily observable environmental features, including the sun and moon, may influence life.	**EB 2** **The student:** Understands how some changes in the observable environment, including the sky, influence life.	**EB 3** **The student:** Understands changes and patterns in different environments and space, and relates them to resource use.
Energy and Change Students understand the scientific concept of energy and explain that energy is vital to our existence and to our quality of life.	**EC F** **The student:** Demonstrates an awareness that energy is present in daily life.	**EC 1** **The student:** Understands that energy is required for different purposes in life.	**EC 2** **The student:** Understands ways that energy is transferred and that people use different types of energy for different purposes.	**EC 3** **The student:** Understands patterns of energy use and some types of energy transfer.
Life and Living Students understand their own biology and that of other living things, and recognize the interdependence of life.	**LL F** **The student:** Recognizes their personal features and communicates basic needs.	**LL 1** **The student:** Understands that people are living things, have features, and change over time.	**LL 2** **The student:** Understands that needs, features, and functions of living things are related and change over time.	**LL 3** **The student:** Understands that living things have features that form systems which determine their interaction with the environment.

continued

Natural and Processed Materials

Students understand that the structure of materials determines their properties and that the processing of raw materials results in new materials with different properties and uses.

	LEVEL 4	LEVEL 5	LEVEL 6	LEVEL 7	LEVEL 8
		NPM F **The student:** Explores and responds to materials and their properties.	**NPM 1** **The student:** Understands that different materials are used in life and that materials can change.	**NPM 2** **The student:** Understands that materials have different uses and different properties and undergo different changes.	**NPM 3** **The student:** Understands that properties, changes, and uses of materials are related.
	EB 4 **The student:** Understands processes that can help explain and predict interactions and changes in physical systems and environments.	**EB 5** **The student:** Understands models and concepts that explain Earth and space systems and that resource use is related to the geological and environmental history of the Earth and universe.	**EB 6** **The student:** Understands how concepts and principles are used to explain geological and environmental change in the Earth and large-scale systems in the universe.	**EB 7** **The student:** Uses concepts and theories in relating molecular and microscopic processes and structures to macroscopic effects within and between Earth and space systems and understands that these systems are dynamic.	**EB 8** **The student:** Uses concepts, models, and theories to understand holistic effects and implications involving cycles of change or equilibrium within Earth and space systems.
	EC 4 **The student:** Understands that energy interacts differently with different substances and that this can affect the	**EC 5** **The student:** Understands models and concepts that are used to explain the transfer and transfor-	**EC 6** **The student:** Understands the principles and concepts used to explain the transfer and transfor-	**EC 7** **The student:** Understands the relationships between components of an energy transfer and	**EC 8** **The student:** Applies conceptual and theoretical frameworks to evaluate relationships between components of

use and transfer of energy.	mation of energy in an energy interaction.	mation of energy that occurs in energy systems.	transformation system and predicts the effects of change.	an energy system and to systems as a whole.
LL 4 **The student:** Understands that systems can interact and that such interactions can lead to change.	**LL 5** **The student:** Understands the models and concepts that are used to explain the processes that connect systems and lead to change.	**LL 6** **The student:** Understands the concepts and principles used to explain the effects of change on systems of living things.	**LL 7** **The student:** Uses concepts and ideas and understands theories in relating structures and life functions to survival within and between systems.	**LL 8** **The student:** Applies their understanding of concepts, models, and theories to interpret holistic systems and the processes involved in the equilibrium and survival of these systems.
NPM 4 **The student:** Understands that properties, changes, and uses of materials are related to their particulate structure.	**NPM 5** **The student:** Understands the models and concepts that are used to explain properties from their microscopic structure.	**NPM 6** **The student:** Understands the concepts and principles used to explain physical and chemical change in systems and families of chemical reactions.	**NPM 7** **The student:** Uses interrelated concepts to explain and predict chemical processes and relationships between materials and families of materials. They use atomic and symbolic concepts in their explanations of macroscopic evidence.	**NPM 8** **The student:** Chooses appropriate theoretical concepts and principles and uses them to conceptualize a framework or holistic understanding in order to explain properties, relationships, and changes to materials.

SOURCE: Western Australia Curriculum Council. Reprinted by permission.

knowledge. The process of collecting evidence to support inferences about what students know is fundamental to all assessments—from classroom quizzes, standardized achievement tests, or computerized tutoring programs, to the conversations students have with their teachers as they work through an experiment (Mislevy, 1996). The NRC's Committee on the Cognitive Foundations of Assessment portrayed this process of reasoning from evidence in the form of what it called the assessment triangle (NRC 2001b, pp. 44–51) (see Figure 5-1).

The triangle rests on cognition, a "theory or set of beliefs about how students represent knowledge and develop competence in a subject domain" (NRC, 2001b, p. 44). In other words, the design of the assessment begins with specific understanding not only of which knowledge and skills are to be assessed but also of how understanding develops in the domain of interest. This element of the triangle links assessment to the findings about learning discussed in Chapter 2. In measurement terminology, the aspects of cognition and learning that are the targets for the assessment are referred to as the construct.

A second corner of the triangle is observation, the kinds of tasks that students would be asked to perform that could yield evidence about what they know and can do. The design and selection of the tasks need to be tightly linked to the specific inferences about student learning that the assessment is meant to support. It is important to note here that although there are a variety of questions that some kinds of assessment could answer, an explicit definition of the questions about which information is needed must play a part in the design of the tasks.

The third corner of the triangle is interpretation, the methods and tools used to reason from the observations that have been collected. The method used for a large-scale standardized test might be a statistical model, while for a classroom

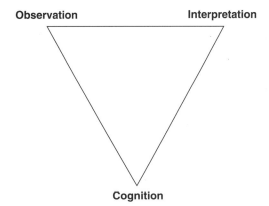

FIGURE 5-1 The assessment triangle.

assessment it could be a less formal, more practical method of drawing conclusions about student understanding based on the teacher's experience. This vertex of the triangle also may be referred to as the measurement model.

The purpose of presenting these three elements in the form of a triangle is to emphasize that they are interrelated. In the context of any assessment, each must make sense in terms of the other two for the assessment to produce sound and meaningful results. For example, the questions that dictate the nature of the tasks students are asked to perform should grow logically from an understanding of the ways learning and understanding develop in the domain being assessed. Interpretation of the evidence produced should, in turn, supply insights into students' progress that match up with those same understandings. Thus, the process of designing an assessment is one in which specific decisions should be considered in light of each of these three elements.

From Concept to Implementation

The assessment triangle is a concept that describes the nature of assessment, but it needs elaboration to be useful for constructing measures. Using the triangle as a foundation, several different researchers have developed processes for assessment development that take into account the logic that underlies the assessment triangle. These approaches can be used to create any type of assessment, from a classroom assessment to a large-scale state testing program. They are included here to illustrate the importance of using a systematic approach to assessment design in which consideration is given from the outset to what is to be measured, what would constitute evidence of student competencies, and how to make sense of the results. A systematic process stands in contrast to what the committee found as a typical strategy for assessment design. These more common approaches tend to focus on the creation of "good items" in isolation from all other important facets of design.

Evidence-Centered Assessment Design

Mislevy and colleagues (see for example, Almond, Steinberg, and Mislevy, 2002; Mislevy, Steinberg, and Almond, 2002; and Steinberg et al., 2003) have developed and used an approach—evidence-centered assessment design (ECD)—for the construction of educational assessment that is based on evidentiary argument. The general form of the argument that underlies ECD (and the assessment triangle discussed above as well as the Wilson construct mapping process discussed below) was outlined by Messick (1994, p. 17):

> A construct-centered approach would begin by asking what complex of knowledge, skills, or other attributes should be assessed, presumably because they are tied to explicit or implicit objectives of instruction or are otherwise valued by

society. Next what behaviors or performances should reveal those constructs, and what tasks or situations should elicit those behaviors? Thus, the nature of the construct guides the selection and construction of relevant tasks as well as the rational development of construct-based scoring criteria and rubrics.

ECD rests on the understanding that the context and purpose for an educational assessment affects the knowledge and skills to be measured, the conditions under which observations will be made, and the nature of the evidence that will be gathered to support the intended inference. Thus, there is recognition that good assessment tasks cannot be developed in isolation, but rather assessment must be designed from the start around the intended inferences, the observations and performances that are needed to support those inferences, the situations that will elicit those performances, and a chain of reasoning that will connect them.

ECD employs a conceptual assessment framework (CAF) that is broken down into multiple pieces (models) and a four-process architecture for assessment delivery systems (see Box 5-4). The CAF serves as a blueprint for assessment design that specifies the knowledge and skills to be measured, the conditions under which observations will be made, and the nature of the evidence that will be gathered to support the intended inferences. Mislevy and colleagues argue that by breaking the specifications into smaller pieces they can be reassembled in differ-

---

BOX 5-4
The Principal Components of the Evidence-Centered Assessment Design Conceptual Assessment Framework and the Four-Process Architecture

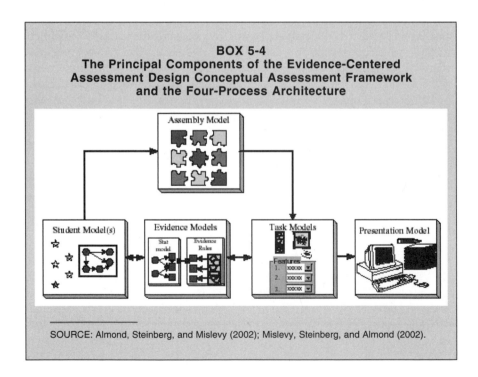

SOURCE: Almond, Steinberg, and Mislevy (2002); Mislevy, Steinberg, and Almond (2002).

ent configurations for different purposes. For example, an assessment that is intended to provide diagnostic information about individual students would need a finer grained student model than would an assessment designed to provide information on how well groups of students are progressing in meeting state standards. ECD principles allow the same tasks to be used for these different purposes (if the task model is written generally enough) but require that the evidence model differ to provide the level of detail that is consistent with the purpose of the assessment.

As discussed throughout this report, assessments are delivered in a variety of ways and ECD provides a generic framework for test delivery that allows assessors to plan for diverse ways of delivering an assessment. The four-process architecture for assessment delivery outlines the processes that the operations of any assessment system must contain in some form or another (see Box 5-4). These processes are selecting the tasks, items, or activities that comprise the assessment (the activity selection process); selecting a means for presenting the tasks to test takers and gathering their responses (the presentation process); scoring the responses to individual items or tasks (response processing); accumulating evidence of student performance across multiple items and tasks to produce assessment (or section) level scores (summary scoring process). ECD relies on specific measurement models that are associated with each task for accomplishing the summary scoring process.

For an example of how the ECD framework was used to create a prototype standards-based assessment, see *An Introduction to the BioMass Project* (Steinberg et al., 2003). The approach to standards-based assessment that is described in this paper moves from statements of standards in a content area, through statements of the claims about students' capabilities the standards imply, to the kinds of evidence one would need to justify those claims, and finally to the development of assessment activities that elicit such evidence (p. 9).

Mislevy has also written about how the ECD approach can be used in a program evaluation context (Mislevy, Wilson, Ercikan, and Chudowsky, 2003). More recently, he and a group of colleagues have been working on a computerized test specification and development system that is based on this approach, called PADI (Principled Assessment Design for Inquiry) (Mislevy and Haertel, 2005).

Construct Modeling Approach

Wilson (2005) also expands on the assessment triangle by proposing another conceptualization—a construct modeling approach—that uses four building blocks to create different assessments that could be used at all levels of an education system (see Figure 5-2). Wilson conceives of the building blocks as a guide to the assessment design process, rather than as a lock-step approach. He is clear that each of the steps might need to be revisited multiple times in the develop-

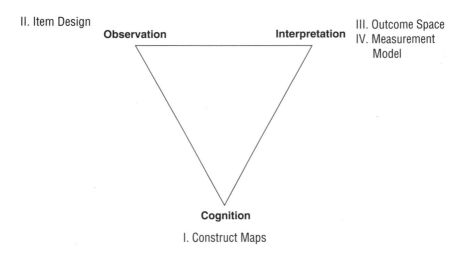

FIGURE 5-2 Assessment building blocks.

ment process in order to refine and revise them in response to feedback. We use these building blocks as a framework for illustrating the assessment design process. The building blocks are:

(1) *Specification of the construct(s)*—the working definitions of what is to be measured.[4]

(2) *Item design*—a description of all of the possible forms of items and tasks that can be used to elicit evidence about student knowledge and understanding embodied in the constructs.

(3) *The outcome space*—a description of the qualitatively different levels of responses to items and tasks (usually in terms of scores) that are associated with different levels of performance (different levels of performance are often illustrated with examples of student work).

(4) *The measurement model*—the basis on which assessors and users associate scores earned on items and tasks with particular levels of performance—that is, the measurement model must relate the scored responses to the construct.

_____

[4]Wilson calls this block "construct maps."

APPLYING THE BUILDING BLOCKS

The committee found that in designing an assessment, the various tasks described by the building blocks would be accomplished differently depending on the purpose of the assessment and who is responsible for its design. For example, in the design of classroom assessment, teachers would most likely be responsible for all aspects of assessment design—from identifying the construct to interpreting the results. However, when a large-scale test is being developed, state personnel would typically identify the constructs to be measured,[5] and professional test contractors might take primary responsibility for item development, scoring, and applying a measurement model—sometimes in collaboration with the state. (Patz, Reckase, and Martineau, 2005, discusses the division of labor in greater detail.)

Specifying the Construct

Key to the development of any assessment, whether it is a classroom assessment embedded in instruction or a large-scale state test that is administered externally, is a clear specification of the construct that is to be measured. The construct can be broad or specific; for example, science literacy is a construct, as is knowledge of two-digit multiplication. Chapter 3 discussed, in the context of assessing inquiry, the difficulty of developing an assessment when constructs are not clearly specified and their meanings not clearly understood.

Any standards-based assessment should begin with the state content standards. However, most standards documents specify constructs using terms such as "knowing" or "understanding." For example, state standards might specify that students will *know* that heat moves in a predictable flow from warmer objects to cooler objects until all objects are at the same temperature, or that students will *understand* interactions between living things and their environment. But, as was discussed in Chapter 4, most state standards do not provide operational definitions of these terms. Thus, a standard that calls for students to "understand" is open to wide interpretation, both about what should be taught and about what would be accepted as evidence that students have met the goal. The committee urges states to follow the suggestions in Chapter 4 for writing standards so that they convey more than abstract constructs.

The committee found that *learning performances*, a term adopted by a number of researchers—Reiser (2002) and Perkins (1998) among others—provide a way of clarifying what is meant by a standard by suggesting connections between the conceptual knowledge in the standards and related abilities and understandings that can be observed and assessed. Learning performances are a way of elabo-

---

[5]In a large-scale testing program the constructs would be specified in the form of a test framework.

BOX 5-5
Scientific Practices That Serve as the Basis
for Learning Performances

Some of the key practices that are enabled by scientific knowledge include the following:

- *Defining and describing.* Defining and describing involves recalling from memory a definition of a concept or principle or describing how one concept relates to other ideas. For example, a student could describe the flow of energy in an ecosystem. Or a student could describe how to use a light probe by telling a fellow student how to use it to measure light reaching a plant.

- *Representing data and interpreting representations.* Representing data involves using tables and graphs to organize and display information both qualitatively and quantitatively. Interpreting representations involves being able to use legends and other information to infer what something stands for or what a particular pattern means. For example, a student could construct a table to show the properties of different materials or a graph that relates changes in object volume to object weight. Conversely, a student could interpret a graph to infer which size object was the heaviest or a straight line with positive slope to mean there was proportionality between variables.

- *Identifying and classifying.* Both identifying and classifying involve applying category knowledge to particular exemplars. In identifying, students may consider only one exemplar (Is this particular object made of wax?) whereas in classifying students are organizing sets of exemplars. For example, they could sort items by whether they are matter or not matter; by whether they are solid, liquid, or gas; or by kind of substance.

- *Measuring.* Measuring is a simple form of mathematical modeling: comparing an item to a standard unit and analyzing a dimension as an iterative sum of units that cover the measurement space.

- *Ordering/comparing along a dimension.* Ordering involves going beyond simple categorization (e.g., heavy vs. light) to conceptualizing a continuous dimension. For example, students could sort samples according to weight, volume, temperature, hardness, or density.

- *Quantifying.* Quantifying involves being able to measure (quantify) important physical magnitudes such as volume, weight, density, and temperature using standard or nonstandard units.

rating on content standards by specifying what students should be able to do when they achieve a standard. For example, learning performances might indicate that students should be able to describe phenomena, use models to explain patterns in data, construct scientific explanations, or test hypotheses. Smith, Wiser, Anderson, Krajcik, and Coppola (2004) outlined a variety of specific skills[6] that

---

[6]Smith et al. (2004) call these "practices."

- *Predicting/inferring.* Predicting/inferring involves using knowledge of a principle or relationship to make an inference about something that has not been directly observed. For example, students can use the principle of conservation of mass to predict what the mass of something should be after evaporation; or they may calculate the weight of an object from knowledge of its volume and the density of a material it is made of.
- *Posing questions.* Students identify and ask questions about phenomena that can be answered through scientific investigations. Young learners will often ask more descriptive questions, but as learners gain experiences and understanding they should ask more relational and cause and effect questions.
- *Designing and conducting investigations.* Designing an investigation includes identifying and specifying what variables need to be manipulated, measured, and controlled; constructing hypotheses that specify the relationship between variables; constructing/developing procedures that allow them to explore their hypotheses; and determining how often the data will be collected and what type of observations will be made. Conducting an investigation includes a range of activities—gathering the equipment, assembling the apparatus, making charts and tables, following through on procedures, and making qualitative or quantitative observations.
- *Constructing evidence-based explanations.* Constructing explanations involves using scientific theories, models, and principles along with evidence to build explanations of phenomena; it also entails ruling out alternative hypotheses.
- *Analyzing and interpreting data.* In analyzing and interpreting data, students make sense of data by answering the questions: "What do the data we collected mean?" "How do these data help me answer my question?" Interpreting and analyzing can include transforming the data by going from a data table to a graph, or by calculating another factor and finding patterns in the data.
- *Evaluating/reflecting/making an argument.* Evaluate data: Do these data support this claim? Are these data reliable? Evaluate measurement: Is the following an example of good or bad measurement? Evaluate a model: Could this model represent a liquid? Revise a model: Given a model for gas, how would one modify it to represent a solid? Compare and evaluate models: How well does a given model account for a phenomenon? Does this model "obey" the "axioms" of the theory?

SOURCE: Smith et al. (2004).

could provide evidence of understanding under specific conditions and provide examples of what evidence of understanding might look like (see Box 5-5).

The following example illustrates how one might elaborate on a standard to create learning performances and identify targets for assessment. Consider the following standard that is adapted from *Benchmarks for Science Literacy* (AAAS, 1993, p. 124) about differential survival: [The student will understand that] *Individual organisms with certain traits are more likely than others to survive and have offspring.* The benchmark clearly refers to one of the central mechanisms of evolution, the concept often called "survival of the fittest." Yet the standard does not indicate which skills and knowledge might be called for in working to attain it. In contrast, Reiser, Krajcik, Moje, and Marx (2003) amplify this single standard as three related learning performances:

• Students *identify and represent mathematically* the variation on a trait in a population.
• Students *hypothesize* the function a trait may serve and *explain* how some variations of the trait are advantageous in the environment.
• Students *predict, using evidence,* how the variation on the trait will affect the likelihood that individuals in the population will survive an environmental stress.

Reiser and his colleagues contend that this elaboration of the standard more clearly specifies the skills and knowledge that students need to attain the standard and therefore better defines the construct to be assessed. For example, by indicating that students are expected to represent variation mathematically, the elaboration suggests the importance of particular mathematical concepts, such as distribution. Without the elaboration, the need for this important aspect may or may not have been inferred by an assessment developer.

Selecting the Tasks

Decisions about the particular assessment strategy to use should not be dictated by the desire to use one particular item type or another, or by untested assumptions about the usefulness of specific item types for tapping specific cognitive skills. Rather, such decisions should be based on the usefulness of the item or task for eliciting evidence about students' understanding of the construct of interest and for shedding light on students' progress along a continuum representing how learning related to the construct might reasonably be expected to develop.

Performance assessment is one approach that offers great potential for assessing complex thinking and reasoning abilities, but multiple-choice items also have their strengths. Although many people recognize that multiple-choice items are an efficient and effective means of determining how well students have acquired basic content knowledge, many do not recognize that they also can be used to measure complex cognitive processes. For example, the Force Concept Inventory (Hestenes, Wells, and Swackhamer, 1992) is an assessment that uses multiple-choice items but taps into higher-level cognitive processes. Conversely, many constructed response items used in large-scale state assessments tap only low level skills, for example by asking students to demonstrate declarative knowledge and recall of facts or to supply one-word answers. Metzenberg (2004) provides examples of this phenomenon drawn from current state science tests.

An item or task is useful if it elicits important evidence of the construct it is intended to measure. Groups of items or series of tasks should be assembled with a view to their collective ability to shed light on the full range of the science content knowledge, understandings, and skills included in the construct as elaborated by the related learning performances.

Creating Items[7] from Learning Performances

When used in a process of backward design, learning performances can guide the development of assessment strategies. Backward design begins with a clear understanding of the construct. It then focuses on what would be compelling evidence or demonstrations of learning (the committee calls these learning performances) and the consideration of what evidence of understanding would look like.

Box 5-6 illustrates the process of backward design by expanding a standard into learning performances and using the learning performances to develop assessment tasks that map back to the standard. For each learning performance, several assessment tasks are provided to illustrate how multiple measures of the same construct can provide a richer and more valid estimation of a student's attainment of the standard. It is possible to imagine that some of these tasks could be used in classroom assessment while others that target the same standard could be included on statewide large-scale assessment. Smith et al. (2004), have illustrated this process more thoroughly in their paper by outlining learning performances for a series of K–8 standards on atomic-molecular theory. Their task sets include multiple-choice and performance items that are suitable for a variety of assessment purposes, from large-scale annual tests to assessments that can be embedded in instruction.

For each assessment task included in Box 5-6, distractors (incorrect responses) that can shed light on students' misconceptions are also shown because distractors can provide information on what is needed for student learning to progress. An item design strategy developed by Briggs, Alonzo, Schwab, and Wilson (2004), which they call Ordered Multiple Choice (OMC), expands on this principle.

A unique feature of OMC items is that they are designed in such a way that each of the possible answer choices is linked to developmental levels of student understanding, facilitating the diagnostic interpretation of student responses. OMC items provide information about the developmental understanding of students that may not be available from traditional multiple-choice items. In addition, they are efficient to administer and to score, thus yielding information that can be quickly and reliably provided to schools, teachers, and students. Briggs et al. (2004) see potential for this approach in creating improved large-scale assessments, but they note that considerable research and development are still needed.

---

[7]Item is used here to refer to any task, condition, or situation that provides information about student understanding or achievement.

BOX 5-6
A Process of Backward Design:
Elaborating Standards Through Learning Performances and Developing Related Assessment Tasks

Standard:
As the result of activities in grades 5–8, all students should develop understanding that substances react chemically in characteristic ways with other substances to form new substances with different characteristic properties (National Research Council, 1996, Content Standard B5-8:1B).[1]

Further clarification of the standard:
Substances have distinct properties and are made of one material throughout. A chemical reaction is a process where new substances are made from old substances. One type of chemical reaction is when two substances are mixed together and they interact to form new substance(s). The properties of the new substance(s) are different from the old substance(s). When scientists talk about "old" substances that interact in the chemical reaction, they call them reactants. When scientists talk about new substances that are produced by the chemical reaction, they call them products. Students differentiate chemical change from other changes, such as phase change, morphological change, etc.

Prior knowledge that students need:
- It is essential that students understand the meaning of properties and that substances have the same properties throughout, no matter from where the sample of the substance is taken.
- Students need to understand the term *substance*.
- Students need to know that a lot of different materials can be made from the same basic materials (this is a grade 3–5 standard).

Possible misconception that students might hold:
- A "new" substance appears because it has been moved from another place (e.g., smoke from wood).
- Matter disappears (e.g., burning, dissolving).
- Chemical reactions occur whenever something changes.
- Phase changes are chemical reactions.
- Mixtures are chemical reactions.
- One substance can be made into any other kind of substance (e.g., straw can be made into gold).

Possible learning performances and associated assessment tasks:
The next learning performance makes use of the skill of identifying. Identifying

---

[1]Understanding this standard requires that students understand a previous standard: As the result of activities in grades 5–8, all students should develop understanding that a substance has characteristic properties, such as density, a boiling point, and solubility, all of which are independent of the amount of the sample. (National Research Council, 1996, Content Standard B 5-8: 1A). This illustrates how new learning builds on previous learning.

involves applying category knowledge to particular exemplars. In identifying, students may consider only one exemplar (Is this particular object made of wax?). Identifying also encompasses the lower range of cognitive performances we want students to accomplish.

Learning performance 1:
Students identify chemical reactions.

Associated Assessment Task #1:
Which of the following is an example of a chemical reaction?
a. tearing a piece of paper
b. cooling a can of soda pop in the refrigerator
c. burning a marshmallow over a fire
d. heating water on a stove

Associated Assessment Task #2:
A class conducted an experiment in which students mixed two colorless liquids. After mixing the liquids, the students noticed bubbles and a gray solid that had formed at the bottom of the container.

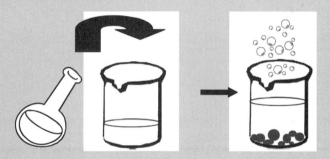

a. What kind of process occurred?
b. Provide evidence supporting how you know this occurred.

Notice Part B goes beyond the learning performance to include justification for one's response.

The next learning performance makes use of the practice of constructing evidence-based explanations. Constructing explanations involves using scientific theories, models, and principles along with evidence to build explanations of phenomena; it might also entail ruling out alternative hypotheses. Developing an evidence-based explanation is a higher order cognitive task.

Learning performance 2:
Students construct a scientific explanation that includes a claim about whether a process is a chemical reaction, evidence in the form of properties of the substances and/or signs of a reaction, and reasoning that a chemical reaction is a process in which substances interact to form new substances so that there are different substances with different properties before compared to after the reaction.

continued

BOX 5-6 Continued

Associated Assessment Task #1:

Carlos takes some measurements of two liquids—butanic acid and butanol. Then he stirs the two liquids together and heats them. After stirring and heating the liquids, they form two separate layers—layer A and layer B. Carlos uses an eye-dropper to get a sample from each layer and takes some measurements of each sample. Here are his results:

Measurements

		Density	Melting Point	Mass	Volume	Solubility in water
Before stirring & heating	Butanic acid	0.96 g/cm³	−7.9 °C	9.78 g	10.18 cm³	Yes
	Butanol	0.81 g/cm³	−89.5 °C	8.22 g	10.15 cm³	Yes
After stirring & heating	Layer A	0.87 g/cm³	−91.5 °C	1.74 g	2.00 cm³	No
	Layer B	1.00 g/cm³	0.0 °C	2.00 g	2.00 cm³	Yes

Write a **scientific explanation** that states whether a chemical reaction occurred when Carlos stirred and heated butanic acid and butanol.

SOURCE: Smith et al. (2004).

Box 5-7 from Briggs et al. (2004) contains a learning progression that identifies common errors. Items that might be used to tap into students' understandings and misconceptions are included. The explanations of answer choices illustrate how assessment tasks can be made more meaningful if distractors shed light on instructional strategies that are needed to reconstruct student misconceptions.

Describing the Outcome Space

As was discussed earlier, assessment is a process of making inferences about what students know based on observations of what they do in response to defined situations. Interpreting student responses to support these inferences requires two things: a scored response and a way to interpret the score. Scoring multiple-choice items requires comparing the selected response to the scoring key to determine if the answer is correct or not. Scoring performance tasks,[8] however, re-

---

[8]The committee uses this term to include any assessment that requires students to generate, rather than select, a response.

quires both judgment and defined criteria on which to base the judgment. We refer to these criteria as a rubric. A rubric includes a description of the dimensions for judging student performance and a scale of values for rating those dimensions. Rubrics are often supplemented with examples of student work at each scale value to further assist in making the judgments. The performance descriptors that are part of the states' achievement standards could be associated with the rubrics that are developed for individual tests or tasks. A discussion of achievement standards is included in Chapter 4.

Box 5-8 is a progress guide or rubric that is used to evaluate students' performance on an assessment of the concept of buoyancy. The guide could be useful to teachers and students because it provides information about both current performance and what would be necessary for students to progress.

Delaware has developed a system for gleaning instructionally relevant information from responses to multiple-choice items. The state uses a two-digit scoring rubric modeled after the scoring rubric used in the performance tasks of the Third International Mathematics and Science Study (TIMSS). The first digit of the score indicates whether the answer is correct, incorrect, or partially correct; the second digit of an incorrect or partially correct response score indicates the nature of the misconception that led to the wrong answer. Educators analyze these misconceptions to understand what is lacking in students' understanding and to shed light on aspects of the curriculum that are not functioning as desired (Box 5-9).

Determining the Measurement Model

Formal measurement models are statistical and psychometric tools that allow interpreters of assessment results to draw meaning from large data sets about student performance and to express the degree of uncertainty that surrounds the conclusions. Measurement models are a particular form of reasoning from evidence that include formal rules for how to integrate a variety of data that may be relevant to a particular inference. There are a variety of measurement models and each model carries both assumptions and inferences that can be drawn when the assumptions are met.

For most of the last century, interpreting test scores was thought of in terms of an assumption that a person's observed score (O) on a test was made up of two components, true score (T) and error (E), i.e., $O = T + E$. From that formulation were derived methods of determining how much error was present, and working backward, how much confidence one could have in the observed score. Reliability is a measure of the proportion of variance of observed score that is attributable to the true score rather than to error. The main portions of the traditional psychometrics of test interpretation, test construction, etc. are built on this basis.

Another commonly used type of measurement model is item response theory (IRT), which, as originally conceived, is appropriate to use in situations where the

BOX 5-7
Ordered Multiple-Choice Items Related to Progress Variable
for Student Understanding of Earth in the Solar System

Level	Description
5 8th grade	Student is able to put the motions of the Earth and Moon into a complete description of motion in the Solar System which explains: • the day/night cycle • the phases of the Moon (including the illumination of the Moon by the Sun) • the seasons
4 5th grade	Student is able to coordinate apparent and actual motion of objects in the sky. Student knows that: • the Earth is both orbiting the Sun and rotating on its axis • the Earth orbits the Sun once per year • the Earth rotates on its axis once per day, causing the day/night cycle and the appearance that the Sun moves across the sky • the Moon orbits the Earth once every 28 days, producing the phases of the Moon COMMON ERROR: Seasons are caused by the changing distance between the Earth and Sun. COMMON ERROR: The phases of the Moon are caused by a shadow of the planets, the Sun, or the Earth falling on the Moon.
3	Student knows that: • the Earth orbits the Sun • the Moon orbits the Earth • the Earth rotates on its axis However, student has not put this knowledge together with an understanding of apparent motion to form explanations and may not recognize that the Earth is both rotating and orbiting simultaneously. COMMON ERROR: It gets dark at night because the Earth goes around the Sun once a day.
2	Student recognizes that: • the Sun appears to move across the sky every day • the observable shape of the Moon changes every 28 days Student may believe that the Sun moves around the Earth. COMMON ERROR: All motion in the sky is due to the Earth spinning on its axis. COMMON ERROR: The Sun travels around the Earth. COMMON ERROR: It gets dark at night because the Sun goes around the Earth once a day. COMMON ERROR: The Earth is the center of the universe.

1	Student does not recognize the systematic nature of the appearance of objects in the sky. Students may not recognize that the Earth is spherical. COMMON ERROR: It gets dark at night because something (e.g., clouds, the atmosphere, "darkness") covers the Sun. COMMON ERROR: The phases of the Moon are caused by clouds covering the Moon. COMMON ERROR: The Sun goes below the Earth at night.
0	No evidence or off-track

Sample ordered multiple-choice (OMC) items based upon Earth in the Solar System Progress Variable

Item appropriate for fifth graders:

It is most likely colder at night because

A. the Earth is at the furthest point in its orbit around the Sun. — Level 3

B. the Sun has traveled to the other side of the Earth. — Level 2

C. the Sun is below the Earth and the Moon does not emit as much heat as the Sun. — Level 1

D. the place where it is night on Earth is rotated away from the Sun. — Level 4

Item appropriate for eighth graders:

Which is the best explanation for why we experience different seasons (winter, summer, etc.) on Earth?

A. The Earth's orbit around the Sun makes us closer to the Sun in summer and farther away in winter. — Level 4

B. The Earth's orbit around the Sun makes us face the Sun in the summer and away from the Sun in the winter. — Level 3

C. The Earth's tilt causes the Sun to shine more directly in summer than in winter. — Level 5

D. The Earth's tilt makes us closer to the Sun in summer than in winter. — Level 4

A unique feature of OMC items is that each of the possible answer choices in an OMC item is linked to developmental levels of student understanding, facilitating the diagnostic interpretation of student item responses. OMC items seek to combine the validity advantages of open-ended items with the efficiency advantages of multiple-choice items. On the one hand, OMC items provide information about the developmental understanding of students that is not available with traditional multiple-choice items; on the other hand, this information can be provided to schools, teachers, and students quickly and reliably, unlike traditional open-ended test items.

SOURCE: Briggs, Alonzo, Schwab, and Wilson (2004). Developed by WestEd in conjunction with the BEAR Center at the University of California, Berkeley, with NSF support (REC-0087848). Reprinted with permission.

BOX 5-8
Progress Guide to Buoyancy

Buoyancy: WTSF
Progress Guide

Level	What the Student Already Knows	What the Student Needs to Learn
RD	**Relative Density** Student knows that floating depends on having less density than the medium, or at least that floating depends on relative density in some way. Mentions the densities of the object and the medium.	
D	**Density** Student knows that floating depends on having less density, or at least that floating is related to density in some way.	To progress to the next level, student needs to recognize that the medium plays an equally important role in determining if an object will sink or float.
MV	**Mass and Volume** Student knows that floating depends on having less mass and more volume, or at least knows that mass and volume work together to affect floating and sinking.	To progress to the next level, student needs to understand the concept of density as a way of combining mass and volume into a single property.

construct is unidimensional (that is, a single underlying trait, such as understanding biology, explains performance on a test item). IRT models make a further assumption, that is, the probability of the observed responses is determined by two types of unobservables, an examinee's ability and parameters that characterize the items. A range of different mathematical models are used to estimate these parameters. When the assumption of unidimensionality is not met, a more complex version of the item response theory model—multidimensional item response theory—is more appropriate. This model allows for the use of items that measure more than one trait, such as both understanding biology and understanding of chemistry.

M V	Mass	Volume	
	Student knows that floating depends on having less mass.	Student knows that floating depends on having more volume.	To progress to the next level, student needs to recognize that changing EITHER mass OR volume will affect whether an object sinks or floats.
UF	**Unconventional Feature**		
	Student thinks that floating depends on an unconventional feature, such as shape, surface area, or hollowness.		To progress to the next level, student needs to rethink their ideas in terms of mass and/or volume. For example, hollow objects have a lot of volume but not a lot of mass.
OT	**Off Target**		
	Student does not attend to any property or feature to explain floating.		To progress to the next level, student needs to focus on some property or feature of the object in order to explain why it sinks or floats.
NR	**No Response**		
	Student did not attempt to answer.		To progress to the next level, student needs to respond to the question.
X	**Unscorable**		
	Student gave a response, but it cannot be interpreted for scoring.		

SOURCE: http://www.caesl.org/conference/Progress_Guides.pdf. Reprinted by permission of the Center for Assessment and Evaluation of Student Learning.

In large-scale assessment programs it is typical for state personnel to decide on the measurement model that will be used, in consultation with the test development contractor. Most often it will be either classical test theory or one of the IRT models. Other models are available (see for example, Chapter 4 of NRC [2001b] for a recent survey), although these have mainly been confined to research studies rather than large-scale applications. The decision about which measurement model to use is generally based on information provided by the state about the inferences it wants to support with test results, and on the model the contractor typically uses for accomplishing similar goals.

BOX 5-9
Delaware Scoring Rubric for Chemical Tests

Question I: Your mixture is made with three chemicals that you have worked with in this unit. You may not have the same mixture as your neighbor. Using two or more senses, observe your unknown mixture. List at least three physical properties you observed. Do not taste the mixture.

This question measures students' ability to observe and record the physical properties of a mixture.

Criterion for a complete response:
1. Identifies and records three different physical properties using two or more senses, e.g., feels soft, like a powder, bumpy, white, has crystals, etc.

Code Response

Complete response
20   Response meets criterion above.
21   Lists three properties and includes one speciic substance, e.g., sugar.

Partially correct response
10   Records two different physical properties using one or more senses.
11   Records two different physical properties using one or more senses, plus adds the name of a chemical (substance).

Incorrect response
70   Records one physical property.
71   Identifies a substance (sugar) rather than any properties.
79   Any other incorrect response.

Non response
90   Crossed out, erased, illegible, incomplete, or impossible to interpret.
99   BLANK

SOURCE: http://www.scienceassessment.org/pdfxls/chemicaltest/oldpdfs/A6.18.pdf.

EVALUATING THE COGNITIVE VALIDITY OF ASSESSMENT

Educators, policy makers, students, and the public want to know that the inferences that are drawn from the results of science tests are justified. To address the cognitive validity of science achievement tests, Shavelson and colleagues (Ayala, Yin, Shavelson, and Vanides 2002; Ruiz-Primo, Shavelson, Li, and Schultz 2001) have developed a strategy for analyzing science tests to ascertain what they are measuring. The same process can be used to analyze state standards and to compare what an assessment is measuring with a state's goals for student learning.

At the heart of the process is a heuristic framework for conceptualizing the construct of science achievement as comprised of four different but overlapping types of knowledge. The knowledge types are:

• *Declarative knowledge* is knowing what—for example, knowledge of facts, definitions, or rules.
• *Procedural knowledge* is knowing how—for example knowing how to solve an equation, perform a test to identify an acid or base, design a study, identify the steps involved in other kinds of tasks.
• *Schematic knowledge* is knowing why—for example, why objects sink or float, or why the seasons change—and includes principles or other mental models that can be used to analyze or explain a set of findings.
• *Strategic knowledge* is knowing how and when to apply one's knowledge in a new situation or when assimilating new information—for example, developing problem-solving strategies, setting goals, and monitoring one's own thinking in approaching a new task or situation.

Using an examinee–test interaction perspective to explain how students bring and apply their knowledge to answer test questions, the researchers developed a method for logically analyzing test items and linking them to the achievement framework of knowledge types (Li, 2001). Each item on a test goes through a series of analyses that are designed to ascertain whether the item will elicit responses that are consistent with what the assessment is intending to measure and if the responses that they elicit can be interpreted to support any intended inferences that the assessor hopes to draw from the results.

Li, Shavelson, and colleagues (Li, 2001; Shavelson and Li, 2001; Shavelson et al., 2004) applied this framework in analyzing the science portions of the Third International Mathematics and Science Study—Repeat (TIMMS-R) (Population 2) and the Delaware Student Testing Program. They found that both tests were heavily weighted on declarative knowledge—almost 60 percent. The remaining items were split between procedural and schematic knowledge. The researchers also analyzed the Delaware science content standards using the achievement framework and found that the state standards were more heavily weighted toward schematic knowledge than was the assessment—indicating that the assessment did not adequately represent the cognitive priorities contained in the state standards. These findings led to changes in the state testing program and the development of a strong curriculum-connected assessment system for improvement of student learning to supplement the state test and provide additional information on students' science achievement (personal communication, Rachel Wood).

BUILDING DEVELOPMENTAL ASSESSMENT AROUND LEARNING

The committee commissioned two design teams that included scientists, science educators, and experts with knowledge of how children learn science to suggest ways of using research on children's learning to develop large-scale assessments at the national and state levels, and classroom assessments that were coherent with them. The teams were asked to consider the ways in which tools and strategies drawn from research on children's learning could be used to develop new approaches to elaborating standards and to designing and interpreting assessments.

Each team was asked to lay out a learning progression for an important theory or big idea in the natural sciences. The learning progression was to be based on experimental studies, cognitive theory, and logical analysis of the concepts, principles, and theory. The teams were asked to consider ways in which the learning progression could be used to construct strategies for assessing students' understanding of the foundations for the theory, as well as their understanding of the theory itself. The assessment strategies (if they developed them) were to be developmental, that is, to test students' progressively more complex understanding of the various layers of the theory's foundation in a sequence in which cognitive science suggests it reasonably can be expected to develop. The work of these two groups is summarized below. Copies of their papers can be obtained at http://www7.nationalacademies.org/bota/Test_Design_K-12_Science.html.

Implications of Research on Children's Learning for Assessment: Matter and Atomic-Molecular Theory[9]

This team used research on children's learning about the nature of matter and materials, how matter and materials change, and the atomic structure of matter[10] to illustrate a process for developing assessments that reflect research on how students learn and develop understanding of these scientific concepts.

Their first step was to organize the key concepts of atomic molecular theory around six big ideas that form two major clusters: the first two form a *macroscopic level* cluster and the last four form an *atomic-molecular level* cluster (Box 5-10 provides further detail on these concepts). The atomic-molecular theory elaborates on the macroscopic big ideas studied earlier and provides deeper explanatory accounts of macroscopic properties and phenomena.

Using research on children's learning, the team identified pathways—*learning progressions*—that would trace the path that children might follow as instruction helps them move from naïve ideas to more sophisticated understanding of atomic molecular theory. The group noted that research points to the challenges

---

[9]Paper prepared for the committee by Carol Smith, Marianne Wiser, Andy Anderson, Joe Krajcik, and Brian Coppola (2004).

[10]These ideas are represented in both the *Benchmarks for Science Literacy* (AAAS, 1993) and *National Science Education Standards* (NRC, 1996).

BOX 5-10
Atomic-Molecular Theory

Children's ability to appreciate the power of the atomic theory requires a number of related understandings about the nature of matter and material kinds, how matter and materials change, and the atomic structure of matter. These understandings are detailed in the standards documents. Smith et al. (2004) organize them around six big ideas that form two major clusters: the first two form a *macroscopic level* cluster and the last four form an *atomic-molecular level* cluster. The first cluster is introduced in the earliest grades and elaborated throughout schooling. The second is introduced in middle school and elaborated throughout middle school and high school. The atomic-molecular theory elaborates on the macroscopic big ideas studied earlier and provides deeper explanatory accounts of macroscopic properties and phenomena.

Six Big Ideas of Atomic Molecular Theory That Form Two Major Clusters

M1. Macroscopic properties: We can learn about the objects and materials that constitute the world through measurement, classification, and description according to their properties.

M2. Macroscopic conservation: Matter can be transformed, but not created or destroyed, through physical and chemical processes.

AM1. Atomic-molecular theory: All matter that we encounter on Earth is made of less than 100 kinds of atoms, which are commonly bonded together in molecules and networks.

AM2. Atomic-molecular explanation of materials: The properties of materials are determined by the nature, arrangement, and motion of the atoms and molecules of which they are made.

AM3. Atomic-molecular explanation of transformations: Changes in matter involve both changes and underlying continuities in atoms and molecules.

AM4. Distinguishing data from atomic-molecular explanations: The properties of and changes in atoms and molecules have to be distinguished from the macroscopic properties and phenomena they account for.

SOURCE: Smith et al. (2004).

---

inherent in moving through the progressions, as they involve macroscopic understandings of materials and substances as well as nanoscopic understandings of atoms and molecules. Box 5-11 contains these progressions as they were conceived by this design team. The team offers the following caveats about this progression. First, learning progressions are not inevitable and there is no one correct order—as children learn, many changes are taking place simultaneously in multiple, interconnected ways, not necessarily in the constrained and ordered

---

BOX 5-11

The Concepts and Foundational Ideas Associated with Atomic-Molecular Theory Illustrate a Possible Learning Progression

1. **Experiences with a wider range of materials and phenomena.** Children extend the range of their experiences with materials, properties of materials, and changes in materials. New experiences often help them to see the limitations of their earlier ideas and to accept new ideas that account for a wider range of phenomena.

2. **Increasing sophistication in describing, measuring, and classifying materials.** Children learn about the limits of their sense impressions and master the use of a wider range of instruments to measure and classify properties of materials and changes in materials. They become aware of properties of materials that are not revealed by casual observation and learn to measure them. They also become aware of the composition of many materials, understanding that even homogeneous materials are mixtures of substances, including different elements and compounds.

3. **Development of causal accounts focusing on matter and mass.** Children move from explanations of changes as events caused by conditions or circumstances to explanations that focus on mechanisms of change and on tracing substances through changes. They come to appreciate that mass is a fundamental measure of the amount of matter, so that changes in mass must be accounted for in terms of matter entering or leaving a system. They learn that gases are forms of matter like solids and liquids; thus gases have mass and can be used to account for otherwise unexplainable mass changes.

---

way that it appears in a learning progression. Second, any learning progression is inferential or hypothetical as there are no long-term studies of actual children learning a particular concept, and describing students' reasoning is difficult because different researchers have used different methods and conceptual frameworks.

For designing assessments to tap into students' progress along this learning progression, the team suggested a three-stage process:

1. Codify the big ideas into learning performances: types of tasks or activities suitable for classroom settings through which students can demonstrate their understanding of big ideas and scientific practices.

2. Use the learning performances to develop clusters of assessment tasks or items, including both traditional and nontraditional items that are (a) connected to principles in the standards and (b) analyzable with psychometric tools.

3. Use research on children's learning as a basis for interpretation of student

4. **Increasing theoretical depth.** Children develop accounts of properties of matter and changes in matter that make increased use of hidden mechanisms and atomic-molecular theory. They are increasingly able to make use of all six big ideas (listed above) and to develop accounts that coordinate four different levels of description:

- *Impressions or perceptual appearances*—what we see and feel—are related to
- *Measurable properties or variables*—mass, volume, density, temperature, pressure, etc.—which are related to
- *Constituent materials* and chemical substances, and finally to
- The *atoms and molecules* of which those substances are composed.

Throughout elementary school, students are working to coordinate the first two levels as they develop a sound macroscopic understanding of matter and materials based on careful measurement. From middle school onward they are coordinating all four levels as they develop an understanding of the atomic-molecular theory and its broad explanatory power.

5. **Understanding the nature and uses of scientific evidence and theories.** Children learn to distinguish between data and models or theories, which can be used to account for many different observations and experiences. They become increasingly able to develop and criticize arguments that involve coordinated use of data and theories. They also become increasingly sophisticated in their understanding of sources of uncertainty and their ability to use conditional and hypothetical reasoning.

SOURCE: Smith et al. (2004).

responses, explaining how responses reveal students' thinking with respect to big ideas and learning progressions.

In creating examples to illustrate their process, the team laid out its reasoning at each step in the development process—from national standards to elaborated standards to learning performances to assessment items and interpretations—and about the contributions that research on children's learning can make at each step. In doing so they illustrate why they believe that classroom and large-scale assessments developed using these methods will have three important qualities that are missing from most current assessments:

• *Clear principles for content coverage.* Because the assessments are organized around big ideas embodied in key scientific practices and content, their organization and relationship to themes in the curriculum will be clear. Rather than sampling randomly or arbitrarily from a large number of individual standards, assessments developed using these methods can predictably include items that assess students' understanding of the big ideas and scientific practices.

• *Clear relationships between standards and assessment items.* Because the reasoning and methods used at each stage of the development process is explicit, the interpretation of standards and the relationships between standards and assessment items is clear. The relationship between standards and assessment items is made explicit and is thus easy to examine.

• *Providing insights into students' thinking.* The assessments and their results will help teachers to understand and respond to their students' thinking. For this purpose, the interpretation of student responses is critically important, and reliable interpretations require a research base. Thus, developing items that reveal students' thinking is far easier for matter and atomic molecular theory than it is for other topics with less extensive research bases.

While this group demonstrates the key role that research on learning can play in the design of high-quality science assessments, they note that for assessors whose primary concern is evaluation and accountability, these qualities may not seem as important as some others qualities, such as efficiency and reliability. They conclude, however, that assessments with these qualities are essential for the long-term improvement of science assessment.

Evolutionary Biology[11]

While the importance of incorporating research findings about student learning into assessment development is widely recognized, research in many areas of science learning is incomplete. The design team that addressed evolutionary biology argued, however, that waiting for research to close all of the gaps would be unwarranted. To illustrate why waiting may not be necessary, the team developed an approach for producing inferences about student learning that apply a contemporary view of assessment and exploit learning theory. Their approach is to use learning theory to more clearly identify what should be assessed and what tasks or conditions could provide evidence about students' understanding, so that inferences about students' knowledge are well founded. The approach has three components.

First, in a standards-based education system, assessment developers rely on standards to define what students should know (the constructs), yet standards often obscure the important disciplinary concepts and practices that are inherent in them. To remedy this, the team suggests that a central conceptual structure be developed around the big ideas contained in the standards as a means to clarify what it is important to assess. Many individual standards may relate to the same

---

[11]Paper prepared for the committee by Kefyn Catley, Brian Reiser, and Rich Lehrer (2005).

big idea, so that focusing on them is a means of condensing standards. Ideally, a big idea is revisited throughout schooling, so that a student's knowledge is progressively refined and elaborated. This practice potentially simplifies the alignment between curriculum and assessment because both are tied to the same set of constructs.

The team also advocates that big ideas be chosen with prospective pathways of development firmly in mind. They note that these are sometimes available from research in learning, but typically also draw on the opinions of master teachers as well as some inspired guesswork to bridge gaps in the research base.

Second, standards are *aligned* with the big ideas, so that they can be considered in the context of more central ideas. This practice is another means of pruning standards, and it is a way to develop coherence among individual standards.

Third, standards are elaborated as *learning performances*. As described earlier, learning performances describe specific cognitive processes and associated practices that are linked to achieving particular standards, and thus help to guide the selection of situations for gathering evidence of understanding as well as clues as to what the evidence means.

The team illustrates its approach by developing a cartography of big ideas and associated learning performances for evolutionary biology for the first eight years of schooling. The cartography traces the development of six related big ideas that support students' understanding of evolution. The first and most important is diversity: Why is life so diverse? The other core concepts play a supporting role: (a) ecology, (b) structure-function, (c) variation, (d) change, and (e) geologic processes. In addition to these disciplinary constructs, two essential habits of mind are included: mathematical tools that support reasoning about these big ideas, and forms of reasoning that are often employed in studies of evolution, especially model-based reasoning and comparative analysis. At each of three grade bands (K–2; 3–5, 6–8), standards developed by the National Research Council (1996) and American Association for the Advancement of Science (1993) are elaborated to encompass learning performances. As schooling progresses, these learning performances reflect increasing coordination and connectivity among the big ideas. For example, diversity is at first simply treated as an extant quality of the living world but, over years of schooling, is explained by recourse to concepts developing as students learn about structure-function, variation, change, ecology, and geology.

The team chose this topic because of its critical and unifying role in the biological sciences and because learning about evolution requires synthesis and coordination among a network of related concepts and practices, ranging from genetics and ecology to geology, so that understanding evolution is likely to emerge across years of schooling. Thus, learning about evolution will be progressive and involve coordination among otherwise discrete disciplines (by contrast, one could learn about ecology or geology without considering their roles in evolution). Unlike other areas in science education, evolution has not been thoroughly researched. The domain presents significant challenges for those who wish to describe the pathways through which learning in this area might develop that could guide assessment. Thus, evolution served as a test-bed for the approach.

CONCLUSIONS

Designing high-quality science assessments is an important goal, but a difficult one to achieve. As discussed in Chapter 3, science assessments must target the knowledge, skills, and habits of mind that are necessary for science literacy, and must reflect current scientific knowledge and understanding in ways that are accurate and consistent with the ways in which scientists understand the world. It must assess students' understanding of science as a content domain and their understanding of science as an approach. It must also provide evidence that students can apply their knowledge appropriately and that they are building on their existing knowledge and skills in ways that will lead to more complete understanding of the key principles and big ideas of science. Adding to the challenge, competence in science is multifaceted and does not follow a singular path. Competency in science develops more like an ecological succession, with changes taking place simultaneously in multiple interconnected ways. Science assessment must address these complexities while also meeting professional technical standards for reliability, validity, and fairness for the purposes for which the results will be used.

The committee therefore concludes that the goal for developing high-quality science assessments will only be achieved though the combined efforts of scientists, science educators, developmental and cognitive psychologists, experts on learning, and educational measurement specialists working collaboratively rather than separately. The experience of the design teams described in this chapter and multiple findings of other NRC committees (NRC, 1996, 2001b, 2002) support this conclusion. Commercial test contractors do not generally have the advantage of these diverse perspectives as they create assessment tools for states. It is for this reason that we suggest in the next chapter that states create their own content-specific advisory boards to assist state personnel that are assigned to work with the contractors. These bodies can advise states on the appropriateness of assessment strategies and the quality and accuracy of the items and tasks included on any externally developed tests.

QUESTIONS FOR STATES

This chapter has described ways of thinking about the design of science assessments that can be applied to assessments at all levels of the system. We offer the following questions to guide states in evaluating their approaches to the development of science assessments:

Question 5-1: Have research and expert professional judgment about the ways in which students learn science been considered in the design of the state's science assessments?

Question 5-2: Have the science assessments and tasks been created to shed light on how well and to what degree students are progressing over time toward more expert understanding?

6

Implementation and Support

There is no single right way to build a science assessment system. There are no step-by-step instructions for developing systems that are well aligned with standards, that clearly communicate valued standards for teaching and learning, and that provide accurate information for decision making. However, certain steps will be invaluable to states that are planning to develop such a system.

This chapter discusses some of these steps and offers some practical ideas for states to consider. Many of these discussions reflect the input of the working groups with whom the committee consulted extensively. This chapter also addresses two other elements of the system—the reporting of results and professional development—that are important for supporting the assessment system and helping it to function as intended. The chapter concludes with a brief discussion of the uses of technology for designing and implementing an assessment system.

NEEDS ANALYSIS

In designing or modifying a coherent science assessment system, states will want to begin with a needs analysis that includes gathering information about what assessment-based information stakeholders need. The needs assessment should include the opinions of a wide range of stakeholders, including students, teachers, school administrators, school district personnel, state policy makers, parents, and the public, as each requires a different array of assessment-based information. A needs assessment can also make clear when and how assessment results should be reported and can identify aspects of the system that will need special monitoring to ensure they are working as intended. It is through such an analysis that the state can consider the role of science assessment in the overall education system and how it will interact with the education and assessment systems in other disciplines.

A needs analysis is just as important for a system that is already operating as it is for one that is being developed. Such an analysis can reveal gaps in an existing system, for example, by identifying the need for information that is not being collected. Understanding how the assessment program is perceived and used can guide improvements in the system, highlight future needs, and help states set targets for the allocation of resources. The results of the analyses can be used to develop a continuous improvement plan for science education and assessment, a plan that should guide future modifications to the system.

States may find it useful to ask school districts and schools to conduct a parallel needs assessment. Results of these local needs assessments can yield information that state-level analyses might not uncover. Local needs assessments also can be used by school districts and schools to identify important gaps in the information that states provide to them as well as strategies for filling those gaps.

The school system of the city of Milwaukee, for example, which had a strong emphasis on developing students' reasoning and problem-solving skills, recognized that the state testing program did not provide them with the information they needed about student achievement in this area. The school district designed and implemented its own local assessment system to supplement the state testing program—incorporating multiple measures of student achievement that included performance assessments administered in classrooms. The state assessment provided the district with both norm-referenced and criterion-referenced data that could be used for some purposes, while the local assessments provided information on higher order thinking and reasoning skills that were not being assessed by the paper-and-pencil tests used by the state (Webb, 2002).[1]

The committee recognizes that, in many instances, the list of needs revealed by a needs analysis will be long and states may have to set short-, intermediate-, and long-term goals for implementing the fully developed assessment systems they want. However, states that are not in a position to develop completely new assessment programs can begin with small steps toward their goals. For example, a state might start addressing needs it has identified by including a small number of open-ended assessment tasks in its large-scale assessment program, or by helping schools and districts to develop standardized, classroom-administered perfor-

---

[1]The Milwaukee example comes from mathematics. The committee notes that a similar system could be developed in science. We include the example to illustrate how local needs can lead to the creation of an assessment system that supplements rather than supplants the state assessment.

mance measures that can shed light on aspects of student achievement that are not assessed by existing tests.

EXPERT ADVICE

Developing a coherent assessment system is a complex and multifaceted task that requires a variety of expertise, both technical and content specific. A network of independent, yet interacting, advisory groups is an invaluable resource, and they should be put in place before system design begins or as early in the process as possible. The committee suggests that the advisory groups should include both permanent and ad hoc members. Permanent committees could be used to generate specific products, such as standards, assessment designs, and state-issued requests for proposals; the ad hoc committees could review these products as necessary. To ensure that the permanent committees maintain continuity, states could rotate new members into the process on a staggered basis. Terms for committee members should be set for no fewer than five years.

One of the advisory groups, sometimes called a Technical Advisory Council (TAC), should advise the state about the technical measurement issues associated with the testing program; other groups should focus on each of the content areas that are part of the state assessment program. Membership for a science content committee should include scientists, science educators, researchers who study science assessment, and individuals with expertise on how people learn science. One or two members of each of the content-specific groups should sit on the TAC to represent the concerns of the discipline. This group will be able to help states evaluate the scientific importance and accuracy of proposed test items before they are included on an assessment as well as respond to comments about the items that are raised after administration.

The membership of the TAC should have expertise in all aspects of test design, development, and implementation, including the assessment of students with special needs. The role of the TAC will vary from state to state and from stage to stage, but it should be able to help the state specify the purpose and use of assessment results, identify potential sources of assessment data (e.g., teacher, portfolio, state test, district test), and evaluate whether or not the proposed methods will achieve the purposes of assessment in a technically sound manner. Throughout the design process, TAC members should help the state write and review specifications to guide the bidding process for the development of specific components of the system. They should also help states to identify strategies for interpreting assessment data to meet identified purposes.

In addition, the TAC could help the state design alignment studies, evaluate the results of the studies, and make recommendations for changes in the system to improve or maintain alignment between standards and assessment as well as across grades and disciplines. It could also help the state monitor and evaluate the overall assessment efforts and recommend changes based on evaluation studies.

Appendix A presents some practical tips for working with a TAC. There are two key recommendations: (1) The TAC should work for the state, not the test publisher, although the test publisher should be held responsible for providing the TAC with all the information it needs to carry out its job—including information on possible problems with the tests or the interpretation of results; and (2) the state should have a plan in place to ensure that the advice of the TAC is considered. Some states, for example, require that the assessment director respond in writing to the advice of the TAC and provide justification for not following particular recommendations.

DEVELOPING THE STRUCTURE

An important step in developing and maintaining a science assessment system is the creation of documents that explain the master plan for the system. These documents should specify the purposes for each assessment in the system, the constructs that each will measure, and the ways the results are to be used. They should provide specific guidance as to who will be tested; where each component will be administered and by whom; who is responsible for developing the component; when the assessments will be administered; and how the results will be scored, combined, and reported for specific purposes. These issues are not mere details, and they can involve a variety of trade-offs and compromises that balance efficiency, cost-effectiveness, technical quality, and the credibility of results.

In developing these documents, states will need to consider:

1. The purposes of the assessment system—how the assessment results will be used at different levels of the education system.
2. The resources that are available to support the assessment system.
3. Which indicators should be included in the assessment system and how they will be combined and reported for each of the identified purposes.
4. Which students should be included in assessments and when, where, and how they should be assessed, given the identified purposes.
5. How the effects of the assessment system should be evaluated.
6. What mechanisms should be put in place to address problems uncovered by the assessment results and the evaluation of the assessment system.

These documents should be reviewed and updated on a regular basis. The state of Maine has developed a variety of documents that specify the components of their assessment system and summarized them in a chart to help policy makers and educators understand the interaction among assessment purposes, development, and scoring (see Table 6-1).

TABLE 6-1 Characteristics of Maine's Assessment System

	Primary Purpose	Selected or Developed by	Scored by
Classroom assessment	Informing teaching and learning	Individual teacher	Individual teacher
School or district assessment	Informing and monitoring	Groups of teachers and administrators	Groups of teachers (and others)
State assessment	Monitoring and evaluating programs to ensure accountability	Groups of adminis-trators, administrators, and/or policy makers	Scorers outside the district
Assessment system	Informing teaching, monitoring and evaluating, certification	District assessment leadership	Both internal and external

SOURCE: Maine Department of Education (2003).

Identification of Purposes

As states identify the purposes that the assessment system will serve, they will need to consider what assessment-based data will be needed for each identified purpose as well as how those data will be reported. The relationship between the results and the decisions must be clear. For example, if a state wishes to know about the progress that all students are making toward achieving state standards, then a large-scale test that is administered to all students and samples broadly from among all of the standards should be included in the system. If a state hopes to provide information that can be used to address individual students' needs, then assessment strategies that permit in-depth assessment of student understanding of a smaller set of knowledge and skills will be needed. If both kinds of information are needed, as is the case with the No Child Left Behind Act (NCLB), then both types of assessment would be needed.

Each assessment that is part of the system should be accompanied by a clear list of purposes for which it could be used—that is, inferences for which it could provide valid evidence. The specific purpose will guide the selection of measures that can elicit evidence of understanding and dictate the circumstances in which they should be used. It is important to note that the *purpose* of testing is not the same as the *type* of test, items, or tasks; there is no specific item type or assessment type that is unique to a particular purpose. For example, well-designed multiple-choice items can be used for formative purposes, just as open-ended performance tasks can be included on tests that are used for accountability or program evaluation purposes. In fact, the same question could be used in assessments designed for different purposes quite successfully.

Although educational measurement experts frequently stress that one test cannot serve all purposes equally well, there need not necessarily be a one-to-one correspondence between the number of tests and the number of purposes, provided the state is cognizant of the trade-offs inherent in using an assessment to serve multiple purposes. Evidence that an assessment is valid for one purpose is insufficient to establish the validity of its use for another purpose (American Educational Research Association, American Psychological Association, and National Council on Measurement in Education, 1999, p. 17). Some evidence exists (Niemi, 1996; Baker, 1997; Baker, Abedi, Linn, and Niemi, 1996) that tests can be designed to yield useful information for various purposes at different levels of the system when the results are reported in different ways. Baker (2003) suggests that system-oriented measures can be turned to instructional improvement purposes in this way. This would be possible if evidence is collected to support the validity of each purpose, or if the different purposes are addressed by aggregating and reporting results in different ways.

The Nebraska STARS (Buchendahl, Impara, and Plake, 2002) and the Maine MeCAS[2] programs have used this approach. In these programs, results of local assessments whose primary purpose is to support teaching and learning in the classroom are being combined with each other and with state-level assessments to support judgments about achievement of the state standards. These judgments are useful to both teachers and policy makers. The programs are built around a strong foundation of professional development that supports teachers in developing technically sound assessments. In each of these states, considerable attention has been paid to establishing the validity of both classroom and district portions of the assessment system for each intended purpose. However, concerns about the comparability of information across districts remain, and further research and experience will be needed to determine how well such strategies will work for different purposes.

At What Level the Assessment Is Administered

Another aspect of the selection of suitable assessment approaches is where the assessment should be administered to maximize its usefulness and provide results that support desired inferences. In a system of assessments, with many ways to implement an assessment strategy, decisions should be based both on the construct to be measured and where the most accurate picture of student learning can be obtained. For example, as discussed in Chapter 3, if a detailed picture of students' abilities to conduct a scientific investigation is needed, this information may be captured best by the teacher while students are actively engaged in inquiry

---

[2]Information about the Maine MeCAS program is available from: http://www.state.me.us/education/mea/index.htm.

activities. Such an assessment should therefore be administered in the classroom (or wherever the activity takes place).

It is also important to consider how the results will be used. There are trade-offs inherent in any decision about where assessment should take place. For example, while ongoing classroom assessment helps teachers make instructional decisions that can enhance student learning, the results of such assessments may not be incorporated easily into an assessment system that is used for accountability purposes because they are not standardized and therefore not easily comparable. By the same token, the results of standardized tests, which are easily absorbed into accountability systems, may not meet the immediate needs of teachers or students.

One strategy for meeting both needs is to ask teachers to incorporate some standardized tasks—which can more easily be used for accountability purposes because their comparability from classroom to classroom can be readily established—into their repertoire of classroom assessment strategies. Such assessment tools would not replace ongoing formative assessment but supplement it (see, for example, the description of New York's and Connecticut's assessment of inquiry in Chapter 3). There is a need for more research on the design and implementation of standardized classroom assessment opportunities. Textbook publishers could assist in this effort by including in their supplementary materials a variety of assessment activities and related scoring rubrics that could be implemented by teachers in the classroom and possibly incorporated into the state's assessment system.

Frequency

Decisions about how frequently to assess depend on how the results are to be used and how stable they need to be over time. For example, tests given at the end of a school year, while useful for providing a snapshot of what students have learned and for evaluating patterns of errors that could be the target of future instructional interventions, do not typically affect the educational experiences of the students who take them. Assessment strategies designed to support students' ongoing learning must provide feedback in time for students and their teachers to benefit from the information. Tests that are used to determine how students are progressing from one grade to the next may only have to be administered once per year. Large-scale assessments, such as the National Assessment of Educational Progress (NAEP) science assessment, that are designed to paint a broad picture of what students in U.S. schools know and can do in science need to be administered even less often. Assessing more frequently than is necessary for a particular purpose is costly and inefficient; assessing too infrequently can provide inaccurate information or may provide information that arrives too late to be useful to support important decisions.

Responsibility for Test Development

In an assessment system the responsibility for developing assessments can be distributed across the system, which makes it more difficult for states to maintain coherence unless there is a plan in place. Roeber (1996) describes a process that states could use in developing a coherent set of assessment practices to meet the information needs of participants at different levels of the education system (Box 6-1). However, he, like the committee, understands that states vary in many ways and that the model is just one possibility among many. We include it in this report to illustrate how such a system could be developed—not as a model for system design.

WORKING WITH A COMMERCIAL TEST PUBLISHER

In creating a high-quality state testing program, many states will work with a commercial test publisher in some way. As Patz et al. (2005) point out, the way a state views the role of professional test development organizations may depend on the way it views the task of assessing student learning. For example, if a state thinks of assessment as primarily an opportunity to capture the success of efforts to pursue key intellectual goals in the schools, then it may see only a limited role for commercial testing contractors. A state that opts for a technically complex, large-scale assessment is likely to depend more heavily on a testing contractor. A system can easily incorporate both kinds of assessment, so that a state may use a contractor only for the development of some components of its assessment system (Education Leaders Council, 2002).

State education and testing industry personnel, working under the auspices of the Education Leaders Council developed a set of standards to guide states as they develop relationships with test publishers. These standards provide guidance on preplanning, design and response strategies for requests for proposals, administration, scoring, reporting, and appropriate uses of data. Although the committee did not evaluate these standards, we think that they raise important considerations for states and their test development contractors.[3]

Appendix A contains a checklist for the preparation of a request for proposals for testing contractors as well as some practical tips for working with them. These are not intended to serve as standards, but rather to highlight aspects of the working relationship that may need attention and to provide some recommendations for improving the collaboration.

Two of the design team papers described in Chapter 2 provide additional guidance for states in working with test contractors. Patz et al. (2005) discuss some basic elements of project management and suggest a variety of ways that

---

[3]The standards are available at: http://www.accountabilityworks.org/publications/ELC_AW_Model_Contractor_Standards_and_State_Responsibilities_for_State_Testing_Programs.pdf.

BOX 6-1
Developing a Coherent Assessment System:
An Illustrative Example

1. The state develops a set of content standards in selected areas with local district input. Most school districts adopt the state standards as their own.

2. In each area, the state coordination team develops an assessment blueprint describing the manner in which the content standards are to be assessed at the state, district, and classroom levels.

3. The state selects subjects for statewide assessments to be administered in certain grades. The purpose of the assessments is primarily to hold schools accountable for student performance. Results are reported to parents, teachers, schools, and districts.

4. Performance standards are created for each area in which the state has created content standards. These standards ensure assessments can be used to judge the performance of students and schools.

5. For each area in which the state has developed content standards, the state coordination team also develops a professional development program to ensure that all local educators are able to address the content standards and help students achieve at high levels.

6. The state creates the assessments that will be used, with the state coordination team overseeing the work to ensure the assessments match the content standards and fulfill the purposes of the overall assessment system.

7. The state creates other assessments (portfolio assessments, performance events, performance tasks, plus more conventional selected-response and open-ended assessments) for use as "off-grades" throughout the school year. These assessments provide information teachers can use to improve the learning of individual students, as well as group information to improve the instructional program at the school and classroom levels.

8. The state sees that the assessments are created, validated, and distributed across the state. As part of this process, the state administers the assessments to a sample of students statewide at each grade level, develops scoring rubrics and training materials for each open-ended or performance measure, and prepares the materials for distribution to school districts.

9. Assessments are tried out in a representative set of classrooms around the state with the results used in several ways: to refine the assessments themselves, to refine the assessment administration directions, and to revise and expand the scoring rubrics.

10. The state provides ongoing information and professional development opportunities to all local school districts. Assessment information collected by classroom teachers is summarized at the building level. District and school summaries are added to provide a more complete picture of student achievement.

SOURCE: Adapted from Roeber (1996).

states could work with test development professionals and test publishers in implementing a science assessment program according to NCLB requirements. Popham et al. (2004) include draft language that could be incorporated (with any desired modifications) into a request for proposals.

REPORTING ASSESSMENT RESULTS

The reporting of assessment results is frequently taken for granted, but consideration of this step is critical in the design of assessment systems and in the use of assessment-based information. The committee recommends that decisions about reporting be made before any assessment design begins.

As we have discussed, information about students' progress is needed at all levels of the system, albeit with varying degrees of frequency and in varying degrees of detail. Parents, teachers, school and district administrators, policy makers, the public, and of course students themselves need clear, accessible, and timely information and feedback about what is taking place in the classroom (Wainer, 1997). Moreover, in a systems approach, many different kinds of information need to be available, but not all stakeholders need the same information. Thus, questions about how various kinds of results will be combined and reported to different audiences and how reporting can support sound, valid interpretations of results need to be considered very early in the process of system design.

NCLB's requirements for the reporting of assessment results are fairly specific. Results that are aligned with the state's academic achievement standards are to be reported for all tested students and disaggregated by major subgroups. The results also are to include "interpretative, descriptive, and diagnostic reports" for individuals that can be used to "help parents, teachers, and principals to understand and address the specific academic needs of students" (P.L. 107-110).

Depending on the needs of different groups for assessment-based information, results can be presented in terms of individual standards or clusters of standards, or in terms of learning progressions that have been defined and made clear and available to all. They can be presented in terms of comparisons of one student's or a group of students' performance to other groups or to established norms. Results can also describe the extent to which students have met established criteria for performance. If descriptions of the skills, knowledge, and abilities that were targeted by the tasks in the assessment are included, users will understand the links between the results and goals for student learning. When these links are clear, users of the results—whether parents, teachers, or policy makers—can see how they could act on what they have learned about student progress.

We note that the reporting of assessment results can take many forms—from graphical displays to descriptive text, and from a series of numbers to detailed analysis of what the numbers mean. Some states report assessment results on a standard-by-standard basis; others provide information keyed to learning objectives for a specific class. In many states in Australia, where learning continua serve as the basis for assessment at all levels of the system, progress maps are used to describe student achievement (see Chapter 5).

NCLB requires that "interpretative" material be included in reports. Interpretive material is supporting text that explains, in a way that is suited to the technical knowledge of the intended audience, the nature and significance of the results. Interpretative material should:

- specifiy the purposes of the assessment.
- describe the skills, knowledge, and abilities being assessed.
- provide sample test questions and sample student responses keyed to performance levels.
- provide a description of the performance levels.
- describe the skills, knowledge, and abilities that a student or group of students have achieved or have not yet achieved.
- describe how the results should be interpreted and used, with a focus on ways to improve student performance.
- describe common misinterpretations of results.
- indicate the precision of scores or classification levels.

Samples of student work are a useful way of illustrating student achievement. When reports include such samples, users can gain further insight as to what it means for a student to be classified at a particular achievement level. Samples can also be used to illustrate the ways in which students need to improve.

Many assessments are designed to generate subscores, that is, detailed results for particular aspects of the domain that has been assessed. Subscores provide an important means of making assessment results more useful. Providing subscores for traditional paper-and-pencil tests, with or without open-ended items, is relatively straightforward; it depends largely on ensuring that a sufficient number of tasks that measure the subdomain have been included and that measurement error for that portion of the assessment has been established. Developing subscores, or perhaps nonnumerical results that address particular aspects of a domain to be measured, is also useful in the context of other kinds of measures, and it fits well with the learning progression model we have presented. However, the development of subscores that can support decisions about curricula or be used in the diagnosis of students' needs relative to state standards is an area that needs further research and development.

Information about the performance of relevant comparison groups can also enhance users' understanding of individual and group results. Other information—for example, about the quality of education and opportunities afforded to students, as well as students' motivation to perform well—can further enhance the validity of score interpretations. The Internet offers the possibility of making a volume of information available to users that might be impractical for paper-based reports. Information can be presented in the context of guidance as to how it can be used and interpreted, and it can be interactive so that users can focus on the areas of greatest relevance to them.

Users need to understand the degree of uncertainty or measurement error associated with assessment results. This is particularly important when a variety of measures are used in a system, although quantitative measures of error can be less straightforward for newer modes of assessment than for traditional tests. Such information can be conveyed using standard error bands, a graphic display, or statements regarding the probability of misclassification (American Educational Research Association, American Psychological Association, and National Council on Measurement in Education, 1999). Regardless of how this is done, each score reported should be accompanied by an indication of its margin of error or other indicators of the measure's degree of precision. This information should be supported by text that makes clear how the precision of the scores should be factored into inferences based on the results. Information on how close individual students or groups of students are to attaining a different performance level can also be reported (Goodman and Hambleton, 2003), along with a description of the skills, knowledge, and abilities represented by each performance level.

Finally, while much research has been done on the design of technically sound assessments, there is little research on ways of reporting results that allow for accurate and meaningful interpretations (Hambleton and Slater, 1997; Jaeger, 1998; Goodman and Hambleton, 2003). Research has indicated that users' preference for a data display and the understandability of a display do not always coincide (Wainer, Hambleton, and Meara, 1999). To ensure that reports communicate clearly and effectively to their intended audiences, different formats should be evaluated to determine which are best understood and most likely to be used accurately by those audiences. This can be accomplished using think-aloud studies and focus groups consisting of members of the relevant audiences. We encourage the U.S. Department of Education to assist states by supporting research on the design of effective assessment reporting tools, including the use of technology for this purpose. We also encourage education policy organizations and professional societies to create opportunities for this issue to be addressed.

PROFESSIONAL DEVELOPMENT

Teachers and students are in the best position to use assessment results directly to improve learning, and teachers need specific knowledge and skills to make sure that this happens. The committee has called on states not to rely exclusively on large-scale assessments, but to use multiple modes of assessment to obtain the kinds of information that are needed to understand and effectively monitor students' science learning. We also call on states to make use of relatively new research findings about the ways in which student learning progresses in the sciences when designing science education systems and science assessments. The demands of such a system on teachers are clearly very great; as a consequence, the responsibility of states to make sure that teachers are supported in this effort, while they are training to enter the profession and throughout their careers, is correspondingly great.

The committee concludes that a strong system of professional development is critical for the proper functioning of a science assessment system, as it is to the success of standards-based reform in general. Many reports and articles have described the nature of high-quality professional development (see, for example, National Research Council, 2001a; Putnam and Borko, 2002; Shepard, 2000; Darling-Hammond, 1998; Hawley and Valli, 1999), and this report does not discuss general principles of effective professional development. Rather we highlight key challenges for professional development that relate to assessment.

Throughout the education system, many individuals and groups—not just teachers—make and influence decisions regarding the use and interpretation of assessment results, and they base their decisions, for good or ill, on the understandings they have of the assessment process. When their understanding is poor, the consequences can be great. It is thus very important that all of these individuals and groups—from elected officials at the highest levels, to school board members, to parents—understand that assessment is integral to the system, not a separate task. These individuals need to have the opportunity, and take the responsibility, to become educated about how assessments work, their goals, and the interpretation of their results.

States rely on both preservice programs (for teachers in training) and in-service programs (for practicing teachers) to provide professional development for their teachers. In general, neither preservice teacher preparation programs offered by colleges and universities, nor in-service programs, which typically are controlled by schools and districts, are currently accomplishing all that they could, particularly with regard to assessment. We focused our attention on the kinds of professional development that are needed to enable teachers and others to use science assessment results to improve student learning outcomes. Just as we see science assessment as an element in a coherent system, we see professional development as an important element for supporting that system.

Whatever form it takes, assessment is a tool that all teachers use every day to obtain information on their students' learning. For classroom assessment to function as it should in a system, it is the teachers who must develop and use means of assessing their students' learning, who must incorporate measurement tools developed by themselves and others into their instruction, and who must prepare students for assessments that will be given outside the classroom setting. Teachers also must absorb and understand the information that all these kinds of assessments can supply, and they have the principal responsibility for using that information to help their students learn and to improve their own instructional strategies.

To accomplish these things, teachers need to understand the principles on which different kinds of assessments are based. Large-scale assessments designed to provide information about many students, for example, often are viewed by teachers as intrusions that bear little relationship to their goals in the classroom, and few teachers are well prepared to make sense of the kinds of results that these assessments typically provide. Yet these assessments are the only means of obtaining important information, including data for evaluating the success of educational approaches, for monitoring trends over time, and for certain accountability purposes. Moreover, if the outside assessments that teachers encounter are designed as parts of the coherent system the committee is calling for, they will be consonant with the assessments used at the classroom level and can provide information about students' progress toward the science standards that teachers can use.

While teachers may not be involved in the design or selection of the large-scale assessment instruments their students take, it is important that they understand the purposes the assessments are designed to serve, the kinds of inferences they were designed to support, and the ways in which the results are to be used. They also need to understand the kinds of data that are produced, and they should have sufficient understanding of the assessment's technical properties to be able to put the data in context and link it to other information they have about their students.

Large-scale assessments are just one tool for obtaining information about what students are learning. Teachers already assess their students constantly. Informally, they gain information through interactions with students—for example, by taking note of the understanding or misconceptions that underlie students' comments and questions and by observing the ways they use resources and approach challenges. More formally, they devise activities, quizzes, tests, and the like to find out how and what students have learned. All of these assessment activities require that teachers have, in addition to a deep understanding of the content domain, a foundation of basic knowledge about how to develop tasks that are valid and useful in the classroom, the ways in which student learning develops, principles of educational measurement, and the subject matter they are teaching.

Teachers need deep understanding of the subject matter they are teaching if they are to develop and use assessment effectively. There is considerable evidence that existing knowledge and beliefs play an important role in how teachers learn to teach, how they teach, and how they think about teaching (Cohen and Ball, 1990; Prawat, 1992; Putnam and Borko, 1997). For example, teachers must understand their discipline deeply to develop assessment opportunities that promote learning and to avoid assessment that encourages rote learning. They need to understand how learning in the subject area develops over time, so that they can assess initial understandings before moving to more complex ideas. Perhaps most important, teachers whose knowledge is incomplete or inaccurate may reinforce, through assessment, incorrect conceptions held by their students.

It is probably unrealistic to assume that in-service professional development opportunities, which schools and districts use for many different purposes, will provide teachers with the skills they need to use and understand assessment effectively. Assessment competence, like competence in any discipline, requires sustained effort and focused instruction accompanied by practice and feedback. The committee therefore calls on colleges and universities that prepare teachers to include in their curricula for teacher education courses on educational measurement that are both general and specific to science. Because the course requirements for teacher preparation programs are largely set by state licensure requirements, the most effective way to encourage these programs to include educational measurement courses is for states to include in their standards for certification and recertification a provision that teachers demonstrate assessment competence as a condition for teacher licensure. Much work is needed to make this a reality. Stiggins (1999) found that only 25 states require assessment competence as a criterion for licensure, and Trevisan (2002) found that only 18 states had any requirements related to assessment literacy for school administrators.

Trevisan points out that, in 1990, the American Federation of Teachers, the National Council on Measurement in Education, and the National Education Association issued *Standards for Teacher Competence in Educational Assessment of Students*. Box 6-2 contains the seven standards these organizations developed for teacher assessment literacy. He calls on states to consider some of these national standards in revising their own licensure requirements. He highlights the work of the state of Washington, which requires all teachers in the state to meet national standards in each field; specifically, teachers are required to meet requirements of the Interstate New Teacher Assessment and Support Consortium (INTASC), which include indicators for assessment literacy.

Education administrators at all levels of the system require assessment competence for (1) assisting teachers in creating and using assessment effectively; (2) providing leadership in the creation and implementation of building- or district-level assessment policies; and (3) using assessment results in their capacity as administrators in making decisions about students, teachers, and instruction; and (4) reporting on assessment results to a variety of stakeholders and constituencies. Box 6-3 includes standards for assessment competency for education administrators that were developed through the collaborative efforts of a number of organizations representing school administrators and the educational measurement community.[4]

---

[4]In 1990, the American Federation of Teachers, the National Council on Measurement in Education, and the National Education Association published the *Standards for Teacher Competence on*

BOX 6-2
Standards for Teacher Assessment Competence

Teachers should be skilled in:

1. choosing assessment methods appropriate for instructional decisions.

2. developing assessment methods appropriate for instructional decisions.

3. administering, scoring, and interpreting the results of both externally produced and teacher-produced assessment methods.

4. using assessment results when making decisions about individual students, planning teaching, developing curriculum, and school improvement.

5. developing valid pupil grading procedures, which use pupil assessments.

6. communicating assessment results to students, parents, other lay audiences, and other educators.

7. recognizing unethical, illegal, and otherwise inappropriate assessment methods and uses of assessment information.

SOURCE: American Federation of Teachers, National Council on Measurement in Education, National Education Association. Available at http://www.lib.muohio.edu/edpsych/stevens_stand.pdf.

While teachers and students can use assessment results directly to improve learning, policy makers and the public use assessment results to allocate resources, set education policy, and advocate for change. All these groups need a better understanding of what assessment results can and cannot tell them about education and student achievement. Several large policy organizations—for example, the National Conference of State Legislatures, the National Association of Secondary School Principals, and the Southern Regional Education Board—have published reports to help their members better understand the uses of assessment results. Similarly, Boston, Rudner, Walker, and Crouch (2003) developed a guide for education journalists to assist them in using and reporting assessment data accurately. The committee urges all who are responsible for using or reporting assessment results to become as informed as possible.

Educational Assessment of Students. The joint committee recommended those standards as a framework for preservice and in-service training for teachers. The committee also recommended that standards be developed for other categories of educational professionals. This document is intended to complement the *Standards for Teacher Competence.*

BOX 6-3
Synthesis of Competency Standards in Student Assessment for Education Administrators

Competencies associated with assisting teachers:

1. Have a working level of competence in the Standards for Teacher Competence in Educational Assessment of Students.

2. Know the appropriate and useful mechanics of constructing various assessments.

Competencies associated with providing leadership in developing and implementing assessment policies:

3. Understand and be able to apply basic measurement principles to assessments conducted in school settings.

4. Understand the purposes (e.g., description, diagnosis, placement) of different kinds of assessment (e.g., achievement, aptitude, attitude) and the appropriate assessment strategies to obtain the assessment data needed for the intended purpose.

5. Understand the need for clear and consistent building- and district-level policies on student assessment.

Competencies needed in using assessments in making decisions and in communicating assessment results:

6. Understand and express technical assessment concepts and terminology to others in nontechnical but correct ways.

7. Understand and follow ethical and technical guidelines for assessment.

8. Reconcile conflicting assessment results appropriately.

9. Recognize the importance, appropriateness, and complexity of interpreting assessment results in light of students' linguistic and cultural backgrounds and other out-of-school factors in light of making accommodations for individual differences, including disabilities, to help ensure the validity of assessment results for all students.

10. Ensure the assessment and information technology are employed appropriately to conduct student assessment.

11. Use available technology appropriately to integrate assessment results and other student data to facilitate students' learning, instruction, and performance.

12. Judge the quality of an assessment strategy or program used for decision making within their jurisdiction.

SOURCE: American Association of School Administrators, National Association of Elementary School Principals, National Association of Secondary School Principals, National Council on Measurement in Education. http://www.unl.edu/buros/bimm/html/article4.html.

INCORPORATING TECHNOLOGY INTO THE SYSTEM[5]

Technology holds great potential to help in efforts to push large-scale testing beyond the paper-and-pencil format, to find ways to measure more kinds of performances, and to transform the way assessments are designed, developed, administered, and scored (Bejar, 1996; Bennett, 1998, 2002; Mislevy, Steinberg, and Almond, 2002). However, that promise has not yet been fully realized in most state testing programs. Despite the fact that multimedia environments offer opportunities to present students with complex, lifelike situations with which they can pursue a sustained investigation, or have opportunities to visualize abstract concepts, or work with large complex data sets, most technology-based assessment is generally used only in technology-based learning environments that have a significant technological infrastructure in place. Thus the application of such assessment approaches has been limited (Quellmalz and Haertel, 2004). More research in this area is critical if technology is to be incorporated into state assessment programs more broadly.

Several groups of researchers are beginning to make progress in this area. For example, Mislevy, Steinberg, Breyer, and Almond (2002) are developing a technology-supported assessment design system through the Principled Assessment Designs in Inquiry (PADI) project (Mislevy et al., 2003). PADI is a system for developing reusable assessment task templates, organized around schemas of inquiry that are based on research from cognitive psychology and science education. The completed system is to have multiple components, including generally stated rubrics for evaluating evidence of inquiry skills, an organized set of assessment development resources, and a collection of schema, exemplar templates, and assessment tasks.

Currently, however, in our review of the use of technology in assessment, we found that most states are using technology primarily for the following purposes: administering assessments; organizing, managing, and analyzing student assessment data; making items, performance tasks, rubrics, and complete tests available to teachers; and scoring and reporting assessment data to various stakeholder groups. Although we found examples of schools and districts that incorporate technology into their instructional and formative assessment activities at a local level, such use has not, for the most part, spread to state assessment programs.

---

[5]For a more in-depth discussion of some of these issues, the committee refers the reader to a paper prepared for the committee by Edys Quellmalz and Geneva Haertel of SRI, International. The paper, "Use of Technology-Supported Tools for Large-Scale Science Assessment: Implications for Assessment Practice and Policy at the State Level" (2004), covers a range of topics related to technology and science assessment.

Online Administration

The *Education Week* report *Technology Counts* (2003) describes how 12 states and the District of Columbia are administering computer-based assessment to students. As testing requirements increase and budgets are tightened, the authors of this document believe that more states will follow suit. It is noteworthy that only four of the states were conducting science assessment on line, and only one was including open-ended questions. But it is also interesting to note that in 2004 Maine made its innovative multiformat science assessment available on laptop computers.

Economics seems to be a primary motivator for the increase in computer-administered assessment. Neuberger (2004) reported that Oregon recovered the cost of developing an online version of its state test within one year. Quellmalz and Haertel (2004) report that vendors estimate that computer-administered tests save half to three-quarters of the administrative costs of paper-and-pencil versions. An added advantage of computer-administered assessments is the potential for immediate feedback that can be used by students and teachers more effectively than results from external assessments that must be sent away for scoring. However, we note that until computer-delivered, large-scale assessment includes opportunities to measure complex thinking and conceptual understanding, its usefulness as a feedback mechanism will be limited.

Scoring

Technology supporting the scoring of responses has been evolving rapidly and has been greatly improved by advances in semantic analysis and computer-based scoring of written text. While a number of commercial products are available to support automatic essay scoring, methods for scoring shorter constructed responses are still being refined.

One effective strategy that has been shown to have a positive effect both on teachers' assessment competence and the quality of their teaching is to involve them in the scoring or evaluation of student test responses. Costs associated with this activity—for example, meeting costs and the costs for transporting the tests and teachers—have limited their use. However, technology can reduce the costs associated with scoring open-ended items (Odendahl, 1999; Whalen and Bejar, 1998). Computer support for live scoring has been developed by commercial testing companies. The supports range from online training and calibration checks to fully online systems in which live conversations between raters are possible and in which all participants can see the same examples, interact with other meeting participants, share comments on the student work samples and rubrics, and amend the scoring rubrics as a group if necessary.

Managing the Data

Most states are already harnessing the power of technology to manage assessment data and to link it with other student information. For example, by providing every student in the state with a unique identification number (as many states are now doing), states can use data analysis programs to view assessment data in multiple ways. Such programs allow educators not only to look at overall achievement and the accomplishments of individual students, but also to disaggregate the information by teacher, by race, by poverty status, and by students with disabilities and those who are learning English. The performance of students who have participated in particular instructional programs can be captured and results can be linked to such factors as the length of time in the school or course-taking patterns. Technology makes these types of analysis easier and more readily available than in the past.

Technology provides an efficient means of storing, managing, and reporting results from multiple assessment opportunities so they can be retrieved, combined, and reported in a cost-effective manner. It also makes possible the creation of databases of student work that can be used by teachers, students, and parents as a guide to expectations for student achievement. These examples of student work, if linked to specific performance levels as described by the state academic achievement standards, could facilitate students' involvement in their own assessment by allowing them to compare their performance with acceptable performance—an important aspect of learning with understanding.

Support for Assessment Development

Many states and school districts have created item banks linked to state standards and made them accessible to teachers and others for use in classroom or district assessment activities. The American Association for the Advancement of Science is actively engaged in developing an item bank of science items that are linked to the *Benchmarks for Science Literacy* and the maps contained in the *Atlas for Science Literacy*. It is also their intention to make these items available to states and researchers through an online delivery system linked to the maps. Item banks are useful tools for teachers and others, but care must be taken to ensure that items drawn from the banks are aligned with state standards and goals. The wide variety among states complicates the sharing of item banks (see Quellmalz and Moody, 2004, for a discussion of some issues involved in operating an item bank).

In sum, the committee found that technology holds great promise for improving science assessment, but further developments in its applications to assessment will be required before that potential can be realized. We urge all concerned to continue to pursue promising strategies.

QUESTIONS FOR STATES

Implementation

Designing an assessment system is an iterative process that cannot be accomplished in one fell swoop. States must build their science assessment systems carefully and deliberately over time, keeping in mind issues of validity and coherence and recognizing that adding new components or eliminating others can create changes in the system that need to be addressed. The committee proposes that in implementing a system, states ask themselves the following questions:

Question 6-1: Has the state brought together important stakeholders and required experts to develop or revise its science assessment system so that it reflects a shared vision of science education?

Question 6-2: Does the state have a written master plan for its science assessment system that specifies which types of assessments are to be used for which purposes; how frequently the different assessments will be administered; who will develop them; who will administer them; at what level of the education system they will be administered; and how the results will be scored, reconciled, and reported?

Question 6-3: Has the state developed both long- and short-term strategies for ensuring that resources are available for assessment development and revision? As part of this process, has consideration been given to such strategies as doing a little bit each year, purchasing curriculum materials that include quality assessments, collaborating with other states that have similar standards to develop assessments or item banks, or developing an assessment system that uses existing personnel and assessment opportunities to assess aspects of science learning that might otherwise be too expensive to assess?

Question 6-4: Is the state's assessment system plan closely aligned with the complete array of its science standards, reflecting the breadth and depth of the science content knowledge, scientific skills and understandings, and cognitive demands that are articulated in the standards?

Question 6-5: Does the state have, and use the support of, both technical and content-specific advisory committees to provide advice and guidance on the design, implementation, and ongoing monitoring and evaluation of the assessment system? Do these advisory committees make recommendations to improve particular aspects of the assessment system, and does the state have in place a plan for considering and responding to their suggestions?

Reporting Assessment Results

Question 6-6: Has consideration been given in designing the assessment system to the nature of the score reports and to the intended inferences that the assessment information will be used to support?

Question 6-7: Have the state and its contractors developed strategies to ensure that reports of assessment results are accessible, relevant, and meaningful to the targeted audiences and that they are provided in a timely manner?

Question 6-8: Do assessment reports include information on the precision of scores and on the accuracy with which the scores can be used to classify students by performance levels? Do they include information about and examples of the appropriate and inappropriate use of the scores and about the kinds of inferences that can and cannot be supported by the results?

Professional Development

Question 6-9: Do the state's teachers, school administrators, and policy makers have ongoing opportunities to build their understanding of current assessment practices and expand their skills in using and interpreting assessment results?

Question 6-10: Do school, district, and state education administrative personnel possess sufficient assessment competence to use assessment information accurately and to communicate it effectively to interested stakeholders?

Question 6-11: Do school, district, and state education administrative personnel have sufficient resources to collect, store, manage, and analyze the data collected through the assessment system?

Question 6-12: Do the state, school districts, and schools include science educators in every step of the assessment process (from the design of the assessments to data collection to the use and interpretation of the results), thereby providing ongoing opportunities for individuals at each of these levels to build their understanding of current assessment practices and expand their skills in using and interpreting assessment results?

Question 6-13: Do the state's teacher licensing regulations for certification and recertification require that all candidates demonstrate assessment competence at a level commensurate with their area of certification?

Question 6-14: Does the state require as part of its certification and recertification standards that all teachers of science possess knowledge of the subjects they teach as well as the knowledge necessary to teach science well?

7

Issues of Equity and Adequacy

The No Child Left Behind Act (NCLB) articulates clear goals for equity in science education and compels states to use data about student achievement to identify any areas in which they may be falling short. By requiring states to disaggregate assessment results for major subgroups and by holding states accountable for achievement across all groups, NCLB makes clear that all students must be given an equitable opportunity to develop science literacy. The law places a premium on the challenge of including all students in assessments, and it highlights the challenges of ensuring that all students' science learning is supported by adequate resources. This chapter explores each of these issues.

OPPORTUNITY TO LEARN

Excellence in science education embodies the idea that all students can achieve science literacy if they are given the opportunity to learn (American Association for the Advancement of Science, 1989; National Research Council, 1996). Although students will achieve understanding of science concepts in different ways and at different depths and at different rates of progress, opportunity to learn implies that all should have the chance to develop the understandings associated with science literacy to the maximum extent possible. The *National Science Education Standards* (National Research Council, 1996) and *Science for All Americans* (American Association for the Advancement of Science, 1989) make this goal a priority, especially for students who historically have not received adequate encouragement and opportunity to pursue science—women, students of color, students with disabilities, and students with limited English language proficiency, for example. The authors of the *National Science Education Standards* made clear their commitment to this goal by advocating that the collection of data about students' opportunity to learn should be included in a science assessment program. NCLB reflects this goal and mandates the interpretation of test-based information in ways that may highlight discrepancies in opportunity to learn among different groups of students, schools, and school districts in a state.

Science education poses particular challenges in meeting the goal of opportunity to learn. Of primary concern is the scarcity of highly qualified science teachers (see for example, National Commission on Mathematics and Science Teaching for the 21st Century, 2000). While NCLB requires that every child have access to highly qualified teachers, there may not be sufficient numbers of these teachers to staff all science classrooms. This is particularly true in rural and urban settings and in the elementary and middle grades, where many teachers are generalists, rather than science specialists. The Council of Chief State School Officers and the National Center for Education Statistics have collected detailed information on the staffing patterns in different schools and subjects that support the committee's observation. (This information is available on the organizations' web sites.)

The fairness of assessments and the validity of interpretations of their results depend on the extent to which students have had sufficient opportunities to learn the knowledge and abilities that are being assessed. Without this information, it is impossible to know whether the results shed light on aspects of the curriculum, instructional strategies, or students' efforts or abilities, or whether they simply indicate that students have not had the chance to learn what has been assessed.

It is particularly important that in interpreting test results, states consider the extent to which students with disabilities and English language learners have had an opportunity to learn the material covered by a science assessment, because instruction in special programs may focus on reading and mathematics rather than science. When students are tested on material that they have not had an opportunity to learn, the test results cannot be interpreted as meaning the same thing as for students who have received instruction in the area.

States have a number of sources of evidence they can use to answer questions about students' opportunity to learn. Collateral information about individual students or groups of students is particularly important when the stakes for individual students are high, as when assessments are used for promotion and graduation, for example. This information can be obtained through questionnaires that ask, for example, whether students were provided with curriculum, instruction, and resources, or whether educators, students, and parents were informed before an assessment was conducted about the knowledge, skills, and abilities that were to be assessed (American Educational Research Association, American Psychological Association, and National Council on Measurement in Education, 1999). Research has suggested that the primary areas that should be considered when examining opportunities to learn are curriculum content, instructional strategies, and instructional resources (Brewer and Stacz, 1996).

Inequities also can exist at a broader level. Differences in performance across groups (e.g., gender, ethnic, or geographic groups) can be confounded with differences in access to curriculum, instruction, and resources. Performance differences from school to school may be confounded with differences in the quality of education, such as the number of advanced course offerings and the quality of educators (American Educational Research Association, American Psychological Association, and National Council on Measurement in Education, 1999). When assessments have high stakes for teachers, inequities with regard to teacher quality may increase; for example, teachers of high quality may choose not to teach in low-performing schools because of the possibility that negative consequences associated with low school performance will affect their careers. Thus, students in these schools, who are typically poor or are members of other subgroups that have been disadvantaged in the past, would not have equal access to high-quality teachers.

In this report we have described assessment strategies that ask students to create responses, rather than choose among a defined set of options. While performance assessments can capture a broad range of complex thinking and problem-solving skills, they are useful only when instruction has provided opportunities for students to be engaged in the kind of skills that are targeted by the assessment. Similarly, assessments that require students to use laboratory materials or other hands-on materials are useful only when students have used comparable materials in the classroom. If innovative item formats are used in the assessment, they should be related to instruction that has provided students with the opportunity to engage in problem solving with these formats. Thus, information about the nature of the instructional program in which each student has been enrolled is an important part of understanding assessment results.

INCLUDING ALL STUDENTS

NCLB requires that all students be included in assessments and that accommodations be offered to students with disabilities and to English language learners as appropriate. States are permitted to provide alternate assessments for students who cannot participate for a variety of reasons in exactly the same assessment as other students. These alternate assessments are either aligned with the same standards as the regular assessments, or, for students who cannot be held to the same standards as other students because of severe cognitive disabilities, are based on alternate achievement standards (U.S. Department of Education, 2004, p. 50).

Issues Related to Accommodations

The challenge for states is complex. Although states are required to provide appropriate accommodations to these two groups of students, the effects of accommodations on test performance and on the inferences based on test results are not clearly understood. Findings from research are not conclusive with regard to the comparability of inferences based on scores obtained under accommodated and nonaccommodated conditions (National Research Council, 2004). Nevertheless, states are expected to include test results for students with disabilities and English language learners in their aggregated reports and to report disaggregated group results for these students, and they may be held accountable for demonstrating that these students are making progress in science.

A principle known as universal design, which was developed by architects and other designers, has been adapted to educational measurement and holds some promise for ameliorating some of the difficulties that testing accommodations present. The principle is that products and buildings—or assessments—should be designed so that the greatest number of people can use them without the need for modification—that is, to eliminate unnecessary obstacles to access. In the case of assessment this might mean, for example, that if all students had more than enough time to complete an assessment task, offering extra time to students who need it because of cognitive disabilities would not provide them with an unfair advantage over other students. The application of universal design principles to assessment has not, however, been fully developed; the committee hopes that with further research it will provide valuable alternatives for states. Further information on this topic is available from the National Center on Educational Outcomes (http://education.umn.edu/NCEO).

Advice to States

Although the research base on the effects of accommodations on the interpretation of test scores and the inferences that can be supported by results is inconclusive, some guidance can be offered for those making decisions about test development and the provision of accommodations. First, states and their test developers should make clear which inferences are to be based on test results. Clear specification of the target skills evaluated and of the ancillary skills required to demonstrate proficiency on the target skills can improve decision making about accommodations. For example, in a written science assessment with open-ended responses, is writing a target skill or an ancillary skill? Is the assessment designed to make inferences about science knowledge, about written expression of science knowledge, or about written expression of science knowledge in English? The answers to these questions can assist with decisions about accommodations, such as whether to provide a scribe to write answers or to provide a translator to translate answers into English. If mathematics is required to complete the assessment tasks, is mathematics computation a target skill or an ancillary skill? Is the desired inference about knowing the correct equation to use or about performing the calculations? (Here, the answers can guide decisions about use of a calculator.) Further discussion about identifying target and ancillary skills and about articulating the intended inferences can be found in *Keeping Score for All: The Effects of Inclusion and Accommodation Policies on Large-Scale Educational Assessments* (National Research Council, 2004, Chapter 6).

Second, states should consider the needs of students with disabilities and English language learners when designing their assessments and making decisions about such issues as time limits, wording of test items, and response formats. For example, one of the most common accommodations is the provision of extra time to complete an assessment. Research has shown that general education students, as well as students with disabilities and English language learners, perform better when time limits are lifted (Zuriff, 2000; Abedi, Hofstetter, Baker, and Lord, 2001; Elliott, Kratochwill, and McKevitt, 2001), which suggests that the time limits set for some assessments may be too stringent. Careful consideration of the amount of time required to complete a test (or whether time limits are needed at all) may reduce the need for extended time accommodations.

Another example is a common accommodation often provided to English language learners referred to as "simplified language," "modified language," or "plain language." This accommodation is intended to reduce the reading level to increase the accessibility of an assessment to a nonnative English speaker. Research has shown that this accommodation helps both English language learners and native English speakers (Abedi, Lord, and Hofstetter, 1998), which suggests that some assessments may use unnecessarily difficult vocabulary. The need to provide this accommodation can be reduced by careful attention to reading level and vocabulary requirements in assessment tasks. Bias and sensitivity reviews should be conducted during the development of assessment items, and reviewers should include individuals with expertise in working with students with disabilities and English language learners who can identify language, noncontent vocabulary, and terminology that causes assessment tasks to be more difficult than intended.

Third, states and their test developers should include samples of students with disabilities and English language learners during the field testing of assessment tasks. Field testing provides critical information about the performance of assessment tasks, and inclusion of students from these groups will help identify problems during the earliest stages of test development.

Many of the measures described in this section were originally devised in the context of traditional assessments; the principles apply to any kind of assessment, although complex questions may arise. The goal of very clearly identifying the construct to be measured and making sure that the assessment does not pose significant challenges that are irrelevant to the intended construct is worthwhile in any assessment context. However, one could choose, for example, to assess students' capacity to conduct a sustained investigation using a set of related standardized tasks to be completed over a period of weeks specifically because it is a way of measuring a complex, multifaceted construct. To complete this assessment, a student may need to be able to document findings with both clear narrative and numerical records, to manipulate equipment, to visually discern subtle changes, and perhaps to collaborate with other students. These are examples of tasks that may pose a particular challenge for some students, and task developers and educators face a challenge in determining which are integral to the construct, and how students with disabilities or English language learners might be accommodated.

RESOURCES

NCLB will focus increased attention on science education in the United States. Indeed, the incremental increase in attention paid to science education is likely to exceed the increase associated with reading and mathematics when annual testing in these subjects became mandatory. While reading and mathematics have been routinely assessed by states for a number of years—decades, in some states—NCLB marks a significantly increased focus on measuring and reporting on science achievement.

The central goal of the assessment component of NCLB is to highlight the areas in which students are not performing at a sufficiently high level and to focus attention on the schools and subjects in which performance targets are not being met. The revelations about inadequacies in science education that are likely to result will have a variety of important implications for schools and states. For example, the increased scrutiny of science education in a state may alter the labor market for teachers, potentially changing the ability of school districts to meet the requirement of NCLB for highly qualified teachers.

The measurement and reporting of science proficiency is likely to lead to an increased focus on science instruction. This reporting also will help to reveal the degree to which schools have supported science education in the past. Numerous authors, including Figlio and Rouse (2004) and Jacob (2003), have indicated that schools tend to focus more attention on the subjects in which performance is measured, particularly when high stakes are attached to results. Therefore, the inclusion of science in an assessment system (and possibly in an accountability system) could lead to a relative increase in the instructional time and staffing devoted to science. This response may be particularly great in schools serving underserved populations, because these schools are the most likely to focus their attention on the high-stakes subjects.

Highlighting Existing Equity and Adequacy Issues

A widespread finding of low science proficiency could indicate that students in a state have not received an adequate level of instruction in science. Such a revelation could have important implications for school finance, as 21 state constitutions have explicit language requiring that states provide for "adequate" levels of school funding. Adequacy standards define a target level of achievement in core subject areas that schools are expected to reach. The minimum adequate level of spending necessary to enable students to attain target achievement levels dictates the basic level of foundation-grant state aid programs, which is by far the most common form of state aid in the United States. A finding of widespread low performance on science assessments could raise constitutional concerns, because definitions of adequate school funding have historically been based on reading and mathematics performance levels, not science ones. Therefore, disappointing science assessment results could indicate that a higher level of school spending is necessary to ensure that the resources allotted for science education are adequate.

Whether such a finding would necessarily raise constitutional concerns is a matter for debate, however. While some interpretations of state adequacy provisions are based on the *realized* levels of student test performance, a more common interpretation is that schools receive adequate funding if students have adequate *opportunity to learn*, regardless of students' actual performance levels. Depending on a state's interpretation of its adequacy provisions, an argument that schools could reach proficiency targets in science with existing resources may be supportable.

A related point is *equity*. A finding of a wide disparity across schools in the rates at which students meet proficiency standards could raise concerns about whether the distribution of school resources across school districts in a state is equitable. The constitution of 20 states supports the notion that school finance in a state must be equitable across school districts. There are two conceptions of equity in school finance: equity for school-age children and equity for taxpayers. In this context, taxpayer equity means that any given tax rate would relate to the same level of per-pupil spending independent of the taxpayer's residential location. The introduction of science testing in a school assessment or accountability system would raise taxpayer equity concerns only if this definition were expanded to imply that any given tax rate would relate to the same level of education *services*, independent of the taxpayer's residential location. If the assessment system helped reveal that the level of science instruction differs across school districts in a state, a state may need to contend with new equity considerations, even if it considers only taxpayer equity.

Children's equity, by contrast, encompasses such questions as whether different groups of children receive similar levels of services. Few interpret state constitutions as mandating equality of outcomes; rather, most interpret equity provisions as requiring equality of opportunity. An equity interpretation of equality of outcomes would suggest that the consequences of testing students in a new subject area are potentially large. However, even the more common conception of equality of opportunity could raise equity concerns if it were found that it is more expensive to produce a certain level of student science achievement in some settings than in others.

In both the equity and adequacy cases, it is not obvious that new science assessments would lead to recommendations for increased science funding. After all, schools' observed science staffing and materials reflect both financial realities and choices made by schools. However, decisions regarding school funding adequacy and equity have been based largely on reading and mathematics performance. The new information provided by science assessments could change the calculus of school finance in many states. Schools already severely constrained fiscally when they were not placing a heavy emphasis on science instruction could become considerably more constrained if they were compelled to shift resources toward science education.

Exacerbating Existing Inequities in School Finance

Beyond simply highlighting the present level of inequities in school finance, new science assessments—especially if incorporated into an accountability system—could exacerbate these inequities through effects on the labor market for science teachers. Clotfelter, Ladd, and Vigdor (2004) and Figlio and Rueben (2001) argue that teachers are responsive to test-based or fiscal accountability systems; also, schools serving lower income or minority students are most likely to have a difficult time retaining high-quality teachers. Therefore, schools with underserved populations—already affected by financing inequities—are likely to be further affected by a disproportionate flight of high-quality teachers.

The rationale behind this argument stems from economic theory. The increased attention paid to science education is likely to increase the demand for qualified science teachers—a tendency reinforced by the "highly qualified teacher" provision of NCLB. At the same time, research has demonstrated that increased accountability pressures decrease the number of teachers—in this case, science teachers—willing to work at any given salary. The result of these two forces is that the market-clearing salary for a science teacher at the current level of quality would necessarily increase as a result of increased accountability pressures. In the absence of salary increases, the consequence of these changes in market forces would be an average lowering of science teacher quality.

The burden of this reduced average level of teacher quality is likely to be borne primarily, if not exclusively, by schools and districts serving minority and economically disadvantaged students. Teachers in schools serving more advantaged populations could be expected to face lower accountability pressure, and these teachers would be less likely to leave science teaching as a result of new science assessments. Hence, the predicted outflow of quality science teachers should be lower in more advantaged schools and districts. Moreover, if these schools are more likely to hire the highly qualified science teachers leaving the less advantaged schools (Clotfelter, Ladd, and Vigdor, 2002), they are also more likely to have provided significant science education to their students prior to the assessment system. Advantaged schools and districts would therefore be expected to experience a smaller increase in the demand for improvement in science education as a result of new assessments. These schools also could be predicted to face a small average reduction in teacher quality at any given salary level. Schools serving more disadvantaged populations, in contrast, are expected to experience larger outflows of qualified science teachers at the same time that their demand for these same teachers is increasing; these schools therefore would sustain larger reductions in average science teacher quality at any given salary level.

The implication of these findings is that teacher salaries are likely to need to increase under heightened accountability conditions in order to maintain—let alone increase—the level of science teacher quality in a state. Moreover, one could expect schools serving minority and low-income populations to need the greatest increase, a situation that would probably exacerbate existing inequities. The increased costs of providing an adequate level of science education, coupled with the likelihood that these increased costs will be borne unequally by schools and districts, suggest that the introduction of science assessments—particularly if high stakes are attached—will raise new equity and adequacy issues in education finance.

The testing provision of NCLB surely will lead to a keener awareness of the state of science education in public schools. Moreover, an increased focus on science assessment is very likely to highlight new school finance issues.

In advance of the implementation of science assessment, states should consider the likely school finance implications—in terms of equity and adequacy—and begin to plan for them. It is not a criticism of NCLB or of science assessment to argue that these assessments are likely to have large school finance implications. Rather, it is important that the school finance system be sufficiently flexible so that states can respond rapidly to new school finance-related issues that are uncovered through the assessment. These ramifications may involve increasing the state's contribution to local education budgets, or they may involve adjusting state aid formulas. With advance warning, states will be better able to cope with these eventualities successfully.

This committee advocates that state science assessments be closely aligned with a set of rigorous, well-defined, and high-quality standards that stress scientific inquiry. The more closely an assessment fully captures these standards, however, the more likely it is to expose existing inadequacies or inequities in the current school finance system. States should be aware that the more closely their assessments are aligned with their standards in the design of science assessments, the more pronounced the potential implications for school finance may be.

The market for high-quality science teachers may change as a result of the introduction of science assessments, and states should be prepared to help increase the incentives for high-quality teachers to remain in the profession and in their schools, following the assessment's introduction. States have many policy options at their disposal for helping to ensure that all students have access to high-quality science teachers. Possible options include targeted bonuses for qualified science teachers to teach or remain in schools serving underserved student populations.

QUESTIONS FOR STATES

Opportunity to Learn

Question 7-1: Is the state's science assessment system constructed to provide information on students' opportunity to learn what is needed to meet the state's goals for science learning? Does the state continually monitor and periodically evaluate its education system to ensure that sufficient opportunity to learn is being maintained for all students?

Including All Students

Question 7-2: Are all components of the state assessment system designed to make them accessible to the widest range of students and to support valid interpretations about their performance? Does the development process for each component include consideration of ways to minimize challenges unrelated to the construct being measured?

Question 7-3: Does the state's science assessment system include alternative assessments that can be used to assess the science achievement of students with significant cognitive disabilities?

Resources

Question 7-4: Has the state set aside resources for making improvements in its science education system to remedy the inequities or inadequacies that may be revealed by assessment and evaluation data? Has it also set aside resources to promulgate exemplary practices that may be revealed by assessment results?

Question 7-5: Does the state monitor the assessment system's effect on the recruitment and retention of high-quality teachers?

8

Evaluation and Monitoring

T he No Child Left Behind Act (NCLB) requires that states provide evidence of how well their assessment systems respond to mandates for establishing a single, statewide system comprised of:

- challenging content standards,
- challenging academic achievement standards, and
- a single, statewide system of annual assessments that are of high technical quality, are aligned with academic content and achievement standards, are inclusive, and are effectively reported.

However, NCLB does not define particular standards of quality with regard to any of these dimensions, nor does it require that the state respond to any evidence of inadequacies with efforts to improve the quality of its assessment systems. Moreover, while NCLB requires states to evaluate various dimensions of their assessment systems, it does not explicitly ask them to evaluate the entire system, or to use accumulated evidence to determine whether and where improvement may be needed. Thus, in attending to the details of the legal requirements, a state may miss the broader question of whether and how well its policies and resources—and specifically its assessment system—are supporting progress in science achievement. NCLB makes clear that evaluation and monitoring are important. In this chapter the committee outlines the role these important functions play in a systems approach: ensuring that the system is well aligned clearly communicates valued standards for teaching and learning and provides accurate data for decision making.

Evaluation is an important feedback mechanism for the education system and must be an integral element in that system. The state must continually monitor and periodically evaluate the effectiveness of the education system as a whole, as well as the effects and effectiveness of each of its components—including the assessment system. The state will need to make sure not only that each component is functioning well independently, but also that the education system as a whole is operating as intended.

The chapter begins with an overview of professional and other standards for assessment quality, goes on to discuss the consequences and uses of assessment systems, and then looks at ways to incorporate evaluation throughout the assessment system.

EVALUATING THE TECHNICAL QUALITY OF ASSESSMENT INFORMATION

Any assessment system must, above all, provide accurate information. Users expect the information to be trustworthy and accurate and to provide a sound basis for actions. *Validity*, the term measurement experts use to express this essential quality of an assessment or an assessment system, refers to the extent to which an assessment's results support meaningful inferences for intended purposes. The validity of such inferences rests on evidence that the assessment measures the constructs it was intended to measure and that the scores provide the information they were intended to provide. Thus, particular assessments cannot be classified as either valid or invalid in any absolute sense; it is the uses to which assessment results are put that are valid to a greater or lesser degree. An assessment that is valid for one purpose, such as providing a general indicator of tested students' understanding of equilibrium, may be invalid for another purpose, such as providing details of students' alternate conceptions about equilibrium that could be used to guide instruction. The same issues apply to the evaluation of assessment systems that produce a variety of information from multiple measures as apply to the use of multiple measures for assessing individuals, although the available methodologies have to be adapted for that purpose.

As discussed earlier, available evidence suggests that the science standards in many states are vague and not sufficiently specific to represent a clear target for assessment development or for curriculum and instruction (Cross, Rebarber, and Torres, 2004). However, the federal requirements do not ask states to revisit or refine their standards. The NCLB Peer Review Guidance (U.S. Department of Education, 2004) asks for evidence that states are improving the alignment of their assessments and standards over time and that they are filling gaps in their coverage of content domains. However, if a state's standards are insufficiently clear for the purpose of determining with any degree of precision whether elements of the system are adequately aligned to them, or for the purpose of establishing priorities for curriculum, instruction, and assessment, then the required evaluations of alignment cannot serve their purpose.

We begin with a look at professional standards for assessment quality.

AERA, APA, and NCME Standards

The most recent edition of *Standards for Educational and Psychological Testing* (American Educational Research Association, American Psychological Association, and National Council on Measurement in Education, 1999) articulates professional standards regarding assessment validity and quality. This document describes specific standards for test construction, evaluation, and documentation; fairness in testing; and test applications. It makes clear that the sponsors of any assessment have the responsibility to ensure that adequate evidence supports the uses intended for the assessment. The *Standards* emphasizes validity as the most fundamental consideration in test development and use, and it identifies the sources of evidence supporting validity. The *Standards* explains that evidence based on analysis of test content, response processes, internal structure, and relations to other variables, as well as evidence based on the consequences of testing, are all important.

The *Standards* addresses other issues as well and provides specific guidance regarding reliability; measurement error; scaling, norms, and score comparability; the process of test development and revision; test administration, scoring, and reporting; and the need for supporting documentation for tests. Separate sections address the rights and responsibilities of test takers and specifically the standards that apply to the testing of those with limited English proficiency and those with disabilities.

The *National Science Education Standards*

The assessment standards defined in the *National Science Education Standards* (National Research Council, 1996), which reflect the views of professional scientists across the country, address many of the same concerns. They highlight four points:

1. Assessments must be consistent with the decisions they are designed to inform.
2. Achievement and opportunity to learn must be assessed.
3. The technical quality of the data collected should be well matched to the decisions and actions taken based on interpretations of those data.
4. Assessment practices must be fair.

Moreover, the standards explicitly include classroom assessments within their purview. The document was innovative in detailing the role of teachers as assessors and the classroom functions of assessment, including improving classroom practice, planning curricula, developing self-directed learners, reporting student progress, and researching teaching practices (National Research Council, 1996).

CRESST Accountability Standards

Responding to the escalating use of assessment for accountability purposes and concerned about the validity of the systems being created, researchers at the Center for Research on Evaluation, Standards, and Student Testing (CRESST), a consortium of university-based experts in educational measurement, have advanced the idea of standards for accountability systems (Baker, Linn, Herman, and Koretz, 2002), specifically advocating that attention be paid to the system as a whole and not just to individual assessments. Drawing on the *Standards for Educational and Psychological Testing* (American Educational Research Association, American Psychological Association, and National Council on Measurement in Education, 1999) as well as their own knowledge and experience and ethical considerations, the developers of the CRESST standards stress that accountability systems should be evaluated on the basis of multiple forms of evidence. Specifically, systems should be supported by rich and varied evidence of the validity of inferences based on assessment results, evidence that all elements of the system are aligned, and evidence that assessment is sensitive to instruction (that is, that good instruction yields higher performance on the assessment than does poor instruction). Standards are presented in five areas—system components, testing standards, stakes, public reporting, and evaluation—and dimensions against which accountability systems could be evaluated are provided for each. With regard to evaluation, the CRESST standards propose that (Baker et al., 2002, p. 4):

> Longitudinal studies should be planned, implemented, and reported evaluating effects of the accountability program. Minimally, questions should determine the degree to which the system:
>
> a. builds capacity of staff;
> b. affects resource allocation;
> c. supports high-quality instruction;
> d. promotes student-equitable access to education;
> e. minimizes corruption;
> f. affects teacher quality, recruitment, and retention; and
> g. produces unanticipated outcomes.
>
> The validity of test-based inferences should be subject to ongoing evaluation. In particular, evaluation should address:
>
> h. aggregate gains in performance over time; and
> i. impact on identifiable student and personnel groups.

Deeper Conceptions of Quality

Other dimensions also need to be considered in the evaluation of assessment systems. We have discussed the developmental nature of science learning and its implications for science assessment. In the committee's view, assessments must be based on solid conceptions of the ways in which science learning develops over time. This grounding in learning deepens the conceptions of quality that can be applied to assessment. Assessment tasks and scoring rubrics that are designed to elicit the knowledge and cognitive processes that are consistent with the nature of learning provide a framework not only for the development of assessments but also for evaluation of the validity of interpretations based on the assessment's results.

For science assessment to support learning, the ways in which learning develops must be considered as the assessment systems are evaluated and monitored. Once a means of designing assessments that are based on models of how student learning develops are put in place, the degree to which these models are reflected in the assessments must be evaluated. Because this deeper conception of what assessment is for has not yet been widely adopted by states, the means of evaluating how effectively an assessment system reflects models of learning are not as well established as other evaluation and monitoring practices. Nevertheless, the committee argues that if a system attempts to incorporate this approach the effectiveness with which it does so needs to be monitored.

EVALUATING THE CONSEQUENCES
AND USES OF ASSESSMENT SYSTEMS

Although states have few sources of guidance as they consider monitoring and evaluating the system as a whole, in several areas considerable efforts have been made that will be helpful.

Validity of Gains

Focusing on an individual test rather than the system as a whole can cause a state to miss unintended consequences of testing. If instruction becomes overly focused on material that is tested on a single test and on the formats used on the test, improved test results may not represent gains in learning or progress toward meeting standards; rather, they may reflect students' improved ability to respond to items on a particular kind of test. In such a case, the meaningfulness of test score gains is in question. Research shows that test scores in the first years after a new test is introduced are likely to show substantial increases, particularly if high stakes are involved, but that improvements tend to level off after that initial stage (Linn, 2003). If students have indeed improved, gains should be evident on other indicators. If not, the gains are suspect. An analysis of test results from the Kentucky Instructional Results System program and those from the National Assessment of Educational Progress and the American College Testing Program (ACT) provides one example of a case in which a state's assessment was not consistent with other indicators (Koretz and Baron, 1998). The Kentucky results showed dramatic upward trends, while the two national assessments showed modest improvement or level performance. Such contrasts raise such questions as whether the state test results reflect real learning or just the effects of test preparation or teaching to the test, and whether the national tests were adequate measures of the Kentucky curriculum.

In another example, California's strong accountability system in reading and mathematics resulted in impressive initial improvement in test scores, with the majority of elementary schools meeting their target goals. Years 2 and 3 of the program saw diminishing returns, with substantially fewer schools reaching their goals, and results from 2004 showed no consistent trends (Herman and Perry, 2002). Some observers believe that patterns such as these illustrate the limits of what can be achieved primarily through test preparation, and that continuing improvement over the long term will require meaningful changes in the teaching and learning process. These findings suggest the need for states to continuously validate their gains and the meaning of their science scores over time.

Reliability of Scores from Year to Year

Ensuring the reliability of scores is another challenge facing those who monitor school performance from year to year. All test scores are fallible. Individual test scores reflect actual student capability but also are subject to errors introduced by students' motivation and state of health on the day of the test, in how attentive they are to the cues and questions in the tests, in how well prepared they are for a particular test format, and in other factors. Test scores at the school level similarly reflect an amalgam of students' actual knowledge and skills and error. Error can be introduced by unpredictable events, such as, for example, loud construction near the school, waves of contagious illness, and other factors that affect which students are actually tested. In addition, there is inevitably substantial volatility in scores from year to year that has nothing to do with student learning, but more to do with variations in the population of students assessed, particularly for smaller schools and schools with high transiency rates. This volatility makes it difficult to interpret changes in test scores from year to year, as these must be interpreted in light of these potential sources of measurement error. For example, in an analysis of Colorado's reading and mathematics assessments, Linn and Haug (2002) found that less than 5 percent of the state's schools showed consistent growth on the Colorado Student Assessment Program of at least 1 percentage point per year from 1997 to 2000, even though schools on average showed nearly a 5 percent increase over the three-year period in the number of students deemed proficient. Combining two years of results for individual schools, as permitted by NCLB, reduces the volatility but does not eliminate the problem.

System Alignment

We have noted the importance of evaluating not only the alignment of the elements of the assessment system but also the elements of the larger system through which science education is delivered. This report has described an assessment system that includes assessments operating at multiple levels and aligned with the broad goals of the overarching system. Thus, alignment, when it is evaluated, must be considered both among the multiple assessment measures and other components of the assessment system, and between the assessment system and the goals of the system. Neither methods for doing this second kind of analysis nor indexes of the overall alignment are readily available. This is an area in which further research would be extremely beneficial.

Even in the absence of a complete research base, however, many aspects of alignment can be investigated. Curriculum and instructional materials, classroom assessments, and other available resources can be coordinated to ensure that they support science learning. Teacher preparation, professional development, and other supports also need to be aligned with standards, as well as students' needs, to ensure that teachers have essential skills and knowledge. The selection of materials, personnel evaluations, preservice requirements, and other essential features of the education system can be coordinated with the defined learning goals and strategies.

Alignment between assessments and standards is a specific type of horizontal coherence. When they are well aligned, they can reinforce the education system's goals for science learning; when poorly aligned, they can distort the standards and the instruction that is used to communicate the standards to students.

While the concept of alignment is straightforward, establishing whether standards and assessments are actually aligned is not. It may be relatively easy to determine whether a test provides an adequate measure of a simple construct, such as two-digit multiplication, but it is exceedingly difficult to measure the degree of alignment between an assessment and standards that include higher order scientific principles. The reason doing this is so difficult is that both the theoretical basis for alignment and the operational procedures for aligning tests and standards are still being developed.

On the theoretical side, evaluating alignment entails establishing the equivalence of the cognitive demands of assessment tasks (often multiple-choice test items) and the cognitive demands of state standards (usually prose statements about student knowledge and skills). On what basis might one decide that the assessment task and the standard are comparable? At present, there is no widely accepted framework for classifying or describing scientific understanding that could serve as a yardstick for comparing assessments and standards.

On the practical side, all existing alignment procedures are based on judgment. Educators look at assessments and standards and try to decide whether a given task (or set of tasks) seems to demand the knowledge and skills described in a given standard or set of standards. Such judgments are difficult and time-consuming to make, and different approaches to the process yield different results. Thus, while alignment is widely regarded as essential in a standards-based system, few are satisfied with current means of measuring it.

A number of researchers have developed practical procedures for judging alignment. Although they differ in specifics, each of the procedures restricts the scope of the comparison by focusing on a small number of key dimensions, and each provides operational definitions and training to improve the reliability of judgments by raters. Overall, many researchers who study alignment have concluded that the state tests they studied were less challenging and narrower in content than their standards. In a paper prepared for the committee, Rothman (2003) summarizes and analyzes six recent alignment studies: Norman L. Webb's studies of alignment between standards and tests in mathematics and science (Webb, 1997, 1999, 2001); Karen K. Wixson's studies of alignment between standards and tests in elementary reading (Wixson, Fisk, Dutro, and McDaniel, 2002); Andrew C. Porter's tools for measuring the content of standards, tests, and instructional materials (Porter, 2002); Achieve's studies of alignment of standards and tests (www.achieve.org); The Buros Center for Testing's study of alignment between commercially available tests and state standards (Impara, 2001; Plake, Buckendahl, and Impara, 2004); and The American Association for the Advancement of Science's Project 2061's studies of standards, textbooks, and textbook tests (2002).

Rothman concludes (p. 16), "Although the six methods differ widely in their criteria for alignment and the procedures used to gauge alignment, they share the conclusion that, with a few exceptions, standards and tests are generally not well aligned. This conclusion contrasts with the results from studies by states and publishers, which typically show a higher degree of alignment."

Further research on alignment is clearly needed. Determining the key dimensions that characterize alignment and examining the validity of methods that are used to set standards for alignment are two issues that should be given high priority by states. Practical procedures need to be developed to improve the reliability of ratings and to reduce the time burden associated with alignment studies. However, these shortcomings should not deter states from making immediate and concerted efforts to bring assessments in line with standards.

We note here that the creation of an assessment system may create additional challenges for alignment studies, although a systems approach could improve the overall alignment between standards and assessments. The designers of a science assessment system select the tests and tasks that constitute the system to align *collectively* with the breadth and depth of state science content standards, to address program monitoring and evaluation needs, and to provide evidence of student competence. In an assessment system, therefore, alignment should be looked at across components. A single assessment may not be well aligned with the standards or the curriculum because it is narrowly focused, but it may be part of a more comprehensive collection of assessments that, as a set, are fully aligned with both.

The goals regarding the development of content and performance standards presented in Chapter 4 address important measures that states can take to improve the alignment between their assessments and standards, but we offer here several further points for states to consider.

First, it is clear that alignment is best addressed not as an afterthought in the development of a standards-based system but as a key goal from the beginning. It is far more effective to build in alignment as the elements of the system are put into place (or modified in response to NCLB requirements) than to try to engineer the elements into alignment after they have been developed (Webb, 1997). Second, the responsibility for ensuring that assessments are aligned to the standards and other aspects of the education system cannot be left to testing contractors and should rest with the states. By updating alignment studies whenever the standards or the tests change, states can monitor a contractor's efforts to ensure alignment.

It is also important to note that improving alignment does not necessarily mean changing tests. Alignment is a characteristic of the relationship between standards and tests and thus can be adjusted by means of changes in either the standards or the tests. Moreover, as a number of alignment studies have shown, standards can be the cause of the problem (Rothman, 2003). If standards are too general, for example, many types of test items could be viewed as fitting under their very wide umbrellas. In such a case, individual items might seem to match standards, but the test as a whole might not measure the full range of knowledge and skills intended in the standards. It is important to consider the effects that any change to tests or standards might have on the comparability of information across years that is based on test results.

INCORPORATING EVALUATION THROUGHOUT THE ASSESSMENT SYSTEM

We turn now to some of the specific challenges of evaluating and monitoring each element of the assessment system.

Assessment Development

Earlier in the report we described the characteristics that assessment systems should have. The first step in developing such an assessment system is to translate standards into assessment frameworks and specifications. These documents should be extensively reviewed to ensure that they are well aligned with the standards. A part of this review should be a determination that assessment of all the standards has been provided for by means of large-scale or classroom-based assessments. The quality of these documents should be reviewed by both teachers and content experts who are not part of the system. Similarly, as assessment tasks are developed, they should be reviewed to be sure they are aligned with the specifications and to monitor the quality of their content, potential bias, and clarity.

Field testing of assessment tasks and tests provides the next step in evaluation, and a variety of types of evidence are needed to show the extent to which the assessments will provide reliable and accurate data and can support valid inferences for their intended purposes. Among the types of evidence that states should look for are the following (American Educational Research Association, American Psychological Association, and National Council on Measurement in Education, 1999):

- item analyses (to reveal relative difficulty and discrimination).
- evidence of score and interrater reliability (to ensure that scoring standards are consistently applied).
- evidence of fairness (e.g., through differential item functioning and content reviews).
- evidence of quality of scaling.
- evidence of the validity of scores (e.g., through qualitative analyses of the ways in which students respond to the assessment items, analyses of the internal structure of the assessment, and analyses of the relationship between assessment performance and other indicators or variables).

An example of this last kind of analysis might be a finding that students' science scores on the statewide test correspond closely to their scores on a classroom measure of science understanding but do not correspond to their scores on a measure of reading. Such a finding would constitute one source of evidence that the state test did in fact measure science skills and knowledge, as opposed to another academic ability. Similarly, if students who had completed a physics course scored higher on a physics test than did students who were otherwise similar but had not taken the course, as one would expect, this would provide evidence for the validity of the physics test. This latter example is particularly important, in that it could be used to document the instructional sensitivity of the assessment, a critical, but too often overlooked, dimension of validity in the context of NCLB. That is, the legislation is premised on the assumption that teachers and schools can improve their teaching and instruction, and that such improvement will show up in higher test scores; however, if tests are not sensitive to the effects of good teaching, they cannot provide evidence of improvement or lack thereof. Such sensitivity cannot be assumed (Baker, Herman, and Linn, 2004).

Before assessments become operational, it is important to ensure that detailed specifications have been met and that the resulting tests are indeed aligned with standards. Various methods for determining alignment have been developed, and all share a similar set of procedures. An independent group of experts, composed of teachers and subject matter experts, is convened and asked to examine each item or task, rate the content focus and level of cognitive demand of the items, and note any extraneous issues—such as language difficulty—that could affect a student's ability to respond. Taking into account the number of items needed to meet minimum measurement criteria, results are then summarized to show the extent of coverage of the standards in question and the balance of coverage (Porter, 2002; Webb, 1997a, 1997b, 1999, 2001, 2002).

Because it is difficult to assess alignment if standards are not clearly articulated and focused, and because alignment studies make clear the limits of what can be assessed in a finite assessment, the results of alignment studies may indicate a need to modify the standards or to take other steps to improve the alignment between standards and assessments. Furthermore, because the committee advocates a system of assessments that supports student learning and development over time, alignment studies will need to address all of the assessments and sources of data that are intended to be part of the system, as well as addressing the alignment of assessments with learning expectations across grades. Methodologies will be needed to judge the alignment of a multilevel system.

Moreover, as states change their actual assessments, or portions of them, from year to year or within years, evidence must be collected to show the extent to which the different test forms are comparable and that the equating from one form to the next has been done correctly. Without this evidence, scores cannot be compared from one administration to the next, because any differences may be caused by differences in the difficulty levels of the two tests or the constructs measured, rather than changes in performance.

Like other aspects of test development, the plan for the reporting of test results requires monitoring, and methods of reporting should be field-tested with each intended audience—parents, administrators, and teachers—to ensure that reports are clear and comprehensible to users, that users are likely to interpret the information appropriately, and that the information is useful. Similarly, standard-setting processes should be monitored to ensure that appropriate stakeholders were included in the process, that the process took into account both empirical data on test performance and qualitative judgments of what kinds and levels of performance can be expected of minimally proficient students, and that there is evidence of the validity and accuracy of proficiency classifications based on the standards. Moreover, methodologies will be needed to ensure that performance standards take into account the results of a system of assessments, some of which are derived from statewide assessments, others from classroom assessments.

Assessment Effects

As noted above, the CRESST accountability standards (Baker et al., 2002) highlight the need for longitudinal studies to examine the effects of any accountability system. If the primary purpose of NCLB science assessments is to improve student achievement overall and to close the achievement gap between high- and low-achieving students, then studies should examine the extent to which the intended benefits are realized. The CRESST researchers suggest that among the intended benefits that should be investigated are the extent to which the system does the following:

- builds the capacity of staff to enable students to reach standards;
- builds teacher assessment capacity;
- influences the way resources are allocated to ensure that students will achieve standards;
- supports high-quality instruction aligned with standards; and
- supports equity in students' access to quality education.

The accountability standards also note potential unintended consequences that should be investigated. These include the possibility of corruption of test scores; adverse effects on teacher quality, recruitment, or retention; and increases in dropout rates. All these unanticipated outcomes have been associated with high-stakes assessments (Klein, Hamilton, McCaffrey, and Stecher, 2000; Madaus, 1998).

The feasibility of the assessment system also merits inquiry. For example, an assessment program may place new burdens on teachers, principals, and districts. It may raise questions about opportunity costs, cost-effectiveness, and the feasibility of performance targets. Thus, evaluation of the feasibility of any targets set for school performance and progress must be part of the process. For example, Linn (2003) uses historical data to suggest that current goals for adequate yearly progress in reading and mathematics represent a level of improvement that is well beyond what the most successful schools have actually achieved.

As noted earlier, when new high-stakes state assessments are put into place, scores typically show an increase over the first several years. But as Koretz (2005) has noted, such gains may be spurious. One way to examine the extent to which gains in test scores represent real improvements in learning—rather than effective test preparation—is to compare the gains shown on the high-stakes test with those shown on other, independent measures of the same or similar construct.

Another study shows the importance of one of the CRESST evaluation recommendations—that the impact of accountability and assessment on subgroups of the student population be monitored (Klein et al., 2000). Reducing the achievement gap in science between historically underachieving minorities and their more privileged peers is an explicit purpose of NCLB. Just as the law requires that results be disaggregated by subgroup, so, too, should studies of the effects of testing look for differential effects on population subgroups. Such effects may suggest different conclusions than those that result from looking only at overall aggregate performance. It is thus important to look not only at multiyear trends in performance overall and by subgroup but also to examine students' longitudinal growth using advanced statistical models and individual-level data. For example, Choi, Seltzer, Herman, and Yamachiro (2004) found that schools with similar overall growth patterns could be differentially effective with students of differing initial ability. In some schools the gap between high-ability and low-ability students could be increasing, while in others with similar overall growth the pattern could be reversed.

Assessment Use

An additional concern is the utility and use of assessment results. A primary purpose of state assessment systems is to provide evidence that will improve decision making and enable states, districts, and schools to better understand and improve science learning. Stakeholders at each level of the educational hierarchy—state departments of education, school districts, schools, and classrooms—need to monitor student performance and take appropriate action to improve it. For example, a district or state may observe trends in student performance in biology, discover that students are performing relatively poorly with particular science concepts, and use these data to institute a new professional program for teachers that develops their capacity to teach and assess understanding of key biology concepts. At the classroom level, a teacher using a classroom assessment to get detailed knowledge of students' understanding of a particular concept, such as buoyancy, can use that information to provide immediate feedback to students, recognizing the need to engage students in additional lab work to overcome their misconceptions. Thus, the consequences and uses of the assessment system at each level need to be evaluated. This analysis should include questions about whether and how the data are actually used, with an eye to both intended and unintended consequences. Surveys, focus groups, observations, and the collection of artifacts are all means of acquiring this kind of information.

CHALLENGES

This report outlines ambitious goals for assessment systems that go beyond current practice in supporting both accountability and student learning, although we recognize that experience with the design requirements of effective standards-based systems is still developing. For example, the committee has stressed, and NCLB requires, that the elements of an assessment and accountability system should be both coherent and aligned with standards. However, the methodology for developing and ensuring such alignment is still evolving, and there is only a limited amount of research to guide states and districts in their efforts to achieve alignment. Similarly, the research base that can support the development of assessments based on current theories of learning is also evolving. Thus, while NCLB is based on the premise that continuous cycles of assessment and improvement are key to helping all students reach high standards, the means of making that a reality are not yet completely evident.

Continual monitoring and periodic evaluation are particularly important in this high-stakes context. If states are able to keep track of the effects and effectiveness of their systems, not only can they avoid unanticipated consequences but they can also make ongoing improvement a genuine element of their systems.

These are the specific challenges facing states:

The time and resources to conduct evaluations are limited in a time of constricted state budgets. Evaluation associated with development and field-testing of assessments should be considered part of the development cost. Evaluation of assessment consequences typically is quite costly and thus has drawn on external funding sources. However, states may be able to look at some important aspects of assessment impact through the routine survey collection of data on students' opportunity to learn.

Funding mechanisms are constrained. States may not be in a position to develop separate contracts for evaluation. Some states have solved this problem by including a requirement for independent evaluation in their requests for proposals for general assessment contracts. Thus, the winners of the contract would contract on behalf of the state for independent technical advisers and others to conduct evaluations.

Sophisticated evaluation skills are required. Expertise in both assessment and evaluation skills is needed; evaluators must be knowledgeable about both qualitative and quantitative procedures.

Appropriate methodologies are still evolving. The most effective ways to assess alignment developmentally, over time, are not entirely evident. Similar concerns are associated with the challenges of assessing the alignment of system components beyond tests and standards; judging the alignment and integration of information across levels (school, district, and state); evaluating instructional sensitivity; and identifying optimal ways to identify and address fluctuations in scores from year to year that are unrelated to student learning.

QUESTIONS FOR STATES

States can use the following questions to consider whether their methods for evaluating and monitoring their assessment systems are sufficient, and to think about ways to move their assessment systems in the directions the committee has described.

Question 8-1: Does the state make use of multiple sources of information to continually monitor the effects of the science assessment system on science learning and teaching in the state?

Question 8-2: Does the state formally evaluate all aspects of its science assessment system, including development, administration, implementation, reporting, use, and both short- and long-term intended and unintended effects? Do the evaluations address the integration of the components of the system and address the major purposes the assessments are intended to serve? Do they include appropriate procedures and incentives? Do they include multiple indicators, such as technical quality, utility, and impact?

Question 8-3: Does the state monitor and evaluate the interactions between its science assessment system and the assessment systems for other disciplines? Does the evaluation address both the intended and unintended effects of the science assessment system on the state's overall goals for K–12 education? Are the content standards, achievement standards, and assessments evaluated together to ensure they work together as a coherent system?

9

Supporting the Design, Implementation, and Evaluation of State Science Assessment Systems

In this report the committee recommends that a coherent assessment system comprised of multiple measures of student achievement is necessary for meeting No Child Left Behind (NCLB) requirements. Moreover, we conclude that such a system is the most effective means for providing decision makers at all levels of the education system with the information they need to support high-quality science education. Throughout this volume we have laid out our reasoning in reaching these conclusions and have provided ideas, not for the creation of an ideal system (which does not exist), but for the creation of systems that change and adapt over time in response to state priorities and circumstances.

As an aid to states in developing, implementing, and supporting assessment systems of high quality as well as for monitoring existing ones, the committee included throughout this report a series of questions to states. These questions represent the committee's advice on the issues that should be attended to as state science assessment systems are developed and put into practice. The questions, which are recapitulated in Box 9-1, are not intended to be answered with a simple yes or no, but rather to serve as yardsticks against which states can measure their efforts. They also serve as a reminder of the importance of thinking systemically about the design of assessment systems. The committee's overarching recommendation to states is that they think carefully about the issues raised by these questions and consider how their systems address the issues that are raised by each.

In asking states to think about the issues raised by these questions, we recognize that we are asking them to rethink long-held assumptions about science

BOX 9-1
Recapping State Considerations

Question 2-1: Does the state take a systems approach to assessment? That is, are assessments at various levels of the system (classroom, school district, state) coherent with each other and built around shared goals for science education and the student learning outcomes described in the state standards?

Question 2-2: Does the state have in place mechanisms for maintaining coherence among its standards, assessments, curricula, and instructional practices? For example, does the state have in place a regular cycle for reviewing and revising curriculum materials, instructional practices, and assessments to ensure that they are coherent with each other and with the state science standards, and that they adhere to the principles of learning and teaching outlined in this report? Does the state conduct studies to formally monitor and evaluate the alignment between its standards and assessments?

Question 3-1: Does the state's science assessment system target the knowledge, skills, and habits of mind that are necessary for science literacy? For example, does it include items, tasks, or tests that require students to describe, explain, and predict natural phenomena based on scientific principles, laws, and theories; understand articles about science; distinguish questions that can be answered scientifically from those that cannot; evaluate the quality of information on the basis of its source; pose and evaluate arguments based on evidence; and apply conclusions appropriately?

Question 3-2: Does the state's science assessment system reflect current scientific knowledge and understanding? For example, does the state have in place mechanisms to ensure that all of the measures that comprise the assessment system are scientifically accurate?

Question 3-3: Does the state's science assessment system measure students' understanding and ability to apply important scientific content knowledge and scientific practices and processes? For example, does it include a focus on assessing students' understanding of the big ideas of science as opposed to recall of isolated facts, formulas, and procedures?

Question 3-4: Has the state conducted an independent review of its content standards to ensure that they articulate both the skills and the content knowledge students need to achieve science literacy?

Question 3-5: Does the state's science assessment system reflect contemporary understandings of how people learn science?

Question 3-6: Is the state's science assessment system consistent with the nature of scientific inquiry and practice as it is outlined in the state standards? For example, are opportunities built into the assessment system to assess students' abilities to conduct extended scientific investigations, if such abilities are included in the state's science standards?

Question 4-1: Have the state's science standards been elaborated to provide explicit guidance to teachers, curriculum developers, and the state testing contractors about the skills and knowledge that are required by the state standards?

Question 4-2: Have the state's science standards been reviewed by an independent body to ensure that they are reasonable in scope, accurate, clear, and attainable; reflect the current state of scientific knowledge; focus on ideas of significance; and reflect current understanding of the ways students learn science?

Question 4-3: Does the state have in place a regular cycle (preferably no longer than 8 to 10 years) for reviewing and revising its standards, during which time is allowed for development of new standards as needed; implementation of those standards; and then evaluation by a panel of experts to inform the next iteration of review and revision? Has the state set aside resources and developed both long- and short-term strategies for this to occur?

Question 5-1: Have research and expert professional judgment about the ways in which children learn science been considered in the design of the state's science assessments?

Question 5-2: Have the science assessments and tasks been created to shed light on how well and to what degree students are progressing over time toward more expert understanding?

Question 6-1: Has the state brought together important stakeholders and required experts to develop and/or revise its science assessment system so that it reflects a shared vision of science education?

Question 6-2: Does the state have a written master plan for its science assessment system that specifies which types of assessments are to be used for which purposes, how frequently the different assessments will be administered, who will develop them, who will administer them, at what level of the education system they will be administered, and how the results will be scored, reconciled, and reported?

Question 6-3: Has the state developed both long- and short-term strategies for ensuring that resources are available for assessment development and revision? As part of this process, has consideration been given to strategies such as doing a little bit each year, purchasing curriculum materials that include quality assessments, collaborating with other states that have similar standards to develop assessments or item banks, or developing an assessment system that uses existing personnel and assessment opportunities to assess aspects of science learning that might otherwise be too expensive to assess?

Question 6-4: Is the state's assessment system plan closely aligned with the complete array of its science standards, reflecting the breadth and depth of the science content knowledge, scientific skills and understandings, and cognitive demands that are articulated in the standards?

continued

BOX 9-1 Continued

Question 6-5: Does the state have, and use the support of, both technical and content specific advisory committees to provide advice and guidance on the design, implementation, and ongoing monitoring and evaluation of the assessment system? Do these advisory committees make recommendations to improve particular aspects of the assessment system, and does the state have in place a plan for considering and responding to their suggestions?

Question 6-6: Has consideration been given in designing the assessment system to the nature of the score reports and to the intended inferences that the assessment information will be used to support?

Question 6-7: Have the state and its contractors developed strategies to ensure that reports of assessment results are accessible, relevant, and meaningful to the targeted audiences and that they are provided in a timely manner?

Question 6-8: Do assessment reports include information on the precision of scores and on the accuracy with which the scores can be used to classify students by performance levels? Do they include information about and examples of the appropriate and inappropriate use of the scores and about the kinds of inferences that can and cannot be supported by the results?

Question 6-9: Do the state's teachers, school administrators, and policy makers have ongoing opportunities to build their understanding of current assessment practices and expand their skills in using and interpreting assessment results?

Question 6-10: Do school, district, and state education administrative personnel possess sufficient assessment competence to use assessment information accurately and to communicate it effectively to interested stakeholders?

Question 6-11: Do school, district, and state educational administrative personnel have sufficient resources to collect, store, manage, and analyze the data collected through the assessment system?

Question 6-12: Do the state, school districts, and schools include science educators in every step of the assessment process (from the design of the assessments to data collection to the use and interpretation of the results), thereby providing ongoing opportunities for individuals at each of these levels to build their understanding of current assessment practices and expand their skills in using and interpreting assessment results?

Question 6-13: Do the state's teacher licensing regulations for certification and recertification require that all candidates demonstrate assessment competence at a level commensurate with their area of certification?

Question 6-14: Does the state require as part of its certification and recertification standards that all teachers of science possess knowledge of the subjects they teach as well as the knowledge necessary to teach science well?

Question 7-1: Is the state's science assessment system constructed to provide information on students' opportunity to learn what is needed to meet the state's goals for science learning? Does the state continually monitor and periodically evaluate its education system to ensure that sufficient opportunity to learn is being maintained for all students?

Question 7-2: Are all components of the states' assessment system designed to make them accessible to the widest range of students, and to support valid interpretations about their performance? Does the development process for each component include consideration of ways to minimize challenges unrelated to the construct being measured?

Question 7-3: Does the state's science assessment system include alternative assessments that can be used to assess the science achievement of students with significant cognitive disabilities?

Question 7-4: Has the state set aside resources for making improvements in its science education system to remedy the inequities or inadequacies that may be revealed by assessment and evaluation data? Has it also set aside resources to promulgate exemplary practices that may be revealed by assessment results?

Question 7-5: Does the state monitor the assessment system's effect on the recruitment and retention of high-quality teachers?

Question 8-1: Does the state make use of multiple sources of information to continually monitor the effects of the science assessment system on science learning and teaching in the state?

Question 8-2: Does the state formally evaluate all aspects of its science assessment system, including development, administration, implementation, reporting, use, and both short- and long-term intended and unintended effects? Do the evaluations address the integration of the components of the system and address the major purposes the assessments are intended to serve? Do they include appropriate procedures and incentives. Do they include multiple indicators, such as technical quality, utility, and impact?

Question 8-3: Does the state monitor and evaluate the interactions between its science assessment system and the assessment systems for other disciplines? Does the evaluation address both the intended and unintended effects of the science assessment system on the state's overall goals for K–12 education? Are the content standards, achievement standards, and assessments evaluated together to assure they work together as a coherent system?

assessment and that we are doing so in the face of a research base that we found to have significant limitations. While current understanding can serve as the foundation for the initial design of assessment systems, more knowledge is needed about the design of these systems as well as the underlying fundamental properties of learning and measurement on which they should be founded.

States working alone cannot accomplish all that is needed to make the design and implementation of effective science assessment systems a reality. Therefore, in this chapter we outline ways in which others can help states in their efforts to create coherent assessment systems. We urge scientists, science educators, cognitive scientists, and educational measurement experts to propose and conduct research on ways in which assessment systems can be designed, implemented, and monitored effectively. We also call on federal funding agencies and others, including professional disciplinary societies, to support this research with funding and expertise and to contribute to the dissemination of findings that can lead to improvements in state science assessment systems. Further, we ask states that have had experience in designing and implementing assessment systems to contribute to these efforts by sharing their experiences with other states. Education policy organizations can assist with these efforts by providing structured opportunities for this sharing to occur.

The committee also calls on institutions of higher education to do their part in supporting high-quality science education and assessment systems. Teachers and others need to understand how children learn science and how assessment can be used to obtain useful information about student competence. Both the initial preparation of teachers and their ongoing professional development should include opportunities to develop a deep understanding of how students learn as well as how to guide students at different levels of understanding. No assessment system, no matter how thoughtfully designed, can function as intended unless all who are responsible for developing assessments and interpreting the results are well prepared.

IMPROVING THE KNOWLEDGE BASE

The committee concluded that the measurement of science achievement would be improved if state assessment systems are founded on research regarding the developmental nature of science learning. However, as has been noted throughout this report, research addressing the nature of student learning in individual science domains is far from complete. While it is possible for states to begin by using well-reasoned conceptions of how students' understanding of science develops over time, research that can confirm or enhance these conceptions is critical if the system is to function as intended. Thus, our first recommendations to those other than states call for such research to be conducted and for funding agencies to support researchers and states in this endeavor.

Recommendation 1: Funding agencies should support research on both: (1) the ways in which students' understanding of the fundamental concepts of science develop over time with instruction, and (2) the ways in which students represent their understanding of these ideas as they develop greater expertise.

Recommendation 2: To assist states in their efforts to make more effective use of assessment results for improving curriculum and instruction and for diagnosing student needs relative to reaching the standards, funding agencies should support research on the ways in which tests could be designed to produce more useful subscores and the ways in which those subscores could be used effectively by teachers and others.

MULTIPLE APPROACHES AND UP-TO-DATE MEASURES

NCLB requires that state science assessments be aligned with state content and achievement standards and that they include multiple up-to-date measures of student achievement that are valid and reliable for the purposes for which they will be used. To meet these requirements, states will need both assistance with developing and validating new forms of assessment and with better incorporating and aligning all aspects of their assessment and education systems while meeting standards for technical quality when systems of assessment are involved.

For example, in an assessment system, assessments and combinations of them would need to be reliable and valid for every level and every purpose for which they are used. Current strategies for thinking about technical quality are not focused on thinking about systems of assessment. New methodologies for judging these concepts across different tests and across different levels (e.g., classroom, school, school district, and state) are needed. Similarly, strategies for conducting alignment studies among multiple components of an assessment system and the state standards are needed. Such strategies need to focus on the collective alignment of all the tests and tasks that constitute the assessment system, yet researchers are still struggling with ways to conduct such studies for a single assessment.

Recommendation 3: Research on the design and validation of science assessment systems should be conducted. Among the subjects investigated should be strategies for using classroom assessments for accountability purposes and instruction and procedures for determining the alignment, reliability, accuracy, and validity of assessment systems composed of multiple measures. Federal funding agencies and others should support these research efforts.

THE ASSESSMENT OF SCIENTIFIC INQUIRY

Most state science standards recommend that students *understand* and *develop* appropriate skills related to scientific inquiry, yet, as we have discussed, many state science assessment systems do not adequately target these skills. Under these circumstances the requirements for alignment between standards and assessments cannot be met. States need assistance with developing valid, reliable, and cost-effective ways to include the assessment of inquiry in their science assessment systems.

Recommendation 4: To support the inclusion of assessment tasks focused on scientific inquiry and investigations in state assessment systems, the U.S. Department of Education, science educators, scientists, and educational measurement experts should help states address issues related to the development, validation, and implementation of such tasks.

INCLUSION

NCLB requires that states include all students in their assessment systems and hold all students accountable for attaining challenging standards. Meeting this requirement has increased the importance of the accommodations that are provided to students with disabilities and those with limited English language proficiency. A previous National Research Council committee found that means for determining which accommodations are suitable under particular circumstances as well as determining that scores obtained under accommodated conditions are comparable to those obtained without accommodations are not well documented. States need help in developing policies and practices related to including these students in their assessments.

Recommendation 5: As an aid to the states in developing science assessments to meet NCLB requirements, federal funding agencies and others should sponsor research on the implications of including students with disabilities and those with limited English proficiency in the science assessment system. Research is needed both on identifying appropriate accommodations and on the validity of inferences that can be drawn from test results obtained under accommodated and nonaccommodated conditions. Research is also needed to support the development of instructional and assessment models, based on learning progressions for students with severe disabilities.

BUILDING PROFESSIONAL CAPACITY

NCLB requirements place a premium on high-quality science teaching, and the committee agrees that this as an essential element in improving science achievement. There is strong evidence that good assessment practices can support student success, but teachers need at least a minimum level of assessment literacy to make effective use of assessments and assessment results. We have already suggested that states provide ongoing professional development opportunities for educators, including participation in all aspects of assessment development and implementation, as a way to build their assessment competence. However, such opportunities are not enough.

Post-secondary institutions that prepare science teachers and state licensing agencies must play a role by assuring that teachers and school administrators enter education with a firm foundation in assessment competence. The committee concluded that if states require new teachers to demonstrate assessment competence as a condition for their certification to teach, then teacher preparation programs will include it. In Chapter 6 of this report we conclude that states should include assessment competence as a requirement for state teacher certification, and here we recommend that institutions of higher education and do their part to support states in their efforts.

Recommendation 6: Post-secondary institutions that prepare science teachers should require that preservice science teachers have appropriate knowledge and skills regarding effective science assessment practices. Such knowledge includes the use of assessment results in promoting student learning and making decisions about instruction, developing and using sound assessments, and understanding the limitations of various types of assessment practices and results. Accomplishing this requires that preservice teachers have a deep understanding of the science they teach.

HIGH-QUALITY STANDARDS

The linchpin of NCLB is the development and implementation of assessments to measure student attainment of high-quality standards, but, as we have discussed, the U.S. Department of Education has not provided guidance on what such standards should look like or how they should be organized. Since standards drive the entire system on which NCLB is built, standards of poor quality will affect every aspect of science education. The committee concludes that the U.S. Department of Education should take a more active role in monitoring the quality of state science standards.

Recommendation 7: The U.S. Department of Education should require that states have an independent body evaluate their academic science standards and submit evidence of their quality as part of the required peer review process. The evaluation should not focus on the specific content that states choose to include, but rather on the degree to which the standards are clear, concrete, and complete; are rigorous and scientifically correct; embody a clear conceptual framework; reflect sound models of the way students learn science; are reasonable in scope; and describe performance expectations for students in clear and specific terms. The results of the evaluation should be made public.

SETTING ACHIEVEMENT STANDARDS

In a standards-based system, both content and achievement standards play a critical part in the educational system. Achievement standards provide targets for instruction and assessment and help students to know what is expected of them so that they can adjust their learning strategies to meet expectations. However, the most consistent finding from the research literature on standard setting is that different methods lead to different results. It is nonetheless incumbent on states to ensure that the methods they use to set standards are defensible. Setting achievement standards for a system of assessment is even more challenging than for a single assessment, and states will need help in this regard. The committee calls on the educational measurement community to conduct research on standard-setting methods that can be used in conjunction with assessment systems. We also urge the U.S. Department of Education to require that states evaluate the methods they currently use.

Recommendation 8: Research on the development of standard-setting strategies that could be used to establish achievement levels when results from multiple assessments are involved should be conducted. Federal funding agencies and others should support this important research.

Recommendation 9: The U.S. Department of Education should require that states have an independent external body evaluate the process they use to develop and set achievement levels. This evaluation should be conducted as early in the development process as possible.

ASSESSMENT SYSTEMS—A PRIORITY

The committee urges states to use NCLB as an opportunity to make science both an educational priority and a responsibility shared by all. At the same time, we urge the federal government and the other bodies mentioned above to take their responsibilities seriously and to join states in considering this an opportunity to bring about substantial improvements in science assessment and student learning.

Recommendation 10: Federal agencies and others should support, with funding and expertise, the development and pilot testing of model assessment systems in order to assist states in their efforts to create such systems.

References

Abedi, J., Hofstetter, C., Baker, E., and Lord, C. (2001). *NAEP math performance and test accommodations: Interactions with student language background.* Los Angeles: National Center for Research on Evaluation, Standards, and Student Testing, University of California.

Abedi, J., Lord, C., and Hofstetter, C. (1998). *Impact of selected background variables on students' NAEP math performance.* Los Angeles: National Center for Research on Evaluation, Standards, and Student Testing, University of California.

Achieve, Inc. (2002). *Staying on course: Standards-based reform in America's schools: progress and prospects.* Washington, DC: Author.

Almond, R.G., Steinberg, L.S., and Mislevy, R.J. (2001). *A sample assessment using the four process framework.* (CSE Technical Report No. 543). Los Angeles: Center for the Study of Evaluation, National Center for Research on Evaluation, Standards, and Student Testing, University of California. Available: http://www.cse.ucla.edu/products/reports_set.htm [acccessed June 2005].

Almond, R.G., Steinberg, L.S., and Mislevy, R.J. (2002). Enhancing the design and delivery of assessment systems: A four-process architecture. *Journal of Technology, Learning, and Assessment, 1*(5). Available: http://www.bc.edu/research/intasc/jtla/journal/v1n5.shtml [accessed June 2005].

American Association for the Advancement of Science. (1989). *Science for all Americans: A Project 2061 report on literacy goals in science, mathematics, and technology.* Washington, DC: Author.

American Association for the Advancement of Science. (1993). *Benchmarks for Science Literacy.* New York: Oxford University Press.

American Association for the Advancement of Science. (2001). *Atlas of Science Literacy.* Washington, DC: Author.

American Educational Research Association, American Psychological Association, and National Council on Measurement in Education. (1999). *Standards for educational and psychological testing.* Washington, DC: Authors.

American Federation of Teachers. (1996). *Making standards matter.* Washington, DC: Author.

American Federation of Teachers (1999). *Making standards matter 1999: An update on state activity.* Available: http://www.aft.org/pubs-reports/downloads/teachers/policy11.pdf [accessed June 2005].

American Federation of Teachers. (2001). *Making standards matter 2001.* Washington, DC: Author.

Archibald, D.A. (1998, July). *The reviews of state content standards in English language arts and mathematics: A summary and review of their methods and findings and implications for future standards development.* Paper commissioned by the National Educational Goals Panel. Available: http://govinfo.library.unt.edu/negp/reports/810fin.pdf [accessed June 2005].

Ayala, C.C., Yin, Y., Shavelson, R.J., and Vanides J. (2002). *Investigating the cognitive validity of science performance assessment with think alouds: Technical aspects.* Paper presented at the annual meeting of the American Educational Research Association. New Orleans, LA.

Baker, E.L. (1997). Model-based performance assessment. *Theory into Practice, 36,* 247–254.

Baker, E.L. (2003, Summer). Multiple measures: Toward tiered systems. *Educational Measurement: Issues and Practice, 22*(2), 13–17.

Baker, E.L., Abedi, J., Linn, R.L., and Niemi, D. (1996). Dimensionality and generalizability of domain-independent performance assessments. *Journal of Educational Research, 89,* 197–205.

Baker, E.L., Linn, R.L. Herman, J.L., and Koretz, D. (2002). *Standards for educational accountability systems.* (Policy Brief No. 5). Los Angeles: National Center for Research on Evaluation, Standards, and Student Testing, University of California.

Baron, J.B. (1990). Performance assessment: Blurring the edges among assessment, curriculum, and instruction. In A.B. Champagne, B.E. Lovitts, and B.J. Calinger (Eds.), *Assessment in the service of instruction: This year in school science* 1990. Washington, DC: American Association for the Advancement of Science.

Baxter, G.P., and Glaser, R. (1998). Investigating the cognitive complexity of science assessments. *Educational Measurement: Issues and Practices, 17,* 37–45.

Baxter, G.P., Elder, A.D., and Glaser, R. (1996). Knowledge-based cognition and performance assessment in the science classroom. *Educational Psychologist, 31*(2), 133–140.

Bejar, I.I. (1996). *Generative response modeling: Leveraging the computer as a test delivery medium.* (ETS Research Report No. 96–13). Princeton, NJ: Educational Testing Service.

Bennett, R. (1998). Reinventing assessment: Speculations on the future of large scale educational testing. Princeton, NJ: Educational Testing Service, Policy and Information Centre.

Bennett, R.E. (2002). *Using electronic assessment to measure student performance.* (Issue Brief). Washington, DC: NGA Center for Best Practices. Available: http://www.nga.org/cda/files/ELECTRONICASSESSMENT.pdf [accessed June 2005].

Blank, R., and Pechman, E. (1995). *State curriculum frameworks in mathematics and science: How are they changing across the states?* Washington, DC: Council of Chief State School Officers.

Blumenfeld, P., Soloway, E., Marx, R., Krajcik, J.S., Guzdial, M., and Palincsar, A. (1991). Motivating project-based learning. *Educational Psychologist, 26*(3 & 4), 369–398.

Bond, L. (2000). *Good grades, low test scores: A study of the achievement gap in measures of quantitative reasoning.* Paper presented at the Fifth Annual National Institute for Science Education Forum, May 22–23, Detroit, MI.

Borko, H., and Elliott, R. (1998). *Tensions between competing pedagogical and accountability commitments for exemplary teachers of mathematics in Kentucky.* (CSE Technical Report No. 495). Los Angeles: Center for the Study of Evaluation, National Center for Research on Evaluation, Standards, and Student Testing, University of California.

Borko, H., and Stecher, B.M. (2001, April). *Looking at reform through different methodological lenses: Survey and case studies of the Washington state education reform.* Paper presented as part of the symposium Testing Policy and Teaching Practice: A Multimethod Examination of Two States at the annual meeting of the American Educational Research Association, Seattle, WA.

Boston, C., Rudner, L., Walker, L., and Crouch, L. (Eds.). (2003). *What reporters need to know about test scores.* Washington, DC: Education Writers Association and ERIC Clearinghouse on Assessment and Evaluation.

Bransford, J.D. (1979). *Human cognition: Learning, understanding, and remembering.* Belmont, CA: Wadsworth.

Brewer, D.J., and Stacz, C. (1996). *Enhancing opportunity to learn measures in NCES data.* Santa Monica, CA: RAND Corp.

Briggs, D., Alonzo, A., Schwab, C., and Wilson, M. (2004). *Developmental assessment with ordered multiple-choice items.* Paper presented at the annual meeting of the American Educational Research Association, San Diego, CA.

Brown, J.S., Collins, A., and Duguid, P. (1989). Situated cognition and the culture of learning. *Educational Researcher, 18*(1), 32–42.

Buckendahl, C.W., Impara, J.C., and Plake, B.S. (2002). District accountability without a state assessment: A proposed model. *Educational Measurement: Issues and Practice, 21,* 6–16.

Catley, K., Reiser, B., and Lehrer, R. (2005). *Tracing a prospective learning progression for developing understanding of evolution.* Commissioned paper prepared for the National Research Council's Committee on Test Design for K–12 Science Achievement, Washington, DC.

Champagne, A.B., and Kouba, V.L. (1996, October). *Science literacy: A cognitive perspective.* Paper presented at the College Board Forum, New York.

Champagne, A.B., and Newell, S. (1994). Directions for research and development: Alternative methods of assessing scientific literacy. *Journal of Research in Science Teaching, 29,* 841–860.

Champagne, A.B., Kouba, V.L., and Hurley, M. (2000). Assessing inquiry. In J. Minstrell and E.H. Van Zee (Eds.), Inquiring into inquiry learning and teaching in science (pp. 447–470). Washington, DC: American Association for the Advancement of Science.

Chi, M.T.H., Feltovich, P.J., and Glaser, R. (1981). Categorization and representation of physics problems by experts and novices. *Cognitive Science, 5*:121–152.

Chi, M.T.H., Glaser, R., and Rees, E. (1982). Expertise in problem solving. In R. Sternberg (Ed.), *Advances in the psychology of human intelligence* (pp. 7–75). Hillsdale, NJ: Lawrence Erlbaum Associates.

Chiu, C.W.T., and Pearson, P.D. (1999). *Synthesizing the effects of test accommodations for special education and limited English proficient students.* Paper presented at the National Conference on Large-Scale Assessment, Snowbird, UT.

Choi, K., Seltzer, M., Herman, J., and Yamachiro, K. (2004). *Children left behind: Focusing on the distribution of student growth in longitudinal studies.* Part of the paper session Using Data Accountability Systems to Judge Schools and Reform Efforts presented at 2004 Annual Meeting of the American Educational Research Association, April 12–16, San Diego, CA.

Clotfelter, C.T., Ladd, H.F., and Vigdor, J.L. (2002). *Who teaches whom? Race and the distribution of novice teachers.* Paper presented at the American Economic Association Annual Meeting, January, Atlanta, GA.

Clotfelter, C.T., Ladd, H.F., and Vigdor, J.L. (2004). *Teacher sorting, teacher shopping, and the assessment of teacher effectiveness.* Available: http://trinity.aas.duke.edu/~jvigdor/tsaer5.pdf [accessed June 2005].

Cohen, D., and Ball, D. (1990). Policy and practice: An overview. *Educational Evaluation and Policy Analysis, 12*(3): 347–353.

Collins, A., and Smith, E.E. (1982). Teaching the process of reading comprehension. In D.K. Detterman and R.J. Sternberg (Eds.), *How much and how can intelligence be increased?* Norwood, NJ: Ablex.

Commission on Instructionally Supportive Assessment. (2001). Building tests that support instruction and accountability: A guide for policymakers. Washington, DC: Author.

Consortium for Policy Research in Education. (1993). *Developing content standards: Creating a process for change.* (Policy Brief No. RB–10–10/93). New Brunswick, NJ: Author, Rutgers University.

Cross, R.W., Rebarber, T., and Torres, J. (2004). *Grading the systems: The guide to state standards, tests, and accountability policies.* Washington, DC: Thomas B. Fordham Foundation.

Darling-Hammond, L. (1998). Teacher learning that supports student learning. *Educational Leadership, 55*(5), 6–11.

Darling-Hammond, L. (1999). *Teacher quality and student achievement: A review of state policy evidence.* Seattle, WA: University of Washington, Center for the Study of Teaching and Policy.

Doherty, K., and Skinner, R. (2003). State of the states. Quality counts 2003 special report. *Education Week, 22*(17), 75–76, 78.

Downing, S., and Haladyna, T.M. (in press). *Handbook of test development.* Mahwah, NJ: Lawrence Erlbaum Associates.

Duschl, R. (2003). Assessment of inquiry. In J.M. Atkin and J.E. Coffey (Eds.), *Everyday assessment* (pp. 41–60). Arlington, VA: National Science Teachers Association Press.

Education Week. (2002). Quality counts 2002: Building blocks for success. *Education Week, 21*(16), 8–9.

Education Week. (2003). Technology counts 2003: Tech's answer to testing. *Education Week, 22*(35), 8–10.

Education Week (2004). Quality counts 2004: Count me in: Special education in an era of standards. 23(17), January 8.

Elliott, S.N., Kratochwill, T.R., and McKevitt, B.C. (2001). Experimental analysis of the effects of testing accommodations on the scores of students with and without disabilities. *Journal of School Psychology, 39*(1), 3–24.

Figlio, D.N., and Rouse, C.E. (2004). Do accountability and voucher threats improve low-performing schools? Available: http://www.aeaweb.org/annual_mtg_papers/2005/0109_0800_0303.pdf [accessed June 2005].

Figlio, D.N., and Rueben, K.S. (2001). Tax limits and the qualifications of new teachers. *Journal of Public Economics, 80*(1), 49–71.

Finn, C.E., and Petrilli, M.J. (2000). *The state of state standards, 2000: English, history, geography, mathematics, and science.* (ERIC Document Reproduction Service No. ED 439 133). Washington, DC: Thomas B. Fordham Foundation.

Firestone, W.A., Camilli, G., Yurecko, M., Monfils, L., and Mayrowetz, D. (2000, April). *State standards, socio-fiscal context and opportunity to learn in New Jersey.* Paper presented at the annual meeting of the American Educational Research Association, New Orleans, LA. Available: http://epaa.asu.edu/epaa/v8n35/ [accessed June 2005].

Firestone, W.A., Mayrowetz, D., and Fairman, J. (1998). Performance-based assessment and instructional change: The effects of testing in Maine and Maryland. *Education Evaluation and Policy Analysis, 20,* 95–113.

Frederiksen, J.R., and Collins, A. (1989). A systems approach to educational testing. *Educational Researcher,* 18(9), 27–32.

Galison, P. (1997). *Image and logic: A material culture of microphysics.* Chicago, IL: University of Chicago Press.

Glaser, R. (1992). Expert knowledge and processes of thinking. In D.F. Halpern (Ed.), *Enhancing thinking skills in the sciences and mathematics* (pp. 63–75). Hillsdale, NJ: Lawrence Erlbaum Associates.

Glaser, R., and Baxter, G.P. (1999). *Assessing active knowledge.* Paper presented at the Center for Research on Evaluation, Standards, and Student Testing Conference Benchmarks for Accountability: Are We There Yet?, September 16–17, University of California, Los Angeles.

Glaser, R., and Chi, M. (1988). Overview. In M. Chi, R. Glaser, and M.J. Parr (Eds.), *The nature of expertise.* Hillsdale, NJ: Lawrence Erlbaum Associates.

Goldberg, G.L., and Rosewell, B.S. (2000). From perception to practice: The impact of teachers' scoring experience on performance based instruction and classroom practice. *Educational Assessment, 6,* 257–290.

Goodman, D.P., and Hambleton, R.K. (2003). *Student test score reports and interpretive guides: Review of current practices and suggestions for future research.* (Center for Educational Assessment Research Report No. 477). Amherst, MA: University of Massachusetts School of Education.

Goodwin, B., Englert, K., and Cicchinelli, L.F. (2003). *Comprehensive accountability systems: A framework for evaluation* (rev. ed.). Aurora, CO: Mid-continent Research for Education and Learning.

Gummer, E., and Champagne, A.B. (2005). Classroom assessment of opportunity to learn science through inquiry. In Lawrence B.Flick and Norman G. Lederman (Eds.), *Scientific inquiry and nature of science: Implications for teaching, learning, and teacher education.* Dordrecht: Kluwer Academic Publishers.

Haertel, E.H., and Lorie, W.A. (2004). Validating standards-based score interpretations. *Measurement: Interdisciplinary Research and Perspectives, 2*(2), 61–103.

Hambleton, R.K., and Slater, S.C. (1997). Reliability of credentialing examinations and the impact of scoring models and standard setting policies. *Applied Measurement in Education, 10*, 19–38.

Hansche, L.N. (1998). *Handbook for the development of performance standards: Meeting the requirements of Title I.* Washington, DC: Council of Chief State School Officers.

Hawley, W.D., and Valli, L. (1999). The essentials of professional development: A new consensus. In L. Darling-Hammond and G. Sykes (Eds.), *Teaching as the learning profession: Handbook of policy and practice* (pp.127–150). San Francisco, CA: Jossey-Bass.

Herman, J. (2003). The effects of testing instruction. In S. Fuhrman and R. Elmore (Eds.), *Redesigning accountability systems for education.* New York: Teachers College Press.

Herman, J., and Golan, S. (1991). *Effects of standardized tests on teachers and learning—Another look.* (CSE Technical Report No. 334). Los Angeles: Center for the Study of Evaluation, National Center for Research on Evaluation, Standards, and Student Testing, University of California.

Herman, J.L., and Klein, D. (1996). Evaluating equity in alternative assessment: An illustration of opportunity to learn issues. *Journal of Educational Research, 89*(9), 246–256.

Herman, J.L., and Perry, M. (2002, June). *California student achievement: Multiple views of K–12 progress.* Menlo Park, CA: Ed Source.

Herman, J.L., Baker, E.L., and Linn, R.L. (2004, Spring). Accountability systems in support of student learning: Moving to the next generation. *CRESST Line,* pp. 1–7. Available: http://www.cse.ucla.edu/products/newsletters/CLspring2004.pdf.

Hestenes, D. (1992). Modeling games in the Newtonian world. *American Journal of Physics, 60*, 732–748.

Hestenes, D., Wells, M., and Swackhamer, G. (1992). Force concept inventory. *The Physics Teacher, 30*, 141–158.

Hoz, R., Bowman, D., and Chacham, T. (1997). Psychometric and edumetric validity of geomorphological knowledge which are tapped by concept mapping. *Journal of Research in Science Teaching, 34*(9), 925–947.

Impara, J.C. (2001). *Alignment: One element of an assessment's instructional unity.* Paper presented at the 2001 annual meeting of the National Council on Measurement in Education. Seattle, WA.

Irvine, S.H., and Kyllonen, P.C. (Eds.). (2002). *Item generation for test development.* Mahwah, NJ: Lawrence Erlbaum.

Jacob, B. (2003). High stakes in Chicago. *Education Next,* Winter, 66–72.

Jaeger, R.M. (1989). Certification of student competence. In R.L. Linn (Ed.), *Educational measurement* (3rd ed., pp. 485–514). New York: Macmillan.

Jaeger, R.M. (1995). Setting performance standards through two-stage judgmental policy capturing. *Applied Measurement in Education, 8*, 15–40.

Jaeger, R.M. (1998). Evaluating the psychometric qualities of the National Board for Professional Teaching Standards' assessments: A methodological accounting. *Journal of Personnel Evaluation in Education, 22*, 189–210.

Jaeger, R.M., Cole, J., Irwin, D.M., and Pratto, D.J. (1980). *An interactive structure judgment process for setting passing scores on competency tests applied to the North Carolina high school competency tests in reading and mathematics.* Greensboro, NC: Center for Education Research and Evaluation, University of North Carolina.

Kane, M.T. (2001). So much remains the same: Conception and status of validation in setting standards. In G.J. Cizek (Ed.), *Setting performance standards: Concepts, methods and perspectives* (pp. 53–88). Mahwah, NJ: Lawrence Erlbaum Associates.

Kingston, N., Kahl, S.R., Sweeney, K., and Bay, L. (2001). Setting performance standards using the body of work method. In G.J. Cizek (Ed.), *Setting performance standards: Concepts, methods, and perspectives*. Mahwah, NJ: Lawrence Erlbaum Associates.

Klein, S.P., Hamilton, H., McCaffrey, D., and Stecher, B. (2000). *What do test scores in Texas tell us?* (Issue paper). Santa Monica, CA: RAND Corp. Available: http://www.rand.org/publications/IP/IP202/ [accessed June 2005].

Koretz, D. (2005). *Alignment, high stakes, and the inflation of test scores.* Center for the Study of Evaluation, Report #655. University of California, Los Angeles.

Koretz, D.M., and Baron, S.I. (1998). *The validity of gains in scores on the Kentucky Instructional Results Information System (KIRIS).* Santa Monica, CA: RAND Corp.

Koretz, D., Barron, S., Mitchell, K., and Stecher, B. (1996). *The perceived effects of the Kentucky instructional results information system.* (MR–792–PCT/FF). Santa Monica, CA: RAND Corp.

Koretz, D., McCaffrey, D., Klein, S., Bell, R., and Stecher, B. (1993). *The reliability of scores from the 1992 Vermont portfolio assessment program.* (CSE Technical Report No. 355). Los Angeles: Center for the Study of Evaluation, National Center for Research on Evaluation, Standards, and Student Testing, University of California.

Kouba, V.L., and Champagne, A.B. (2002). Can external assessments assess science inquiry? In Robert W. Lissitz (Ed.), *Optimizing state and classroom tests: Implications of cognitive research for assessments of higher order reasoning in subject-matter domains.* College Park: University of Maryland.

Kozma, R., and Russell, J. (1997). Multimedia and understanding: Expert and novice responses to different representations of chemical phenomena. *Journal of Research in Science and Teaching, 43*(9), 949–968.

Krajcik, J.S., Mamlok, R., and Hug, B. (2000). Modern content and the enterprise of science: Science education in the twentieth century. In L. Corno (Ed.), *Education across a century: The centennial volume.* (One-hundredth yearbook of the National Society for the Study of Education). Chicago, IL: University of Chicago Press.

Lane, S., Parke, C.S., and Stone, C.A. (2002). The impact of a state performance-based assessment and accountability program on mathematics instruction and student learning: Evidence from survey data and school performance. *Educational Assessment, 8*(4), 279.

Lane, S., Stone, C.A., Parke, C.S., Hansen, M.A., and Cerrillo, T.L. (2000). *Consequential evidence for MSPAP from the teacher, principal and student perspective.* Paper presented at the annual meeting of the National Council on Measurement in Education, April, New Orleans, LA.

LaPointe, A.E., Mead, N.A., and Phillips, G.W. (1989). *A world of differences: An international assessment of mathematics and science.* Princeton, NJ: Educational Testing Service.

Larkin, J.H. (1981). Enriching formal knowledge: A model of learning to solve textbook physical problems. In J. Anderson (Ed.), *Cognitive skills and their acquisition.* Hillsdale, NJ: Lawrence Erlbaum Associates.

Larkin, J.H. (1983). The role of problem representation in physics. In D. Gentner and A. Stevens (Eds.), *Mental models.* Hillsdale, NJ: Lawrence Erlbaum Associates.

Latour, B. (1999). *Pandora's hope: Essays on the reality of science studies.* Cambridge, MA: Harvard University Press.

Lerner, L.S. (1998). *State science standards: An appraisal of science standards in 36 states.* Washington, DC: Thomas B. Fordham Foundation. Available: http://lsc-net.terc.edu/do.cfm/paper/8070/show/page-3/use_set-l_standards [accessed June 2005].

Lerner, L.S. (2000). The state of state standards in science. In C.E. Finn and M.J. Petrilli (Eds.), *The state of state standards 2000.* Washington, DC: Thomas B. Fordham Foundation.

Lester, F.K., Jr., Masingila, J.O., Mau, S.T., Lambdin, D.V., dos Santon, V.W., and Raymond, A.M. (1994). Learning how to teach via problem solving. In D. Aichele and A. Coxford (Eds.), *Professional development for teachers of mathematics* (pp. 152–166). Reston, VA: National Council of Teachers of Mathematics.

Li, M. (2001). *A framework for science achievement and its link to test items.* Unpublished doctoral dissertation, Stanford University.

Li., M., and Shavelson, R.J. (2001). *Examining the links between science achievement and assessment.* Paper presented at the annual meeting of the American Educational Research Association, Seattle, WA.

Li, M., Shavelson, R.J., Kupermintz, H., and Ruiz-Primo, M.A. (2002). On the relationship between mathematics and science achievement: An exploration of the Third International Mathematics and Science Study. In D.F. Robitaille and A.E. Beaton (Eds.), *Secondary analysis of the TIMSS data* (pp. 233–249). Boston, MA: Kluwer Academic.

Linn, R.L. (2003). Accountability: Responsibility and reasonable expectations. *Educational Researcher, 32*(7), 3–13.

Linn, R.L., and Haug, C. (2002). Stability of school building accountability scores and gains. *Educational Evaluation and Policy Analysis, 24*(1), 29–36.

Little, J.W. (1994). Teachers' professional development in a climate of educational reform. *Educational Evaluation and Policy Analysis, 15*, 129–151.

Loucks-Horsley, S., Hewson, P., Love, N., and Stiles, K. (1998). *Designing professional development for teachers of science and mathematics.* Thousand Oaks, CA: Corwin Press.

Madaus, G. (1998). The distortion of teaching and testing: High-stakes testing and instruction. *Peabody Journal of Education, 65*, 29–46.

Marzano, R., Pickering, D., and Pollack, J. (2001). *Classroom instruction that works.* Alexandria, VA: Association of Supervision and Curriculum Development.

Masters, G., and Forster, M. (1996). *Progress maps. Assessment resource kit.* Victoria, Australia: Commonwealth of Australia.

Mazur, E. (1997). *Peer instruction: A user's manual.* Upper Saddle River, NJ: Prentice Hall.

McDonnell, L.M., and Choisser, C. (1997). *Testing and teaching: Local implementation of new state assessments.* (CSE Technical Report No. 442). Los Angeles: Center for the Study of Evaluation, National Center for Research on Evaluation, Standards, and Student Testing, University of California.

Messick, S. (1994). The interplay of evidence and consequences in the validation of performance assessments. *Education Researcher, 23*(2), 13–23.

Mestre, J.P. (1994). Cognitive aspects of learning and teaching science. In S.J. Fitzsimmons and L.C. Kerpelman (Eds.), *Teacher enhancement for elementary and secondary science and mathematics: Status, issues and problems* (NSF 94–80, pp. 3-1–3-53). Arlington, VA: National Science Foundation.

Mestre, J.P. (Ed.). (2005). *Transfer of learning from a modern multidisciplinary perspective.* Greenwich, CT: Information Age.

Metzenberg, S. (2004). Science and mathematics testing: What's right and wrong with the NAEP and the TIMSS? In W.M. Evers and H.J. Walberg (Eds.). *Testing student learning, evaluating teacher effectiveness.* Stanford, CA: Hoover Institution Press.

Millman, J., and Greene, J. (1993). The specification and development of tests of achievement and ability. In R.L. Linn (Ed.), *Educational measurement* (3rd ed., pp 335–366). New York: American Council on Education.

Minstrell, J. (2001). The role of the teacher in making sense of classroom experiences and effecting better learning. In D. Klahr and S. Carver (Eds.), *Cognition and instruction: 25 years of progress.* Mahwah, NJ: Lawrence Erlbaum Associates.

Mislevy, R.J. (1996). Test theory reconceived. *Journal of Educational Measurement, 33*(4), 379–416.

Mislevy, R.J., and Haertel, G. (2005). *Overview of the PADI assessment design system.* Paper presented at the American Educational Research Association Annual Meeting, April, Montreal.

Mislevy, R.J., Steinberg, L.S., and Almond, R.G. (2002). On the structure of educational assessments. *Measurement: Interdisciplinary Research and Perspectives, 1,* 3–67.

Mislevy, R.J., Wilson, M., Ercikan, K., and Chudowsky, N. (2003). Psychometric principles in student assessment. In T. Kellaghan and D.L. Stufflebeam (Eds.), *International handbook of educational evaluation* (pp. 489–532). Dordrecht, The Netherlands: Kluwer Academic.

National Assessment Governing Board. (2004, November). *NAEP 2009 science framework development: issues and recommendations.* Washington, DC: Author.

National Center for Education Statistics. (2001). *Teacher preparation and professional development: 2000.* Available: http://nces.ed.gov/pubs2001/2001088.pdf [accessed June 2005].

National Commission on Excellence in Education. (1983, April). *A nation at risk: The imperative for educational reform. A report to the nation and the Secretary of Education United States Department of Education.* Available: http://www.ed.gov/pubs/NatAtRisk/index.html [accessed June 2005].

National Commission on Mathematics and Science Teaching for the 21st Century. (2000). *Before it's too late: A report to the nation from the National Commission on Mathematics and Science Teaching for the 21st Century.* Jessup, MD: Education Publications Center.

National Council on Educational Standards and Testing. (1992). *Raising standards for American education.* Washington, DC: U.S. Government Printing Office.

National Education Goals Panel. (1993). *Promises to keep: Creating high standards for American students.* (Report on the Review of Educational Standards from the Goals 3 and 4). Washington, DC: Author, Technical Planning Group.

National Research Council. (1990). *Fulfilling the promise: Biology education in the nation's schools.* Committee on High School Biology Education, Board on Biology, Commission on Life Sciences. Washington, DC: National Academy Press.

National Research Council. (1996). *National science education standards.* National Committee on Science Education Standards and Assessment. Center for Science, Mathematics, and Engineering Education. Washington, DC: National Academy Press.

National Research Council. (1999a). *How people learn: Brain, mind, experience, and school.* J.D. Bransford, A.L. Brown, and R.R. Cocking (Eds.), Committee on Developments in the Science of Learning, Commission on Behavioral and Social Sciences and Education. Washington, DC: National Academy Press.

National Research Council (1999b). *Testing, teaching, and learning: A guide for states and school districts.* R.F. Elmore and R. Rothman (Eds.), Committee on Title I Testing and Assessment, Board on Testing and Assessment, Commission on Behavioral and Social Sciences and Education. Washington, DC: National Academy Press.

National Research Council. (2000a). *Educating teachers of science, mathematics, and technology: New practices for the new millennium.* Committee on Science and Mathematics Teacher Preparation, Center for Education. Washington, DC: National Academy Press.

National Research Council. (2000b). *How people learn: Brain, mind, experience, and school: Expanded edition.* Committee on Developments in the Science of Learning, J.D. Bransford, A.L. Brown, and R.R. Cocking (Eds.) with additional material from the Committee on Learning Research and Educational Practice. M.S. Donovan, J.D. Bransford, and J.W. Pellegrino (Eds.), Commission on Behavioral and Social Sciences and Education. Washington, DC: National Academy Press.

National Research Council. (2000c). *Inquiry and the national science education standards: A guide for teaching and learning.* Committee on Development of an Addendum to the National Science Education Standards on Scientific Inquiry, Center for Science, Mathematics, and Engineering Education. Washington, DC: National Academy Press.

National Research Council. (2001a). *Classroom assessment and the national science education standards*. Committee on Classroom Assessment and the *National Science Education Standards*. J. M. Atkin, P. Black, and J. Coffey (Eds.). Center for Education. Washington, DC: National Academy Press.

National Research Council. (2001b). *Knowing what students know: The science and design of educational assessment*. Committee on the Foundations of Assessment. J. Pellegrino, N. Chudowsky, and R. Glaser (Eds.). Board on Testing and Assessment. Center for Education. Division of Behavioral and Social Sciences and Education. Washington, DC: National Academy Press.

National Research Council. (2002). *Learning and understanding: Improving advanced study of mathematics and science in U.S. high schools*. Committee on Programs for Advanced Study of Mathematics and Science in American High Schools. J.P. Gollub, M.W. Bertenthal, J.B. Labov, and P.C. Curtis (Eds.). Center for Education, Division of Behavioral and Social Sciences and Education. Washington, DC: National Academy Press.

National Research Council (2003). *Assessment in support of instruction and learning: Bridging the gap between large-scale and classroom assessment*. Committee on Assessment in Support of Instruction and Learning. Board on Testing and Assessment. Committee on Science Education K–12, Mathematical Sciences Education Board. Center for Education, Division of Behavioral and Social Sciences Education. Washington, DC: The National Academies Press.

National Research Council. (2004). *Keeping score for all: The effects of inclusion and accommodation policies on large-scale educational assessments*. Committee on Participation of English Language Learners and Students with Disabilities in NAEP and Other Large-Scale Assessments. J.A. Koenig and L.F. Bachman (Eds.). Board on Testing and Assessment, Center for Education. Division of Behavioral and Social Sciences and Education. Washington, DC: The National Academies Press.

National Science Board Commission on Precollege Education in Mathematics, Science and Technology. (1983). *Educating Americans for the 21st century: A report to the American people and the National Science Board*. Washington, D.C.: Author.

National Science Teachers Association. (1992). *Scope, sequence, coordination. The content core: A guide for curriculum designers*. Washington, DC: Author.

National Staff Development Council. (2001). *Standards for staff development* (Rev. Ed.). Oxford, OH: Author.

Neill, M., and Medina, N.J. (1989). Standardized testing: Harmful to educational health. *Phi Delta Kappan, 70,* 688–697.

Neuberger, W. (2004). *Online assessment in Oregon: The technology-enhanced student assessment*. Presented at the No Child Left Behind Leadership Summit, March, St. Louis, MO.

Niemi, D. (1996). Assessing conceptual understanding in mathematics: Representation, problem solutions, justifications, and explanations. *Journal of Educational Research, 89,* 351–363.

Odendahl, N. (1999). Online *delivery and scoring of constructed-response assessments*. Paper presented at the American Educational Research Association Annual Meeting, Montreal.

Olson, L. (1998). An "A" or a "D": State rankings differ widely. *Education Week*, April 15.

Oswald, J.H., and Rebarber, R. (2002). *State innovations priorities for state testing programs*. Washington, DC: Education Leadership Council.

Patz, R., Reckase, M., and Martineau, J. (2005). *Building NCLB science assessments: Psychometric and practical considerations*. Commissioned paper prepared for the National Research Council's Committee on Test Design for K–12 Science Achievement, Washington, DC.

Perkins, D. (1992). *Smart schools: From training memories to educating minds*. New York: Free Press.

Perkins, D. (1993). Teaching for understanding. *American Educator: The Professional Journal of the American Federation of Teachers, 17*(3), 28–35.

Perkins, D. (1998). What is understanding? In M.S. Wiske (Ed.), *Teaching for understanding: Linking research with practice*. San Francisco: Jossey-Bass Publishers.

Phillips, S.E., and Rebarber, T. (2002). *Model contractor standards and state responsibilities*. Washington, DC: Education Leadership Council.

Plake, B.S., Buckendahl, C.W., and Impara, J.C. (2004). *Classroom-based assessment system for science: A model.* Commissioned paper prepared for the National Research Council's Committee on Test Design for K–12 Science Achievement, Washington, DC.

Poggio, J.P., Glasnapp, D.R., and Eros, D.S. (1981). *An empirical investigation of the Angoff, Ebel, and Nedelsky standard setting methods.* Paper presented at the American Educational Research Association Annual Meeting, April, Los Angeles, CA.

Popham, J., Keller, T., Moulding, B., Pellegrino, J., and Sandifer, P. (2004). *Instructionally supportive accountability tests in science: A viable assessment option? An analysis.* Commissioned paper prepared for the National Research Council's Committee on Test Design for K–12 Science Achievement, Washington, DC.

Porter, A.C. (2002). Measuring the content of instruction: Uses in research and practice. *Educational Researcher, 31*(7), 3–14.

Prawat, R. (1992). Teachers' beliefs about teaching and learning: A constructivist perspective. *American Journal of Education, 100,* 354–395.

Putnam, R., and Borko, H. (1997). Teacher learning: Implications of new views of cognition. In B.J. Biddle (Ed.), *International handbook of teachers and teaching* (pp. 1223–1296). Boston, MA: Kluwer Academic.

Putnam, R.T., and Borko, H. (2002). What do new views of knowledge and thinking have to say about research on teacher learning? In B. Moon, J. Butcher, and E. Bird (Eds.), *Leading professional development in education* (pp. 11–29). London: Routledge and Falmer.

Quellmalz, E.S. (1984). Designing writing assessments: Balancing fairness, utility, and cost. *Educational Evaluation and Policy Analysis, 6,* 63–72.

Quellmalz, E.S., and Haertel, G.D. (2004). *Use of technology-supported tools for large-scale science assessment: implications for assessment practice and policy at the state level.* Commissioned paper prepared for the National Research Council's Committee on Test Design for K–12 Science Achievement, Washington, DC.

Quellmalz, E.S., and Kreikemeier, P. (2002). The alignment of standards and assessment: Building better methodologies—Validities of science inquiry assessments: a study of the alignment of items and tasks drawn from science reference exams with the *National Science Education Standards.* Paper presented at American Educational Research Association Symposium, New Orleans, LA.

Quellmalz, E.S., and Moody, M. (2004). *Models for multi-level state science assessment systems.* Commissioned paper prepared for the National Research Council's Committee on Test Design for K–12 Science Achievement, Washington, DC.

Raizen, S.A., and Kaser, J.S. (1989). Assessing science learning in elementary school: Why, what, and how? *Phi Delta Kappan, 70*(9), 718–722.

Reckase, M., and Martineau, J. (2004). *The vertical scaling of science achievement tests.* Commissioned paper prepared for the National Research Council's Committee on Test Design for K–12 Science Achievement, Washington, DC.

Reiser, R.A. (2002). A history of instructional design and technology. In R.A. Reiser and Dempsey, J.V. (Eds.), *Trends and issues in instructional design and technology.* NJ: Merrill, NJ: Prentice Hall.

Reiser, B.J., Krajcik, J., Moje, E., and Marx, R. (2003). *Design strategies for developing science instructional materials.* Paper presented at the National Association for Research in Science Teaching Annual Meeting, March, Philadelphia, PA.

Resnick, L.B. (1995). From aptitude to effort: A new foundation for our schools. *Daedalus, 124*(4), 55–62.

Roeber, E. (1996). *Designing coordinated assessment systems for Title I of the Improving America's Schools Act of 1994.* Washington, DC: Council of Chief State School Officers.

Rothman, R. (2003). *Imperfect matches: The alignment of standards and tests*. Commissioned paper prepared for the National Research Council's Committee on Test Design for K–12 Science Achievement, Washington, DC.

Rudolph, J.L., and Stewart, J.H. (1998). Evolution and the nature of science: On the historical discord and its implications for education. *Journal of Research in Science Teaching, 35*, 1069–1089.

Ruiz-Primo, M.A., Shavelson, R.J., Li, M., and Schultz, S.E. (2001). On the cognitive validity of interpretations of scores from alternative concept-mapping techniques. *Educational Assessment, 7*(2), 99–141.

Rutherford, F.J., and Ahlgren, A. (1989). *Science for all Americans: American Association for the Advancement of Science, Project 2061*. New York: Oxford University Press.

Salomon, G., and Perkins, D.N. (1989). Rocky roads to transfer: Rethinking mechanisms of a neglected phenomenon. *Educational Psychologist, 24*(2), 113–142.

Schoenfeld, A.H. (1983). *Problem solving in the mathematics curriculum: A report, recommendation, and annotated bibliography*. (MAA Notes No. 1). Washington, DC: Mathematical Association of America.

Schoenfeld, A.H. (1985). *Mathematical problem solving*. Orlando, FL: Academic Press.

Schum, D.A. (1994). *The evidential foundations of probabilistic reasoning*. New York: Wiley.

Senge, P. (1990). *The fifth discipline: The art and practice of the learning organization*. New York: Currency Doubleday.

Shapin, S., and Shaffer, S. (1985). *Leviathan and the air-pump: Hobbes, Boyle, and the experimental life*. Princeton, NJ: Princeton University Press.

Shavelson, R.J., and Ruiz-Primo, M. A. (1999). On the assessment of science achievement. *Unterrichts Wissenschaft, 2*(27), 102–127.

Shavelson, R.J., Li, M., Ruiz-Primo, M.A., Wood, R., and Martin, K. (2004, July) *On Delaware's Assessment of Science Achievement: II Audit Test Development, Reliability and Validity* (second of two unpublished reports on Delaware's Assessment of Science Achievement).

Shepard, L.A. (2000). The role of assessment in a learning culture. *Educational Researcher, 29*(7), 4–14.

Sibum, H.O. (2004). Beyond the ivory tower: What kind of science is experimental physics? *Science, 306*, 60–61.

Simon, H.A. (1980). Problem solving and education. In D.T. Tuma and R. Reif (Eds.), *Problem solving and education: Issues in teaching and research* (pp. 81–96). Hillsdale, NJ: Lawrence Erlbaum Associates.

Sireci, S.G., Li, S., and Scarpati, S. (2003). *The effects of test accommodations on test performance: A review of the literature*. (Center for Educational Assessment Research Report No. 485). Amherst, MA: University of Massachusetts School of Education.

Smith, C., Wiser, M., Anderson, C.W., Krajcik, J., and Coppola, B. (2004). *Implications of research on children's learning for assessment: matter and atomic molecular theory*. Commissioned paper prepared for the National Research Council's Committee on Test Design for K–12 Science Achievement, Washington, DC.

Smith, M.L., and Rottenberg, C. (1991). Unintended consequences of external testing in elementary schools. *Educational Measurement: Issues and Practices, 10*, 7–11.

Smylie, M.A., Allensworth, E., Greenberg, R.C., Harris, R., and Luppescu, S. (2001). *Teacher professional development in Chicago: Supporting effective practice*. Chicago, IL: Consortium on Chicago School Research.

Stecher, B., and Barron, S. (1999). *Quadrennial mile-post accountability testing in Kentucky*. (CSE Technical Report No. 505). Los Angeles: Center for the Study of Evaluation, National Center for Research on Evaluation, Standards, and Student Testing, University of California.

Stecher, B., Barron, S.L., Chun, T., and Ross, K. (2000). *The effects of the Washington state education reform on schools and classroom.* (CSE Technical Report No. 525). Los Angeles: Center for the Study of Evaluation, National Center for Research on Evaluation, Standards, and Student Testing, University of California.

Stecher, B., Barron, S., Kaganoff, T., and Goodwin, J. (1998). *The effect of standards-based assessment on classroom practices: Results of the 1996–1997 RAND survey of Kentucky teachers of mathematics and writing.* (CSE Technical Report No. 482). Los Angeles: Center for the Study of Evaluation, National Center for Research on Evaluation, Standards, and Student Testing, University of California.

Steinberg, L.S., and Almond, R.G. (2003). On the structure of educational assessments. *Measurement: Interdisciplinary Research and Perspectives, 1,* 3–67.

Steinberg, L.S., Mislevy, R.J., Almond, R.G., Baird, A.B., Cahallan, C., Dibello, L.V., Senturk, D.,Yan, D., Chernick, H., Kindfield, A.C.H. (2003). *Introduction to the Biomass Project: An illustration of evidence-centered assessment design and delivery capability.* (CSE Technical Report No. 609). Available: http://www.cse.ucla.edu/reports/R609.pdf [accessed June 2005].

Stiggins, R.J. (1999). Evaluating classroom assessment training in teacher education programs. *Educational Measurement: Issues and Practice, 18*(1), 23–27.

Sylvester, R. (1995). *A celebration of neurons: An educator's guide to the human brain.* Alexandria, VA: Association for Supervision and Curriculum Development.

Thompson, S.J., Blount, A., and Thurlow, M.L. (2002). *A summary of research on the effects of test accommodations—1999 through 2001.* Minneapolis, MN: National Center on Educational Outcomes.

Tindal, G., and Fuchs, L. (2000). *A summary of research on test accommodations: An empirical basis for defining test accommodations.* (ERIC Document Reproduction Service No. ED 442 245). Lexington, KY: Mid-South Regional Resource Center.

Trevisan, M.S. (2002, June). The states' role in ensuring assessment competence. *Phi Delta Kappan, 83*(10), 766–771.

U.S. Department of Education. (2000). *Before it's too late: Report to the nation from the National Commission on Mathematics and Science Teaching for the 21st Century.* Washington, DC: Author.

U. S. Department of Education. (2004). *Standards and assessments peer review guidance: Information and examples for meeting requirements of the No Child Left Behind Act of 2001.* Available: http://www.ed.gov/policy/elsec/guid/saaprguidance.pdf [accessed June 2005].

Van Valkenburgh, B., Wang, X., and Damuth, J. (2004). Cope's rule, hypercarnivory, and extinction in North American canids. *Science, 306,* 101–104.

Vygotsky, L.S. (1978). *Mind in society.* Cambridge, MA: Harvard University Press.

Wainer, H. (1997). Improving tabular displays: With NAEP tables as examples and inspirations. *Journal of Educational and Behavioral Statistics, 22,* 1–30.

Wainer, H., Hambleton, R.K., and Meara, K. (1999). Alternative displays for communicating NAEP results: A redesign and validity study. *Journal of Educational Measurement, 36,* 301–335.

Webb, N.L. (1997a). *Criteria for alignment of expectations and assessments in mathematics and science education.* (Research Monograph No. 6). Madison, WI: National Institute for Science Education.

Webb, N.L. (1997b, January). *Determining alignment of expectations and assessments in mathematics and science education. NISE Brief* 1(2). Madison: University of Wisconsin–Madison, National Institute for Science Education.

Webb, N.L. (1999). *Alignment of science and mathematics standards and assessments in four states.* Research monograph #18. Madison: University of Wisconsin–Madison, National Institute for Science Education.

Webb, N.L. (2001). Alignment analysis of STATE F language arts standards and assessments, grades 5, 8, and 11. Paper Prepared for the Technical Issues of Large-Scale Assessment Group of the Council of Chief State School Officers. November 30.

Webb, N.L. (2002). *Assessment literacy in a standards-based urban education setting.* Paper presented at the AERA Annual Meeting, New Orleans.

Whalen, S.J., and Bejar, I.I. (1998). Relational databases in assessment: An application to online scoring. *Journal of Educational Computing Research, 18,* 1–13.

Wiggins, G.P. (1998). *Educative assessment: designing assessments to inform and improve student performance.* San Francisco, CA: Jossey-Bass.

Wiggins, G.P., and McTighe, J. (1998). *Understanding by design.* Alexandria, VA: Association for Supervision and Curriculum Development.

Wiliam, D., and Black, P. (2004). *International approaches to science assessment.* Commissioned paper prepared for the National Research Council's Committee on Test Design for K–12 Science Achievement, Washington, DC.

Wilson, M. (2004). Assessment tools: Psychometric and statistical. In J.W. Guthrie (Ed.), *Encyclopedia of education,* 2nd ed. New York: Macmillan Reference USA.

Wilson, M. (2005). *Constructing measures: An item-response modeling approach.* Mahwah, NJ: Lawrence Erlbaum Associates.

Wilson, M., and Draney, K. (2002). A technique for setting standards and maintaining them over time. In S. Nishisato, Y. Baba, H. Bozdogan, and K. Kanefugi (Eds.), *Measurement and multivariate analysis* (pp. 325–332). Proceedings of the International Conference on Measurement and Multivariate Analysis, Banff, Canada, May 12–14, 2000. Tokyo, Japan: Springer-Verlag.

Wilson, M., and Draney, K. (2004). Some links between large-scale and classroom assessments: The case of the BEAR Assessment System. In M. Wilson (Ed.), *Towards coherence between classroom assessment and accountability.* One-hundred-third Yearbook of the National Society for the Study of Education, Part II. Chicago: University of Chicago Press.

Wilson, M., and Sloane, K. (2000). From principles to practice: An embedded assessment system. *Applied Measurement in Education, 12*(2), 181–208.

Wixson, K.K., Fisk, M.C., Dutro, E., and McDaniel, J. (2002). *The alignment of state standards and assessments in elementary reading.* CIERA Technical Report. Ann Arbor, MI: Center for the Improvement of Early Reading Achievement.

Wolf, S.A., and McIver, M.C. (1999). When progress becomes policy: The paradox of Kentucky state reform for exemplary teachers. *Phi Delta Kappan, 80,* 401–406.

Zuriff, G.E. (2000) Extra examination time for students with learning disabilities: An examination of the maximum potential thesis. *Applied Measurement in Education, 13*(1), 99–117.

Appendixes

A

Practical Tips

In the December 1, 2004, issue of *Education Week*, writer Lynn Olson described the No Child Left Behind Act (NCLB) as a bounty for test publishers. Citing a General Accounting Office study indicating that anywhere from $1.9 to $5.3 billion will be spent on test development and administration by 2010, Olson details the rapid growth in both the number of test publishers and in the number of contracts being let by states to testing companies and their subcontractors. In 2002, Matt Gandal (Achieve, 2002) indicated that more than 200 new tests in required subjects at appropriate grade levels would have to be developed by the testing industry just to meet NCLB requirements, and they would have to do it in a window of approximately five years. Partnerships between states and test publishers are key to getting the task done. In an effort to stimulate thinking about a number of important issues, members of the assessment directors and state science supervisors working groups that collaborated with the committee asked us to outline some of these issues in our report.

The information contained in this appendix is drawn from the experiences of members of the committee, the working groups, and the design teams as well as from conversations that took place in June 2004 at a meeting sponsored by the U.S. Department of Education in Boston, at which test developers and state testing directors had a chance to discuss issues of mutual interest related to science assessment. In addition, we drew from the design team report, "Building Partnerships," in which the authors discuss what test developers need from states to build quality assessments. We encourage readers to consider these ideas, and we hope to stimulate thinking but make no claims that the issues we raise are an exhaustive list or that other approaches to working with contractors might not be successful.

We would like to see more systematic attention paid to helping states and testing companies work together effectively, and we encourage such organizations as the Council of Chief State School Officers to organize regular opportunities for states to discuss these types of issues and to share perspectives with each other and with test publishers, state contracting officers, and representatives from state technical advisory committees.

WRITING STATE ASSESSMENT REQUESTS FOR PROPOSALS

The request for proposals (RFP) is the way that states communicate to test publishers what they expect in the design of their state science assessments. Miscommunication at this stage can lead to costly mistakes in the testing process. Below are a series of questions that states should consider before letting a contract via RFP.

General

One approach is to call for a prime contractor who will be responsible for the performance of any subcontractors. This approach has the advantage of allowing state staff to deal with one contractor, who in turn handles any problems, issues, and communication with subcontractors. This approach may be essential if the state does not have enough staff or the capacity to manage multiple vendors. It is particularly efficient in eliminating any issues among vendors about hand-offs at times of transitions—whether the first vendor met the timeline, whether the material was in final form, etc., as the prime contractor is responsible for meeting the overall deadlines and quality requirements. A prime contractor approach may also work with more than one vendor if the testing program is divided into several stand-alone projects in which each vendor has full responsibility for an entire section of a testing program, for example, an entire grade level or subject. This assumes that students receive multiple score reports for each tested subject.

If there are sufficient state staff and capacity to manage multiple vendors, there may be several advantages: vendors with particular specialties would bid on the part of the program for which they are uniquely qualified, potentially offering a higher quality proposal. The potential cost competition among vendors bidding on only one piece of a larger program may result in a lower overall price for the assessment. Small vendors or vendors with innovative approaches that may otherwise not be part of a prime contractor's package may bring interesting ideas and cost savings to the project. Finally, state staff would need to communicate directly with each vendor, thus reducing the potential for miscommunication of directions and decisions. In addition, state staff would potentially have access to multiple teams of psychometricians and other test development staff to provide a variety of potential solutions to problems and issues that may arise.

The following are some of the important issues that states should consider when entering into contractual agreements for the development of assessments.

Questions

Eligible Offerers

1. What types of entities are allowed to bid?
2. What is the basic product/service to be provided?
3. Is the assessment to be paper-and-pencil or online?
4. How many contracts will be awarded? For what products/services?
5. Is the state calling for a prime contractor with subcontractors under its direction, or will individual contractors be permitted to bid on a piece of the assessment?

Contract Period

1. When will the work start?
2. When does the contractor assume authority for the administration of tests?
3. What is the total length of the contract?

Budget

1. What is the amount available or allocated, if there is a certain sum?
2. Will the contract run beyond the state annual budget cycle, and, if so, what are the expectations for continuation?

Authority

1. Who has sign-off authority in the state department of education?
2. Who will be the primary contact in the state department of education?

Applicable Laws, Rules, and Guidelines

1. What are the controlling state/federal laws or rules governing the testing program in the state?
2. What are the controlling state/federal laws or rules governing test security and student confidentiality?

Ownership of Test Items

1. Who owns test items?
2. Who is responsible for obtaining copyright permission for the state to use copyrighted material or art?

3. If any copyrighted material or art will be publicly released, who is responsible for obtaining the necessary permissions?

Test Development

Technical and quality standards to be met:
1. What is the state's test development process? Describe steps: who is involved in each step, who approves each step, what are the time frames for each step, and who sets performance standards and how?
2. Specify standards for technical quality: Will the contractor adhere to the standards developed by the American Psychological Association, American Educational Research Association, and National Council on Measurement in Education? If not, which standards will be used?

Specification of Products

1. Grade levels and subjects must be specified.
2. Specify numbers of students to be tested annually by grade level.

Timeline

1. What is the timeline for test development?
2. When are first live tests to be administered?

Background and Contextual Information

The state should provide as much information as possible about expectations for the basic content of the assessment. If curriculum standards are very general or banded in multiple grade levels, a considerable amount of work will need to be done to make decisions about the content of the assessment, as the curriculum standards may be too general to assess directly. Questions to be answered include: Will the assessment cover a single grade's content or be a cumulative assessment of multiple grades, and what balance of content versus process is desired? States should think through the issue of the number of standards to be assessed versus the length of the test—a general guideline is 3–4 test items for each objective tested. If there are 200 standards to be tested, this would mean an 800-item test.

The question of how much the test is expected to drive instruction should also receive consideration. Bidders need to plan for additional training, telephone assistance, and other resources if, for example, a state desires a majority of the assessment to be composed of performance tasks in which physical items need to be supplied and used in the assessment in a situation in which the majority of teachers were not teaching in this manner on a regular basis.

Questions

Purpose of the Assessment

1. Is it high stakes for students? If so, what are the consequences?
2. Are multiple administrations expected for each student? If so, over what life span for each student? What type of historical files will be required or are maintained for each student? Will the contractor be expected to match individual student files over multiple years or across multiple districts?
3. Are the tests high stakes for districts or campuses? If so, what are the consequences?

Standards Being Assessed

4. What content standards are being assessed? (These should be attached or links provided.)
5. If standards are long or not conducive to direct assessment, have assessment objectives been established and specific test-eligible content determined? If not, what responsibilities would the contractor have in the process to make this determination?
   a. Describe special issues that may arise in the development of objectives.
   b. List state groups that need to be involved and the expected numbers of reviewers, responders to drafts, etc.
   c. What is the expected length of time for objectives to be developed and finalized?

Interface with the Current Assessment Program

6. Is this a stand-alone program, or will it be another assessment in an ongoing assessment program?
7. If the latter, what requirements are there to produce an assessment that "looks like" the existing assessments?
8. What requirements are there to produce the same type of score reports as the existing program? Is there an expectation to have a separate set of score reports, or will score reports be integrated with other subject area score reports?
9. Is this program to be integrated into the existing program?
10. If not integrated, what is expected in terms of coordination with the existing contractor?

11. Is this a contract that will "take over" from an existing contractor? If so, what are the timelines? Will the existing contractor be expected to transfer files? What other transition or phase-out arrangements are planned?

Any Anticipated Changes

12. What are the planned changes to the program over the life of the contract?
13. What are the potential changes to the program once it is started (e.g., state board or legislative changes that are on the horizon that may affect the contractor's work plan)?
14. What are the state growth rates in terms of numbers of students, additions of new educational entities (e.g., charter schools), and other infrastructural issues that the contractor will be required to address?

ADDITIONAL DETAILS

Questions

Test Development

1. What is the basic test design desired (e.g., 1-parameter, 3-parameter)? Are tests expected to be vertically linked or aligned between grade levels (elementary, middle, and high school)? Are scores on one test expected to be correlated to scores on another?
2. What is the anticipated blueprint and length of the test?
3. Is a custom test or an augmented norm-referenced test desired?
   Note: If an augmented norm-referenced test is planned, an alignment study of the "base" test items should be required. The RFP should require a test design, including how many items will be provided for each curriculum standard and the anticipated blueprint. The contractor's experience in developing augmented assessments and a sample design of how it will be accomplished for the state should be required.
4. Is the test expected to be released to the public? How often? The complete test or just a sample of the items? Are answer keys required to be provided with the released tests? Must test items be coded as to which curriculum objective is being tested on the released test? Is any other information expected to be made available?
5. What item types are expected?
   a. Performance items, multiple choice, constructed response?
   b. Who writes the items? Who reviews them?
   c. Who trains the item writers?
   d. What are the item specifications? How will they be developed?
   e. How will universal design or alternative assessments be incorporated?

6. Is a field test expected?
   a. What sample size is expected?
   b. Will it be separate or embedded?
   c. Who is required to solicit district or student participation?
7. If performance items are expected:
   a. Who provides materials, the district or the contractor?
   b. How will the contractor know how many and where to send the materials?
   c. Is the contractor responsible to reship by the test day if the materials don't arrive?
   d. Are the items restocked each year?
   Note: States should consider that the more open-ended items and performance items that are included, the more costly the test.
8. For item review procedures prior to live use:
   a. Does the contractor or the state call meetings? What is the purpose of the meetings? How many times is each group expected to meet and for what purpose?
   b. Who selects the participants?
   c. What are the parameters of selection? Who is expected to participate—teachers, university professors, parents, members of the public, etc?
   d. How many people are expected to participate? How long are the meetings expected to be, and where are they expected to be held?
   e. What is the frequency of the meetings?
9. What stipulations are there for linguistic or cognitive demands in the items (e.g., English and Spanish, universal design, "plain language")?
10. Is an item bank expected to be made available? If so, what are the specifications? Must it be query-able? By what parameters should the items be coded (e.g., curriculum objective, field test statistics, etc.)?
11. Quality of test instruments: What is the expected standard for graphics, print quality, paper weight, ancillary materials and equipment, etc.? What are the expectations for "sealing" sections of the test booklets? What oversight or review is expected by state staff or outside reviewers prior to final production? What are the quality control procedures, checks for test production, accuracy, etc.? Who has the final sign-off on page proofs and test booklet production? What is the anticipated timing or timeline for these critical review tasks?
12. Quality of scaling or equating: describe the procedures for conducting studies for scaling or equating custom tests, and describe the plan to ensure accuracy of scaling or equating of augmented tests. What review or oversight is expected on these procedures by state staff or outside experts? What is the anticipated timeline for these studies?

Test Administration

1. Timing of the test:
   a. When is the test to be given? If dates are not yet decided, what is the process for deciding and when will the decision be made? Is the test a single day or a testing window? Is the test to be secure or not?
   b. Who must be tested? How many students are anticipated on any single day? Are there any student exemptions? How will accommodations be handled? Is the contractor expected to provide customer service phones on test day? What types of questions will need to be prepared for?
   c. What sampling procedures (if applicable) will be used?
   d. How will shipping of the proper supply of materials or online connections be handled? How will the contractor obtain enrollment data?
2. Who is responsible at the local level? What are the administration instructions, the procedures for security of materials, the procedures for checking quantity and obtaining additional materials, if needed? What are the procedures for problem resolution (paper-and-pencil and online testing have different issues)?
3. Training at local level: Who is eligible for testing, data collection procedures, standardization of administration, allowable accommodations? How is the return of materials handled? What are the procedures for breaches of test security?
4. Test security and confidentiality of student information include:
   a. Current procedures in place at the local level.
   b. Explanation of the procedures the vendor will follow, including confidentiality procedures, secure storage requirements, numbering and sealing test booklets, the disposition of answer documents and test booklets at the end of administration, and records storage over multiple years.

Scoring and Reporting

1. What is the expectation for standard setting? Identify the procedure, if it has been decided, or have bidders provide a plan for recommendation.
2. Consider overall data collection needs: coordination with existing state collections, coordination with any other vendors, and coordination with other state assessments.
   a. What scores or data are to be reported and to whom?
   b. What data elements (e.g., demographic information) need to be collected with individual assessment responses?
   c. What form must score reports take: paper, online, or a combination?

    d. Do score reports need to be joined to other assessments (either current or historical) or vendors (or both)?

    e. What are the deadlines for scores to be returned?

    f. What are the form and content of data files that are expected to be provided to the state? What are the procedures for updating data or error correction?

    g. Appeals: Can district personnel or parents ask for rescoring? If so, what is the process for maintaining confidentiality, and who pays?

3. Scoring procedures, especially open-ended scoring:

    a. When will the standards be set? How, and by whom?

    b. Will they use the whole test or subtest scores?

    c. What rubrics will be used?

    d. What training is planned?

    e. Will it be done online, scanned, or on paper?

    f. What are the procedures to ensure interrater reliability?

    g. What are the quality control procedures, including internal tracking procedures, to ensure that the correct score is transferred to the correct student's score report?

4. Quality control procedures should include:

    a. Delineation of who has sign-off authority for equating and production of score reports.

    b. Ensuring correct scoring.

    c. Ensuring correct output to reports.

    d. Ensuring accurate equating.

    e. How the score reports will be shipped and delivered to the district, the campus, and the student.

    f. Customer service.

5. What public relations arrangements have been made?

Contractor Issues

1. Stipulate as much detail as possible or consider a two-stage process with a request for information first.

2. Provide ways for bidders to acquire more information or to clarify areas of potential misunderstanding; have a vendor conference, allow for published Q&A documents, and give plenty of time between clarification and due dates.

3. Articulate the proposal review process: specify the timelines for review and selection and who has ultimate authority to enter into a contract.

4. Identify all costs for which the contractor will be responsible, including travel for committees; when the contractor staff must be available on-site; etc.

5. Determine the cost basis expected: per student or based on the activity deliverable?
6. Clearly specify activities in detail. A cost for a fixed set of services or products may provide the best cost comparison among bidders. However, if the state has not specified every detail of the expected services, then a set of costs by bidders detailing what would be provided at multiple cost levels may be more helpful.
7. Identify areas in which the contractor may (or must) offer services to districts for a fee, if any.
8. Identify issues of potential marketing conflict or prohibitions.
9. Specify possible financial penalties or incentives for the vendor for missing or making deadlines, etc.
10. Identify how changes of plan or modifications of the contract can occur: who has authority, whether notice is required, etc.
11. Identify any current amounts allowed or expected for specifications that may be helpful, for example, current square footage of warehouse space, number of toll-free customer service phone lines, meeting space requirements, location, and amount of office space, if required.

Other Questions

1. Public relations: describe any documents or materials expected to be developed to explain the testing program to various audiences, such as parents, the media, legislators, etc. Describe the media expected and the time frame and quantity anticipated.
2. Legal defensibility:
    a. Describe whether the contractor is expected to assist with legal defense under the current contract or if this possibility would mean an addendum to the contract.
    b. If the former, describe the potential types of assistance that would be expected, for example, explaining how the test development process met applicable legal and psychometric standards.
3. Required reports: describe any and all reports expected, the audience for each, the interval expected for the reports, and the medium and quantity expected (technical digest, program activities, status reports, etc.)
4. Committees:
    a. Technical advisory committee
        i. A technical advisory committee (TAC) is needed if it is a high-stakes testing program.
        ii. It can be convened for other purposes, for example, review of tests against psychometric standards, item development or item review decision procedures, research and options for a variety of issues, and support for decisions that are necessary for sound

testing but not popular or accepted by policy makers or the public.

    iii. Describe how many members, whether the committee is expected to be in-state or national, whether the vendor is expected to make arrangements for meetings, etc.

  b. Ad hoc technical committees: describe if any are expected to be needed for such areas as hand scoring, evaluation of the program as a whole, advice on laboratory equipment use in the testing process, accommodations for students with disabilities or English language learners, etc.

5. Management:

  a. What are the expectations for communication between the state staff and the contractor?

    i. How often are face-to-face meetings expected? (Once a month is typical but could be more or less frequent depending on the project complexity.)

    ii. What staff are expected to be available?

    iii. Are there other meetings or events for which the contractor staff is expected to be available (legislative committees, board meetings, teacher or administrator association meetings, testing conferences, training seminars, etc.)?

  b. Specify a timeline of project deliverables: anticipated events, completions, due dates—or require bidders to propose one.

  c. Require regular reports (and specify how often) against the project deliverables.

  d. Require regular reports on problems or issues to be resolved.

  e. Require names and résumés of the key staff to be dedicated to the project; require staff approval for changes.

GETTING THE BEST FROM TEST CONTRACTORS

Test contractors are key to getting a state testing program into operation. Even states that plan to design their own unique assessment systems often work with test contractors or consultants who are responsible for many aspects of test design. Here we provide suggestions for making the relationship work.

1. Try to set up a collegial, not adversarial, relationship with the publisher. Do things to engender communication and cooperation.

2. Staffing is very important. There need to be project managers on both sides (at the state and at the contractor) who can easily reach each other to make the day-to-day decisions. Both parties should be experienced and knowledgeable about testing and measurement.

3. Specify a framework for the decisions that can be made at this management level and those that cannot. Set up some kind of decision-making hierarchy so that tough decisions can be taken to a higher level. This is

important for both sides (state and contractor). The state project manager should be clear about what sorts of decisions he or she expects to be involved in. The state manager should not micromanage—let the publisher do its job—but should be specific about the things the state wants to weigh in on.

4. Communication and cooperation are key. Make sure the project managers on both sides communicate on a regular basis. Set up opportunities for staff (at all levels) on each side to meet with each other and talk about the test. Stress the teamwork aspect of the project.

5. It often helps to familiarize the contractor with the state—its priorities, students, and teachers—to humanize the process for them. Do whatever it takes to remind them that this is about children and learning, not the bottom line. (Some states told us that they invite representatives from the publisher to visit classrooms, meet teachers, and talk with students and parents.)

6. The state project manager should visit the test publisher's office regularly (2–3 times a year) to check on affairs, to see firsthand how things are managed, to meet staff, and to emphasize their interest in the project. It was suggested that states arrange for a kickoff meeting when the contract is assigned, two regular meetings, as well as a kickoff meeting each year, and a postadministration meeting.

7. Review the contract carefully and have everything specified in detail in writing. There is no detail that is too small to specify. (Think about the contract as if you were spending your own money; study it in the same way you would study a lease or a home sale contract).

8. If you expect a publisher to do something, put it in writing. For instance, if you expect to have a postadministration report and want it in writing, specify it as well as the topics to be covered, the general length of the report, and the deadline. Some states find it useful to build in time for the project manager to review and comment on first drafts of the report before it goes to the higher levels.

9. Make sure that the appropriate subject matter experts are working on the test. You have a right to know about the staff assigned to your project, meet them, review their credentials, etc. Several states mentioned that it is imprudent to accept a nonscience expert, even if only temporarily, unless the length of temporary replacement is specified.

10. Review the proposed staffing plan very carefully. Look at who is on the project and what their credentials are and pay close attention to the time allocations. If they have put a well-known person in the staffing plan (e.g., to do the equating), make sure they've allocated enough time for the person to actually do the work and not just delegate it.

11. Try to negotiate the right to have final approval of all staff working on a project. This is tough to get. Most of the time the best you can get is to be

informed about the staffing and their credentials and to be informed in advance of any changes to be made. However, most publishers will agree to inform you in advance of a change to be made in the project manager. Sometimes they allow the state to comment and offer suggestions, although they won't always take them.

12. There are a variety of alignment procedures; make sure they use one. Ask them how they plan to evaluate the alignment between your science standards and the test items. Get specifics: What strategy will they use, who will be involved, how will they analyze the results? There should be some alignment sessions; ask to observe or participate. If it makes sense, involve teachers from the state in the process.

13. Insist that they use teachers in as many ways as possible and appropriate. Teachers can be involved in alignment studies, they can help write or review items, they can score constructed responses. This is a tremendous enrichment opportunity for teachers (but be sure that you pay teachers or give them administrative leave in exchange for their help). If the contractor is out of state, consider asking them to maintain office sites in your state, so they can easily run item writing, item reviewing, and scoring sessions in the state. (Having teachers write and review items can be problematic because of test security issues, but there are ways to do it.)

14. Find out exactly how they plan to handle item development. How many items will they use from their existing item banks? How many do they plan to write? Who are their item writers? Who are the item reviewers? What is the acceptance ratio for items? If it is too high (e.g., they accept most items that are written), they may not be reviewing the items carefully enough. What are the criteria for determining if an item is acceptable or not? If they're using external item writers, specify in the contract to receive a list. This is important if you decide to change contractors. Using the same item writers over time provides continuity to the testing program; and you want to be sure that the contractor won't claim the list of item writers is proprietary.

15. Find out exactly how they plan to handle setting achievement standards (basic, proficient, advanced): What method will they use, who will participate, how it will be handled? Again, insist that they involve teachers to the extent possible and feasible. Insist on observing the process. One of the key statistics that comes out of state testing programs is the percentage of students who are proficient. The integrity of this statistic depends on how the process is handled.

16. Equating seems to be the area in which problems occur with state tests (e.g., New York's equating error). Understanding equating procedures requires specialized knowledge. Pay careful attention to the proposed plans and solicit outside expert opinion about the plans.

17. Invest in a technical advisory committee (TAC). A TAC is absolutely essential. This should be a group of people to advise the state about the more technical measurement issues associated with a testing program.

18. Specify in the contract that the publisher is required to participate in TAC meetings. Some states require the publisher to organize the meetings, develop the agenda, hold the meetings, and prepare the minutes. This can save state personnel a great deal of time, but be sure the meetings serve the state's needs and answer its questions.

19. Make sure that neither the state nor the contractor holds back important information at TAC meetings, information that might forewarn about potential errors. Foster the teamwork aspect of the project and make sure everyone sees the TAC meetings as a way to improve the testing program, not a way to find fault with the contractor.

20. There are crucial times during test development when states need to pay close attention to the contractors' work, i.e., during the initial stages of getting a program up and running. TAC members or other outside experts should be called in to help if necessary in order to provide close oversight of what the contractor is doing.

PERSPECTIVES FROM TEST PUBLISHERS

The following material was drawn from presentations made at a U.S. Department of Education–sponsored meeting on science assessment for NCLB that was held in Boston in June 2004. At that meeting, test publishers agreed that partnerships with states are key to developing an effective system. They described, from their perspectives, things that states could do to help test publishers do an effective job. We list these below.

1. States should clearly articulate, in advance of developing assessment systems, what type of data they want the system to generate so that the assessments can be designed to meet the goals and provide the needed results.

2. States should begin the assessment development process by describing what reports the assessment system needs to generate once it is in place.

3. States should take care to make their RFPs clear and precise. At a minimum, in their RFPs, states should:

   a. Be very explicit as to what content standards need to be assessed, including which grade levels should be tested.

   b. Describe what types of items should be in the assessment and how many of each type of item is desired.

   c. Stipulate whether or not the assessment should include the use of manipulatives.

   d. Tell the test developers if the state wants them to do validity studies.

   e. Define who will develop items and who will train the item developers.

    f. Describe what the needs are for data from the assessment system, including how the data will be reported and to whom. If some types of data are not needed, then that should be included in the RFP as well.

    g. Specify the level of cognitive demand and the dimensions of performance that are to be assessed.

    h. Articulate the minimum needs and where there is room for fresh ideas or creative approaches.

4. States should keep all bidders informed during the submission process. Some strategies that have worked include:

    a. Hosting a forum at which there are ongoing opportunities to clarify and ask questions about the RFP.

    b. Establishing a process by which prospective bidders can access all of the questions that are asked by other bidders and that are answered by state assessment officials.

    c. Avoiding making last-minute changes to the RFP after it has been released, but if changes need to be made, do not make them close to the submission deadline and make sure all prospective bidders have access to them.

5. States should develop a realistic timetable for the RFP and the decision-making process.

    a. Make sure there is enough time between when the RFP is released and when the proposals need to be submitted.

    b. Leave sufficient time between the end of the question-and-answer period and the final submission deadline.

    c. Do not change the length of the proposal review period or final vendor selection deadline. This makes it difficult for the test development companies to plan and staff accordingly.

6. States should consider using a two-stage process in deciding on a contractor.

    a. If a state has a lot of uncertainty about its assessment system, then it should consider releasing first a request for information that can later help it to shape an RFP.

    b. States should consider awarding a small contract to a developer to help them define components of their RFP or assessment system that are new.

B

Background Papers

As explained in the report, the committee asked groups of experts to write papers on several aspects of assessment systems, children's learning, and related topics. The titles and authors are listed below. The papers are available online at http://www7.nationalacademies.org/bota/Test_Design_K-12_Science.html.

DESIGN TEAMS

"Building NCLB Science Assessments: Psychometric and Practical Considerations"
Richard J. Patz, Aptos, CA (leader)
Mark Reckase, Michigan State University, East Lansing
Joseph Martineau, Michigan State University, East Lansing
Contact: rpatz@mindspring.com

"Classroom-Based Assessment System for Science: A Model"
Barbara S. Plake (team leader), Buros Center for Testing, University of Nebraska–Lincoln
Chad W. Buckendal, Buros Center for Testing, University of Nebraska–Lincoln
James C. Impara, Buros Center for Testing, University of Nebraska–Lincoln
Contact: bplake@unl.edu

"Instructionally Supportive Accountability Tests in Science: A Viable Assessment Option?"
W. James Popham, University of California, Los Angeles (leader)
Paul D. Sandifer, South Carolina Department of Education, Chapin, SC (retired)
Thomas E. Keller, Maine Department of Education, Augusta*
Brett Moulding, Utah Office of Education, Salt Lake City*
James W. Pellegrino, University of Illinois at Chicago**

Consulting Scientists
James Beall, St. John's College, Annapolis
Henry W. Heikkinen, University of Northern Colorado, Greeley
Smith L. Holt, Oklahoma State University, Stillwater
John Layman, University of Maryland, College Park
A. Truman Schwartz, Macalester College, St. Paul, MN
Christos Zahopolous, Northeastern University
Contact: wpopham@ucla.edu

"Models for Multi-Level State Science Assessment Systems"
Edys S. Quellmalz, SRI International, Menlo Park, CA
Mark Moody, Baltimore
Contact: edys.quellmalz@sri.com
Moody.mark@verizon.net

ASSESSMENT AND RESEARCH ON LEARNING

"Implications of Research on Children's Learning for Assessment: Matter and Atomic Molecular"
Carol L. Smith, University of Massachusetts, Boston
Marianne Wiser, Clark University
Charles W. Anderson, Michigan State University, East Lansing (leader)
Joseph Krajcik, University of Michigan, Ann Arbor**
Brian P. Coppola, University of Michigan, Ann Arbor
Contact: carol.smith@umb.edu
andya@msu.edu

"Tracing a Trajectory for Understanding Evolution"
Kefyn Catley, Vanderbilt University
Brian J. Reiser, Northwestern University
Richard Lehrer, Vanderbilt University**
Contact: kefyn.catley@vanderbilt.edu

---

*Working group member liaison
**Committee member liaison

OTHER TOPICS

"Imperfect Matches: The Alignment of Standards and Tests"
    Robert A. Rothman, Brown University

"International Approaches to Science Assessment"
    Dylan Wiliam, Educational Testing Service, Princeton, NJ
    Paul Black, King's College, London

"Use of Technology-Supported Tools for Large-Scale Science Assessment:
    Implications for Assessment Practice and Policy at the State Level"
    Edys S. Quellmalz, Center for Technology in Learning, SRI International,
        Menlo Park, CA
    Geneva D. Haertel, Center for Technology in Learning, SRI International,
        Menlo Park, CA

"The Vertical Scaling of Science Achievement Tests"
    Mark Reckase, Michigan State University, East Lansing
    Joseph Martineau, Michigan State University, East Lansing

SCOPE OF WORK:
MODEL SCIENCE ASSESSMENT SYSTEMS DESIGN TEAMS

Overview

The National Research Council's Committee on Test Design for K–12 Science Achievement requests that each design team prepare a paper that lays out its conception of a model for a state system of science assessments. At a minimum, the model should meet the requirements of the No Child Left Behind Act of 2002 (NCLB). Accordingly, the assessment system should adhere to the following terms specified in the legislation:

1. States must have challenging academic content standards in science. Science content standards may be grade-specific, cover more than one grade, or may be course-specific at the high school level.

2. States must administer science assessments, which are to be aligned with the state's science standards and *involve multiple up-to-date measures of student academic achievement*, including measures that assess higher-order thinking skills and understanding, at least once each in grades 3–5, 6–9, and 10–12.

3. Assessments may include either (or both) criterion-referenced assessments or augmented norm-referenced assessments. The assessments may be comprised

of a uniform set of assessments statewide or a combination of state and local assessments.

4. At least three achievement levels should be specified (e.g., basic, proficient, and advanced).

5. The same assessment system should be used to measure the achievement of all children, and the system should provide for participation of all students. Reasonable adaptations and accommodations should be made for students with disabilities and limited English proficient students.

6. Assessment results should be reported in aggregate for the full group of test takers, disaggregated for specified population groups, and at the individual level. Reports should include both descriptive and diagnostic information.

The committee encourages design teams to move beyond these specific requirements in proposing a model for building a system of high-quality science assessments that is standards-based and strives to improve science learning among the nation's students.

Specific Workplan

Each design team will have approximately six months to prepare a 50- to 75-page paper laying out its conception of a model for a state system of science assessments.

Key Components of Model Assessment Systems

The committee will lay out a conceptual frame of questions and issues that each design team will need to consider in creating its model. Each team will have some latitude in developing the specific details for its model; however, all models should be standards-based and should focus on promoting science learning. The committee's conceptualization of each team's charge will likely include the components described in the following sections. Each design team will be asked to focus on a specific model for designing a system of science assessments and may be asked to emphasize certain aspects of the model. However, it is important that none of the key components of a system be ignored. For all aspects of the model, the team should keep costs as well as states' limited resources in mind and should propose ways to develop systems in an efficient and cost-effective manner. In addition, the team should provide estimates of the timeline required for developing and implementing the various components of the proposed science assessment system.

In developing the model, the design team should consider that states are in various stages with regard to their systems of science assessments. Some may have an established system, and their efforts may involve moving to a new system that meets the requirements of NCLB. Others may be in the earliest stages of developing a system. The design team should therefore describe procedures by which a state might adapt its current system to move toward the proposed system as well as procedures for implementing the system from the ground up.

Design teams should lay out an explicit theory of action about how the system would work and how the pieces (state, local, school/classroom—assuming levels in addition to the state would be involved) would be expected to fit together to achieve alignment with state science standards and to support student learning. There should be explicit examples of "pieces" at various levels and how they fit together.

Instructional, Curricular, and Content Issues

The design team should lay out a strategy by which the state can develop a system of science assessments in which curriculum, instruction, and assessments across grade levels and topics are aligned with each other and with state science standards. For the purposes of this report and to provide a common basis for describing this process, the design team should use the *National Science Education Standards* to exemplify how the strategy might be implemented. The paper should describe the process for identifying the competencies to be covered on the assessment and should detail the steps to be taken to ensure consistency among material covered by the assessments and curriculum and instruction. The system should include mechanisms by which results from large-scale assessments can inform instruction and classroom practice with the ultimate objective of improving science learning. As part of this discussion, the design team should also specify the process for developing and setting performance standards. In addition, the design team should consider the potential negative consequences associated with the system (e.g., narrowing of science curriculum to teach to the test) and describe ways to circumvent these potential unintended consequences.

Concrete examples should be included in the description of the model assessment system. To assist with this, the committee will negotiate with each team the selection of a conceptually related cluster of standards (e.g., conservation of matter, science and technology, personal and social relation of science) to develop examples at each of the grade levels. The design team should include exemplar items for the cluster of standard(s) at each grade span, and describe how evidence from that cluster could be combined with evidence from other clusters to classify students into one of NCLB achievement levels. Exemplar items must be scientifically accurate, age appropriate, and measure students' understanding of important concepts. In addition, for exemplar open-ended items or performance assessment tasks, the team should provide exemplar scoring rubrics.

Development of the Assessment System

The design team should specify the process for developing the assessment system used at each grade level as well as the strategies they use to ensure alignment between levels and across topics. Design teams should be as specific as possible about test specifications and the rationale for their test blueprints.

In addition to procedures for identifying the skills, content, and competencies to be evaluated, there should be discussion of the procedures for determining the item format(s) to be used on the assessments. Consideration should be given to a variety of available item formats, such as multiple choice, constructed response, performance assessments, portfolios, etc. In addition, consideration should be given to assessment tasks that rely on teachers' ongoing appraisals of performance in the classroom. Further, the design team should specify the process used for determining the developmental appropriateness and scientific accuracy of the tasks to be included at each grade span. The design team should discuss how the various formats might be incorporated into a comprehensive system of assessments targeted at measuring a wide range of cognitive skills across grade levels. Design teams should suggest ways that district-wide or local classroom assessments that are aligned to state standards, curriculum, instruction, and the large-scale state assessment can be used in conjunction with the large-scale assessment to inform instruction.

Design teams should include a description of processes and procedures to be used to conduct bias, sensitivity, and technical reviews of items and tasks. The proposed processes and procedures should include the methods for reviewing items and for involving teachers, other educators, and science experts in the review process. The review process should pay special attention to ways to ensure that items and tasks are accessible to students with disabilities and English language learners. In addition, technical reviews should include a plan for ensuring that items and tasks are scientifically accurate and age appropriate.

The model should also include a plan for developing scoring procedures. For example, if the system includes open-ended items, the plan should include discussion of ways to develop a scoring rubric for open-ended items and the mechanism for training scorers and conducting the scoring process.

In developing the model, the design team should consider that one potential objective of science assessments under future legislation will likely be to track performance trends over time. Thus, the proposed model should include discussion of ways to implement appropriate scaling and equating procedures that will enable maintenance of performance trends.

Given that NCLB calls for reporting results according to performance standards, the model should include discussion about processes for determining and setting performance levels.

Involving Teachers

The model should include a variety of mechanisms for involving teachers in the design and development of the assessment system, both to help the assessment system function well, and to help the teachers learn how to use the assessment system to improve their instructional practices. The design team should consider ways in which teachers can participate in item writing, item review, scoring, and other assessment development activities. In describing these plans, the design team should outline the ways in which teachers would be trained to participate in these activities.

Professional Development

The model should include plans for ensuring that teachers and administrators are fully informed about the assessment system—the content and skills evaluated, the means for evaluating mastery of these skills, and the ways results are reported. Details should be included for ways to provide professional development activities that educate teachers and administrators about how best to prepare students for the assessment, understanding assessment results, and using them to make instructional decisions.

Including and Accommodating Students with Special Needs

In developing its model, the design team should keep in mind that a primary objective of NCLB is to include all students in the assessment system and should propose ways for accomplishing this objective. The discussion should include procedures for developing assessments so as to reduce the need for accommodations, e.g., making sure time limits are reasonable, using plain language. In addition, the plan should include discussion of procedures for specifying the kinds of accommodations that should be offered to students with disabilities and English language learners.

Reporting Assessment Results

The design team should develop a plan for reporting assessment results to a wide variety of audiences, including students, parents, teachers, schools, school districts, and states. The proposed model should include examples of reports that are appropriate for each of these audiences. In developing samples of reports, the design team should consider the ways the reported information might be used and develop sample reports that are appropriate, given these uses. The committee is particularly interested in examples of reports that would be useful for teachers and school administrators in planning instructional programs.

Use of Assessment Results

Although science assessment does not currently fall under the accountability measures of NCLB, design teams should consider the ways that the reported assessment information might be used in an accountability system. In addition, design teams should discuss and provide examples of the ways in which reported assessment results can be used by teachers and principals to evaluate students' achievement and inform instructional practice.

Meeting Standards for Technical Quality

Design teams should consider and incorporate professional technical standards for content and testing as detailed in the *National Science Education Standards* (National Research Council, 1996) and in *Standards for Educational and Psychological Testing* (American Educational Research Association, American Psychological Association, and National Council on Measurement in Education, 1999).

Use of Technology

In designing its model, the team should consider ways in which technology can be used in the assessment system to make the system more efficient. In particular, the design team should outline ways technology could be used to enhance evaluation of skills, to utilize innovative item formats, to provide accommodations to students with special needs, to score open-ended responses, and/or to enhance score reporting.

C

Biographical Sketches of Committee Members, Staff, and Working Group Members

COMMITTEE MEMBERS AND STAFF

Mark R. Wilson (*Chair*) is a professor of policy, organization, measurement, and evaluation cognition and development in the Graduate School of Education at the University of California, Berkeley. He is also a convenor of the Berkeley Evaluation and Assessment Research Center. His research focuses on educational measurement, survey sampling techniques, modeling, and assessment design. He is currently advising the California State Department of Education on assessment issues as a member of the Technical Study Group. He has served as a member of the National Research Council's Committee on the Foundations of Assessment. He has a Ph.D. in measurement and educational statistics from the University of Chicago.

J. Myron Atkin is professor emeritus of education and human biology at Stanford University, where he specializes in science curriculum and teaching. A former science teacher at the elementary and secondary school levels, he focuses on innovations in science education in the United States and other countries, as well as teachers' roles in formulating educational policy for curriculum and teaching, including assessment and evaluation. His publications include *Everyday Assessment in the Science Classroom* (with Coffey), *Inside Science Education Reform: A History of Curricular and Policy Change* (with Black), and *Changing the Subject: Innovations in Science, Mathematics, and Technology Education* (with Black). He has served on several National Research Council committees, including Assessment in Support of Instruction and Learning: Bridging the Gap Between Large-Scale and Classroom Assessment; Science Education K–12; and Next Steps in

Education Research, Practice, and Progress: Strategic Planning at the National Academies. He has a Ph.D. in science education from New York University.

Meryl W. Bertenthal (*Study Director*) is a senior program officer in the Board on Testing and Assessment of the National Research Council. Previously, she served as a senior research associate with the Committee on Equivalency and Linkage of Educational Tests and the Board on Testing and Assessment. She also served as a senior program officer with the Committee on Programs for Advanced Study of Mathematics and Science in American High Schools and as study director for the Committee on Assessment in Support of Instruction and Learning. Before joining the NRC staff she worked in public education as a teacher and as a curriculum and instructional supervisor. Her areas of interest include student assessment, educational reform, and education policy. She has an M.A.Ed from Clark University and completed a post master's degree program in counseling education at the University of Virginia.

Audrey B. Champagne is a professor in the Department of Educational Theory and Practice in the School of Education and in the Department of Chemistry in the College of Arts and Sciences at the University at Albany, State University of New York. She also serves as coprincipal investigator of the Students' Construction of Scientific and Mathematical Explanations Project and of the local systemic initiative, Assessment in the Service of Learning. Previously, she served as a senior scientist and project director of the Learning Research and Development Center at the University of Pittsburgh. Her involvement in U.S. and international activities in the assessment of science achievement has included membership on advisory committees for the National Assessment of Educational Progress (NAEP) and the Trends in International Mathematics and Science Study. She is a fellow of the American Association for the Advancement of Science. She participated in the development of the National Science Education Standards and served as chair of the National Research Council's Working Group on Science Assessment Standards. Champagne is a member of the planning committee charged with the design of the 2006 NAEP Science Framework. She has a Ph.D. in science education from the University of Pittsburgh.

David N. Figlio is the Knight-Ridder professor of economics at the University of Florida and research associate at the National Bureau of Economic Research. He also serves as associate of the Institute for Research on Poverty and has previously served on the faculty at the University of Oregon. His work focuses on education and public finance and includes investigations of the quality of public and private schools and the relationship between teacher pay and teacher quality. He has also worked in Chile, Sweden, Tanzania, Thailand, and other countries to help design and evaluate school policies. His work on school accountability and education policy has been published or is forthcoming in the *American Economic Review*, the

Journal of Public Economics, the *Journal of Law and Economics,* and the *Journal of Urban Economics,* and as chapters in books. He has a Ph.D. in economics from the University of Wisconsin–Madison.

Gregory B. Hall is the assistant superintendent for assessment and research for the Office of Superintendent of Public Instruction for the state of Washington. Previously, he served as assistant director for achievement testing and an assessment specialist in the department of education of the Province of Alberta in Canada. He has also served as a principal of a grade K–9 school and as a teacher of science, physics, and mathematics in Alberta's public school system. His postsecondary teaching and workshop leadership across the United States have focused on the topics of developing classroom and performance assessments, particularly for use in improving student learning. He has a B.S. in physics and a B.E. in science, both from the University of Alberta.

Joan Herman is codirector of the National Center for Research on Evaluation, Standards, and Student Testing at the University of California, Los Angeles. Her research has explored the effects of testing on schools and the design of information systems to support school planning and instructional improvement. Her recent work has focused on the validity and utility of alternative forms of assessment, with particular emphasis on opportunity to learn and portfolio assessment, as well as evaluation of technology and school reform. A former teacher, she has served in leadership positions with both the California Educational Research Association and the American Educational Research Association. Her numerous publications include *Tracking Your School's Success: A Guide to Sensible School-Based Evaluation* and *A Practical Guide to Alternative Assessment.* She has an Ed.D. in learning and instruction from the University of California, Los Angeles.

Heinrich D. Holland is Harry C. Dudley research professor of economic geology at Harvard University in the Department of Earth and Planetary Sciences. His research interests include the chemistry of the atmosphere and oceans, particularly the controls on atmospheric oxygen and carbon dioxide and on the composition of seawater; the chemical evolution of the atmosphere and oceans, particularly the evolution of the oxygen and carbon dioxide content of the atmosphere and of the major cations and anions in seawater; the origin and composition of ore-forming fluids and the formation of hydrothermal ore deposits; and the chemical contamination of the atmosphere, rivers, and lakes. He has taught science in the elementary grades, has served on school committees in New Jersey and Massachusetts, and has been active in education issues at the undergraduate and graduate levels. He is a member of the National Academy of Sciences and has served as a member of the National Research Council's Associateship Programs Advisory Committee and panels on Earth and Atmospheric Sciences and Geochemical Cycles. He has a Ph.D. in geology from Columbia University.

Joseph Krajcik is professor of educational studies in the School of Education at the University of Michigan and a member of the Center for Highly Interactive Classrooms, Curriculum and Computing in Education. He works with teachers in science classrooms to bring about sustained change by creating classrooms in which students collaborate to find solutions to important intellectual questions that subsume essential curriculum standards and use new technologies as productivity tools. He also seeks to discover what students learn in such environments, as well as to explore challenges that teachers face in enacting such complex instruction. With colleagues he is designing and testing the next generation of middle school curriculum materials to engage students in developing deep understandings of science content and practices. He is a fellow of the American Association for the Advancement of Science and has served as president of the National Association for Research in Science Teaching and as a reviewer for the National Science Foundation, as well as many professional journals. His National Research Council service has included membership on the Department of Education OERI Visiting Scholars Review Panel and the Ford Foundation Minority Postdoctoral Review Panel on Education. He has a Ph.D. in science education from the University of Iowa.

Suzanne Lane is a professor of research methodology in education in the School of Education at the University of Pittsburgh. Her research interests focus on measurement issues, including the technical quality and validity of large-scale assessments and performance-based assessments, item response models for test design, and generalizability theory. She has directed research on the consequences of the Maryland State Performance Assessment Program and directed the assessment division of the project Quantitative Understanding: Amplifying Student Achievement and Reasoning (QUASAR). She was president for the National Council of Measurement in Education and vice president for Division D of the American Educational Research Association. She has served as consultant to the American Institutes for Research, the College Board, the Educational Testing Service, and the Delaware, Kentucky, New Jersey, New York, and Pennsylvania departments of education. She has a Ph.D. in educational psychology from the University of Arizona.

Richard Lehrer is a professor at Vanderbilt University in the Peabody College Department of Teaching and Learning, and coeditor of *Cognition and Instruction*. Previously he worked at the University of Wisconsin, Madison, where he was associate director of the National Center for Improving Student Learning and Achievement in Mathematics and Science. He collaborates with teachers to craft, implement, and assess modeling of mathematics and sciences in the elementary grades. He has also formulated innovative geometry instruction for primary- and elementary-grade students that is guided by longitudinal study of student thinking about space. He is a former high school science teacher and has pioneered classroom research that investigates cognitive technologies as tools for thought in mathematics, science, and literacy. He has served as a member of the National Research Council's Committee on the Foundations of Assessment. He has a Ph.D. in educational psychology and statistics from the University of New York, Albany.

Sharon Lewis is director of research for the Council of the Great City Schools, where she is responsible for developing and maintaining a research program that articulates the status, needs, attributes, operation, and challenges of urban public schools and their students. She previously served in the Detroit Public Schools as assistant superintendent for the Department of Research, Development and Co-ordination and as director of the Office of Research, Evaluation and Testing. She has also served as an international education consultant to the U.S. Department of Defense Dependents Schools and as a Michigan delegate to the Soviet Union and the People's Republic of China. Her National Research Council service has included membership on the Board on International Comparative Studies in Education, the Committee on the Evaluation of National and State Assessments of Educational Progress, and the Committee on Appropriate Uses of Educational Testing. She has an M.A. in educational research from Wayne State University.

James W. Pellegrino is distinguished college professor in psychology and educa-tion and codirector of the Center for the Study of Learning, Instruction, and Teacher Development, at the University of Illinois at Chicago. Previously, he served as the Frank W. Mayborn professor of cognitive studies and dean of the Peabody College of Education at Vanderbilt University. His research focuses on human cognition, cognitive development, individual differences, and applica-tions of cognitive research and technology to instructional and assessment design issues. His National Research Council service includes the Panel on Learning and Instruction (chair), the Committee on the Foundations of Assessment (cochair), the Committee on the Evaluation of the National Assessment of Educational Progress (chair), the Committee on Learning Research and Educational Practice (cochair), the Board on Testing and Assessment, and the Committee on Improv-ing Learning with Information Technology. He has a Ph.D. in experimental and quantitative psychology from the University of Colorado.

Brian Stecher is a senior social scientist in the education program at the RAND Corporation. His research focuses on the development, implementation, quality, and impact of educational assessment and curriculum reforms. His current work includes two large-scale studies of the implementation of standards-based ac-countability. He has directed research on the impact of class size reduction, the effects of state assessment systems on classroom practices, the relationship be-tween mathematics and science teaching reforms and student achievement, and the use of performance-based assessments in large-scale testing programs. He recently served as a member of the National Research Council's Steering Committee for the Workshop on Taking Stock of the National Science Education Standards: The Research. He has a Ph.D. in education from the University of California, Los Angeles.

Gerald M. Stokes is the director of the Joint Global Change Research Institute, a collaborative enterprise of the Pacific Northwest National Laboratory and the University of Maryland. Previously he served in several positions at the Pacific Northwest National Laboratory and as the chief scientist of the Atmospheric Radiation Measurement program at the U.S. Department of Energy. A fellow of the American Association for the Advancement of Science, he has served as president of the board of the Columbia River Exposition of History, Science, and Technology and as a member of the board of the Association for the Advancement of Science through Astronomy. His primary research interests include climate and the design of large-scale field research facilities. His National Research Council service includes membership on the Committee on Support for Thinking Spatially: The Incorporation of Geographic Information Science Across the K–12 Curriculum and the National Committee on Science Education Standards and Assessment. He has a Ph.D. in astronomy and astrophysics from the University of Chicago.

Rachel Wood is currently serving as head of school at the Alternative School for Math and Science, and her additional responsibilities include teaching science to sixth, seventh, and eighth graders. Prior to assuming this role, she was education associate at the Science Resources Center of the Delaware Department of Education, where she served as state science supervisor with the responsibility for leading implementation of its science standards. Her previous responsibility had been as cochair of the Delaware Department of Education Science Curriculum Framework Commission to develop the elementary and secondary science standards, after serving as a junior and senior high school science teacher. She has led the state of Delaware's efforts to create a comprehensive assessment program. Her National Research Council service includes membership on the Committee on Science Education K–12, the Committee on Classroom Assessment and the *National Science Education Standards*, and the Working Group on Teaching Evolution. She has a B.S. in biology and an M.S. in earth science from Salisbury University.

WORKING GROUP MEMBERS

Amitabha Basu is a teacher of biology and science at George Washington Carver High School of Engineering and Science in Philadelphia. He has also recently served as an adjunct lecturer in ecology at Drexel University, a consultant and lecturer in the biotechnology laboratory technician program of the Community College of Philadelphia and The Wistar Institute, and a consultant to the science and technology curriculum committee of the Pennsylvania Department of Education. In Bangalore, India, he served as scientific officer and faculty in the field of biological electron microscopy at the Indian Institute of Science. He has a Ph.D. in biology from the University of Calcutta and an M.S. in education from Drexel University, where he is working toward a Ph.D. in environmental science.

Conni Crittenden is a teacher at Williamston Explorer Elementary School in Williamston, Michigan, where she established and directs the McAuliffe Lab for the Integration of Science, Math, and the Arts for kindergarten through fifth-grade students. Throughout the district and the state, she has served as a mentor teacher, science consultant, and chair of elementary and K–12 science, and has developed and provided professional development activities for teachers. In the College of Education at Michigan State University, she teaches a course for intern teachers on teaching for understanding. Her awards include a McAuliffe Fellowship and the Presidential Award for Excellence in Elementary Science Teaching, and she has participated with other presidential award recipients in workshops sponsored by the Space and Rocket Center Education Division of the National Aeronautics and Space Administration. She has an M.S. in fisheries and wildlife–environmental education from Michigan State University.

Diane Hernandez is the science consultant in the Standards and Assessment Division of the California Department of Education. Her responsibilities center on the planning, development, implementation, monitoring, reporting, and evaluation of the science tests required by or administered through the Standardized Testing and Reporting Program, the Golden State Exams, the National Assessment of Educational Progress, and the No Child Left Behind Act. Previously she served as a teacher of mathematics and science at various grade levels. She has also served as a national consultant and facilitator for the Activities Integrating Math and Science Education Foundation. She has an M.A. in mathematics and science with emphasis on curriculum and instruction from Fresno Pacific University.

Hector Ibarra is a teacher of science at West Branch Middle School, in West Branch, Iowa. His teaching approaches include field-based research and encouraging student involvement in the community. His numerous awards include Fulbright Study Abroad in Japan and Russia, as well as the Presidential Science Teaching Award, a Christa McAuliffe fellowship, the Milken National Educator Award, and the U.S. Environmental Protection Agency Educators' Environmental Excellence Award. He has served as president of both the National Association of Presidential Awardees in Science Teaching and the National Middle Level Science Teachers Association. He has an M.S. in science education with emphasis in geology from the University of Iowa and has completed course work toward a Ph.D. there.

Linda Jordan is the science coordinator at the Tennessee Department of Education. Previously she served as a high school teacher of biology, chemistry, and ecology, as well as a middle school teacher of physical science. She has provided national, state, and regional leadership for science educators by numerous means, including the Council of State Science Supervisors (executive board), the Tennessee Science Teachers Association (executive board), and the Appalachian Educational Laboratory Eisenhower Math/Science Consortium (regional steering committee). She has an M.S. in science education and an educational specialist degree, both from the University of Tennessee, Knoxville.

Thomas E. Keller is a science specialist and regional education services team member at the Maine Department of Education. He has also served as an instructor in the College of Education at the University of Southern Maine and as a high school science teacher, as well as president of the Council of State Science Supervisors. He has worked to align local comprehensive assessment systems with state standards, make teacher certification more standards-based, and help school districts to integrate curriculum programs and instructional materials with state and national standards and assessments. His service with the National Research Council includes membership on the Committee on Science Education and the Committee on Assessment in Support of Instruction and Learning: Bridging the Gap Between Large-Scale and Classroom Assessment. He has an Ed.D. in teacher preparation and curriculum studies from the University of Massachusetts.

Shelley A. Lee is the science education consultant in the Wisconsin Department of Public Instruction. She facilitates development of the state science academic content standards as well as the Wisconsin Student Assessment System in science with the assessment division and a commercial testing company. In addition, she conducts item and data analysis, assists school districts with making decisions about local curriculum and programs, and provides interpretations about the state science academic standards. Previously she served as a ninth-grade science teacher and as president of the National Science Teachers Association. Her publications include *Beyond 2000—Teachers of Science Speak Out.* She has a B.S. in education from Southeastern Oklahoma State University and is doing course work toward a master's degree in curriculum and instruction.

Patricia LeGrand is a teacher at Guilford County Middle College High School in Jamestown, North Carolina. Previously, with Enterprise City Schools in Alabama, she served as the science department chair, and while teaching at Dudley High School and with Greensboro City Schools, she taught academically gifted science and advanced placement chemistry as well as general chemistry. She has received awards in recognition of her teaching and is a national board-certified teacher who shares her strategies for success and leads efforts to improve instruction. Her doctoral research involved reaching and teaching capable, yet poorly performing students. She has an Ed.D. in curriculum and instruction from the University of North Carolina at Greensboro.

Shelley Loving-Ryder is assistant superintendent for assessment and reporting at the Virginia Department of Education. Previously she coordinated testing in the Virginia Department of Education, which included criterion-referenced and norm-referenced programs, as well as the National Assessment of Educational Progress. She has also taught high school mathematics. She has an M.S. degree in psychology from the University of Richmond and has done doctoral study in clinical psychology at the Virginia Commonwealth University.

John McKinney is a teacher of earth science at Mountain Ridge Middle School in Colorado. He uses research-based practices, data collection, and assessment methods, as well as creative instruction, and has been involved in writing district standards, developing district-wide performance assessments in science, and creating interesting curricula that meet district standards. He is a master teacher and curriculum textbook author and has received numerous awards for excellence and leadership in science education, including a Milken National Educator of the Year Award for teaching. He has an M.S. in earth sciences from the University of Northern Colorado.

Valdine McLean is a teacher of physics, chemistry, biology, and student leadership at Pershing County High School in Lovelock, Nevada. She has served in such leadership roles as president of the Nevada State Science Teachers Association and as a presenter and facilitator for workshops with a technology focus. Her innovative teaching style seeks to serve all children and has been recognized by several awards, including Master Teacher of the Year from the National Teacher Training Institute, Nevada Teacher of the Year, the state and national Presidential Award for Mathematics and Science Teaching, and the national Teaching Excellence Award from the Horace-Mann and National Education Association Foundation for Improving Education. She is a member of the National Research Council's Teacher Advisory Council. She has a B.S. in biology from Humboldt State University and is working toward an M.S. in science education.

Herman W. Meyers is associate professor in the Department of Education at the University of Vermont, where he has also held the position of department chair. Previously he was deputy commissioner of the Vermont State Department of Education (2000–2004). His other University of Vermont responsibilities have included directing the design and management of field-based, preservice and in-service teacher education in the Teacher Corps Projects. His research projects and evaluations have included study of the extent of gender and family background equity in school outcomes, a project to attract minority students to teacher education, evaluations of Mathematics and Science Partnership programs for Vermont and Massachusetts, and the first implementation year of the Vermont assessment system. He has a Ph.D. in higher education administration from the University of Connecticut.

Brett Moulding is the state science specialist for the Utah State Office of Education. He provides leadership and direction for science education policy and programs, including development and implementation of Utah's Science Core Curriculum, the Core Science Assessment, and statewide science professional development of K–12 teachers. Previously he was a high school chemistry teacher and received the Presidential Award for Excellence in Mathematics and Science Teaching. He is president-elect of the Council of State Science Supervisors and serves as a member of the science advisory committee of the National Assessment of Educational Progress. He has an M.A. in education with emphasis on science from Weber State University.

Pat Roschewski is the director of statewide assessment at the Nebraska Department of Education. Previously she served in a school district as director of curriculum as well as in other administrative positions, and during most of that time also served as a teacher, primarily in a middle school classroom. She has also worked at the district level with classroom- and school-based assessment systems. Her doctoral dissertation was entitled "Promising Practices, Processes and Leadership Strategies in Building Quality Local Assessment." She has a Ph.D. in curriculum and administration from the University of Nebraska, Lincoln.

Carol A. Shestok is the K–5 science coordinator of curriculum and instruction and mentor training coordinator of the Westford Public School System in Westford, Massachusetts. She has served as an elementary school teacher, an instructor at Fitchburg State College, a member of the Massachusetts Science Curriculum Frameworks and the Massachusetts Comprehensive Assessment Development committees, and a national board certification national standards delegate to Australia, New Zealand, and the People's Republic of China. She has received the Presidential Award in Excellence in Mathematics and Science Teaching and the Environmental Educator Award of the U.S. Environmental Protection Agency. She has an M.Ed. from Kutztown University and is studying for a Ph.D. in leadership and schooling at the University of Massachusetts.

Ann Smisko (retired) served as the associate commissioner for curriculum, assessment, and technology at the Texas Education Agency, where she provided leadership and oversight to the areas of curriculum, student assessment, advanced academic services, textbook administration, and educational technology. She has been responsible for developing and implementing the state assessment program, including the Texas Assessment of Knowledge and Skills, instructional materials adoptions, and educational technology to ensure alignment with the Texas Essential Knowledge and Skills assessment. She has worked in formulating education policy as well as in special education, school support services, governmental relations, and professional staff development. She has served as a supervisor of student teachers at Boston College and as a teacher of students with disabilities at the Perkins School and the Boston Public Schools. She has a Ph.D. in education administration from the University of Texas, Austin.

C. Scott Trimble (retired) served as the associate commissioner in the Office of Assessment and Accountability of the Kentucky Department of Education. Previously he served in the Kentucky Department of Education's Office of Curriculum Assessment and Accountability as director of the Division of Assessment Implementation. He also served in the Office of Research and Planning as director of the Division of Evaluation, director of the Testing Unit, and education research analyst in the Division of Research. He has an M.A. in international and comparative education from Michigan State University.

Marsha Winegarner is a K–12 science program specialist and consultant in the Bureau of Curriculum, Instruction and Assessment of the Florida Department of Education, where she provides leadership in state initiatives in curriculum, standards, and professional development. Previously she served as a high school science teacher, as well as a Fulbright Memorial Fund Teacher Program delegate to Japan, a participant in the Leadership Institute of the National Research Council, and a teaching fellow at the Research Science Institute, the Massachusetts Institute of Technology, the University of California, and George Washington University. Her honors include the Presidential Award for Excellence in Science Teaching. She has an M.A. in zoology from the University of South Florida.

Index